**Community Care
Practice Handbooks**

General Editor: Martin Davies

The Essential
Social Worker

Community Care
Practice Handbooks

General Editor: Martin Davies

The Essential Social Worker

A Guide to Positive Practice

Martin Davies

*With an Appendix on
'Law and the Social Worker' by
Caroline Ball, Barrister-at-law*

SECOND EDITION

Gower

To my father,
Tom Brett Davies

Published by
Gower Publishing Company Limited,
Gower House,
Croft Road,
Aldershot,
Hants GU11 3HR,
England

Gower Publishing Company,
Old Post Road,
Brookfield,
Vermont 05036,
U.S.A.

First edition published in 1981 by
Heinemann Educational Books Ltd.,
Reprinted 1983
Filmset by Witwell Ltd, Liverpool, England.

ISBN 0566 00985 4 Hardback
ISBN 0566 00986 2 Paperback

Contents

Preface

The Essential Social Worker has two purposes. First, I have tried to provide a short but readable account of social work practice in Britain. It is, I hope, unpretentious but not uncontroversial. I have deliberately adopted a generic perspective, taken an overall view, although the coverage is inevitably influenced by the balance of material available in the literature and by my own interests and experience. I believe that *The Essential Social Worker* will provide its readers with a broad perspective on professional practice in the 1980s, warts and all.

Secondly, the book represents a personal view of a sphere of activity with which I have been associated for 25 years. I thought it was time for me to stand back and take a look at social work from the sidelines. So much has changed, so rapid still are the changes, and so multifarious are the pressures on social work, that – especially for a teacher of the profession's next generation – an occasional pause in the mad dash towards eternity can be salutary if not beneficial. And so I have put together a portrait of where I think social work has reached.

The book is intended for newcomers to the subject and for would-be practitioners; but, as an essay on the nature of social work, it is also intended as a contribution to the debate within the profession – a contribution which, in particular, emphasises the critical nature of the relationship between social work and the state. I don't ask or expect people to agree with me; I do hope that they will treat the subject as seriously and as sympathetically as I have tried to do.

Norwich,
July 1980

Preface to the Second Edition

Although, it is only four years since *The Essential Social Worker* was first published, this new edition has required major amendment. Professional practice continues to evolve rapidly, and the text's reliance on empirical evidence has meant that due consideration has had to be given to the impact of new developments on the social work scene. 'Patch', permanency and privatisation are terms which found no place in the 1981 index but which cannot now be ignored. One of the best-received chapters of the first edition – that on client perspectives – has been given a spring-clean, and is now much tighter in the balance of its argument. Large sections of the book have been revised, especially in Chapters 4, 5, 6 and 11.

The structure of the text has been revised and, I think, simplified. It is now effectively in two parts. The first represents a firming-up of my attempt to provide a theoretical framework for an understanding of social work in the statutory sector of a mixed economy. The second brings together various ideas about the nature of social work skill and pays increased attention to the importance of day-care and environmental support systems.

Because *The Essential Social Worker* is designed as a portrait of where social work is at, it necessarily reflects both social reality and one person's perspective upon it. Both the reality and my view of it have moved on since 1981, and this second edition is designed to convey something of that movement. My own position has strengthened. I remain firmly convinced that there is a clear role for social work in any urban society laying claim to democratic principles, and, despite the concern which I express in Chapter 13 about current threats to a consensus model of politics, the personal social services (both in local authorities and the penal system) have come through a difficult period remarkably well. Social work continues to fulfil a commitment by the state to provide humane safeguards for its most vulnerable citizens, though the clarity of its role is still insufficiently felt or appreciated by many students.

The main conceptual change in this edition is to be found in my move towards an out-and-out attempt to postulate a theory of maintenance as a way of explaining social work's place in the political system. Other elements in the professional sphere of practice – the achievement of change, the fulfilment of responsibility and (an additional one) the pro-active involvement of the worker in the community – are now supersumed by the idea that social work is concerned first and foremost with maintaining otherwise vulnerable individuals *and* with maintaining the state in a relatively stable position. The theory is not yet complete, but it has been supported by a number of research accounts of practice that have been published since the first edition of this book.

I have changed the key terminology in Chapter 5: in place of 'power' wielded by the social worker, I now talk about the worker's designated 'responsibility'. I still think that it is important for the practitioner to bear in mind that the client tends to think in terms of the social worker's power – it is terribly easy for us to lose sight of that – but I accept that social workers do not *feel* very powerful and that their agencies are nervous about them *becoming* too powerful. The term that I used in the first edition, though deliberately provocative, sometimes seemed to obstruct serious discussion about the nature of social work responsibilities. That should not now happen.

I have again deliberately – some would say wilfully – sought to present a confident, assertive view of social work practice. Last time, for example, I picked up and made use of Olive Stevenson's (1974) seductive phrase about social workers being 'brokers in shades of grey'. That chapter has gone. Social workers have no monopoly of such a role, and too often the idea can be misconstrued and used self-indulgently to justify indecision, buck-passing or theoretical squeamishness. The truth is that social workers are employed to do a wide-ranging but quite specific job, which necessarily involves them in risk-taking, decision-making and the exercise of judgment. They cannot expect always to be right or regularly to receive public plaudits. But they should nonetheless determine to be knowledgeable in relevant spheres, adept at fulfilling their ascribed roles, sensitive to personal and occupational limitations, and appropriately active in service of the client. If they achieve that, then social workers will deservedly earn the respect of the community. It is the aim of this book to help them to do so.

Norwich,
December 1984

Permissions

The author and the publishers would like to thank the following for kind permission to reproduce their material in this book (numbers of the pages where this material occurs are given in brackets): Grace Batey (184–5); Richard J. Bealka (170–1); British Journal of Social Work (179–80); Community Care (147–8, 169–70, 184–5); Beryl Day (84–5); Her Majesty's Stationery Office (178–9); John Jamieson (169–70); Nottinghamshire County Council (147); Social Work Today (163–4, 156–7); C. E. Wakefield (147–8).

Acknowledgements

The Essential Social Worker is very much a personal statement about my relationship with a particular subject, and it is right that I should acknowledge the influence on me of three men and one woman over the two decades that preceded its composition. Tom Simey at Liverpool University imbued me with a critical sensitivity to the dangers of social work dogma that has never deserted me; Peter Westland and Arthur Rogers, then probation officers, taught me how to combine academic awareness with a commitment to and a feeling for the clients' lives in practice; and Jean Heywood, in Manchester University, at a critical time reinforced for me the conviction that good social work must combine intelligence and warmth. Both qualities are crucial: without intelligence or critical sensitivity social work loses its way; without warmth, commitment or feeling, it loses its identity.

More recently, my thinking has been stimulated by the responsibility of designing from scratch a new social work course (the MA at the University of East Anglia), by discussions with my students and colleagues at Norwich, and especially by conversations with my friend, David Howe. I have drawn heavily on contemporary journals – *Community Care, Social Work Today* and the *British Journal of Social Work* – and it is a cause for considerable satisfaction that the state of British practice is now so readily reflected with relatively little time-lag. I have consulted with and am grateful to Juliet Cheetham, Tony Hall, Nancy Hazel, Rudolf Klein, Bill McWilliams, Rolf Olsen and Colin Pritchard.

I am grateful to UEA for providing me with a term's study leave, and to my wife, Judy, for tolerating the strange hours of work that authorship entails.

PART I

The Theory and Practice of Maintenance

1 Moving Beyond the Myths

Two myths are commonly held about social work, and there are those within the profession or on its fringes who believe that one or other – or even both – are necessary to justify its existence. This book argues that is not so.

The first myth claims that social work is all about politics and politicking, and that all social workers must therefore accept the role of policy campaigners and party activists. Those who propagate this myth are normally in no doubt about the party which must claim the social worker's allegiance. The second myth holds that social work is primarily concerned with client therapy. Both myths are borne of the idea that the social worker is first and foremost an agent of change; and there is evidence that they flourish because of the personal needs or the evangelical fervour of many of those who enter the profession. If the reader is looking to have such myths reinforced, then he would be advised to turn elsewhere for his shot of reassurance; there are many alternative social work writings that provide it in fulsome measure.

Some other false emphases will similarly find little favour in the pages that follow, and it might be as well to dispose of them at the outset:

1 *Social work is an impossible job, and it leads to personal burnout.* It isn't, and, properly practised, it shouldn't.
2 *Social workers need to be in tune with their inner selves in order to cope with the complex problems found in other peoples' lives.* Certainly a balanced personality and a degree of self-awareness are important professional qualities in any job but a narcissistic concern with self-knowledge is not a prerequisite for effective social work practice.
3 *Social workers are better than other human service professionals at understanding the problems of their clients.* Not so. They simply see their clients' problems from a different perspective.
4 *All social workers are socialists, or should be.* The first assertion is simply incorrect, and the second depends on the validity of the political myth. The functions of the social worker do not depend on political conformity for their satisfactory performance, though empathy with, and sensitivity to, the feelings of the underprivileged

citizen *are* prerequisites for effective practice, and there is as a result a natural tendency for the majority of social workers to be politically left of centre.

In so far as there are common elements in social work they are best described by the general notion of *maintenance:* society maintaining itself in a relatively stable state by making provision for and managing people in positions of severe weakness, stress or vulnerability; and society maintaining its own members by virtue of social work's commitment to humanist endeavour and its emphasis on the idea of respect for the client, optimism for the future, and faith in the essential, or at least potential, unity of society. The pragmatically humane approach to social policy has had an impact on twentieth century Western society that should not be underestimated. Most social workers would recognise and support Julian Huxley's assertion (1961) that 'existence can be improved, that vast untapped possibilities can be increasingly realised, that greater fulfilment can replace frustration'; they might disagree on the kinds of effort required of the social worker to activate the client's and society's potential, but a fundamental belief in the capacity of man to improve his own circumstances without necessarily doing so at the expense of others is central to the social worker's philosophy of practice.

Social work, like tourism, computer programming and the leisure industry, has emerged in a particular historical context. Its existence reflects the economic buoyancy of twentieth century industrial societies, coupled with the growing recognition by the state of its obligation to provide for the deviant and the disadvantaged, the depressed and the disabled, the child at risk and the elderly, and to do so in terms and according to standards which avoid the degradation and dismissiveness of the past and of less humane societies. This recognition remains common to all political parties, though there is disagreement about the extent to which governments should encourage and subsidise private commercial initiative in the welfare sector, and about the scale of public expenditure on the personal social services.

Social work can usually be characterised as operating in response to human needs. But that is not to say that social work is always and everywhere available as a free service to those who demand it. For the *needs* might as often be those of society as of the individual-in-distress. It will be a frequent theme in the pages that follow that social work's obligations to the state are as legitimate as its obligations to the client, and that, indeed, the end-product of social work is necessarily a negotiated settlement between the state and the various individuals with whom the social worker is deputed to deal. The conflicts and tensions that exist in any open society will impinge on the social worker's field of action, but it is unlikely that any one influence will emerge as carrying undue force.

It is a central argument of this book that social work can only be understood by observing what it does and then by reflecting upon the contribution that those activities make to the way society ticks. As good a way to begin as any is to demonstrate how today's social workers operate from the cradle to the grave; indeed they are involved before the cradle is bought and after the body is buried.

Thirteen varieties of social work – from the cradle to the grave

1. The social worker counsels pregnant women who apply to have an abortion. He may prepare a report which could influence the decision of the consultant gynaecologist

Practice may vary according to policy variations in gynaecology departments. In one Lancashire town where requests for abortion are almost never refused, the social worker merely fulfils a counselling and advisory function. In another, where a more restrictive policy applies, social workers have to assess carefully the social and psychological circumstances of the applicant and make a recommendation in the light of this. If, in the social worker's opinion, there is no reason why the woman should not give birth to the baby and raise it satisfactorily, the recommendation is likely to be negative.

2. The social worker has almost absolute power to facilitate or prevent the process of adoption. He selects adoptive parents, advises the natural mother, and allocates the child

Adoptions may involve the transfer of a child to a complete stranger, with one social worker counselling the natural mother, allocating the child to a previously selected adoptive family and then superintending the exchange, and another social worker carrying out a review of the adoption arrangements and presenting a report to the court with a firm recommendation: yes or no. Other adoptions may involve the assumption of full parental rights by relatives of the mother's – her parents, for example. In such cases the social worker will, as before, have the responsibility of reporting the arrangements to the court and making a recommendation.

3. The social worker is expected by the community to play a key role in preventing child abuse. He has the power to recommend the removal of a child whom he believes to be at risk of being harmed

Prevention has become a fashionable concept in social work but its theoretical foundations are somewhat shaky. Nevertheless both the NSPCC (with *prevention* encased in its title) and other social work agencies are expected to take such steps as they consider appropriate in order to avoid child abuse. Detailed manuals are provided which set out the steps required by local authority departments, and case conferences abound. A small but growing number of children are now removed from their parents at birth. But it seems reasonable to fear that social workers will find it difficult to improve on their recent record in prevention: even with regular visiting and close knowledge of a delicate situation, deaths and child abuse will continue to occur; and, however much the sequence of events can be thought to have been predictable with the benefit of hindsight, it is foresight that matters. No social worker will ever be able to claim 100 per cent certainty in that.

4. The social worker works in day centres designed to provide non-custodial facilities for juvenile or adult offenders

The centres offer education, social skills training, crafts or sporting activities, and groupwork or counselling often designed to focus on the participants' law-breaking behaviour. Intermediate treatment (IT) for juveniles provides a virtual *carte blanche* for social workers to develop their own creative ideas in youth work, although social services departments vary in the scale of their budgetary commitment. Day centres for adult offenders are becoming more numerous, but there is controversy over the extent to which they should incorporate a strictly disciplined regime: on the one hand, such an approach may be alien to social work principles; on the other, it may be essential if the courts are to be persuaded to use them as an alternative to prison or youth custody.

5. In respect of families with mentally handicapped children, the social worker expects to play a significant part in helping the child make the transition from childhood to adulthood

There may be an attempt to help the child find a job in the real world if the handicap is not too severe, or arrangements may be made for attendance at a day centre or sheltered workshop. There is evidence from a number of research studies to suggest that there is considerable room for improvement in practice – both so far as the frequency of

social work help is concerned, its relevance and sensitivity, and in the degree of commitment shown by the social worker, not only to the handicapped teenager but to the family bearing the heavy burden of caring for him day-in-day-out.

6. The social worker organises the community service programme for offenders, whereby men and women of all ages do useful work under supervision instead of going to prison or being otherwise punished for crimes committed

The Community Service for Offenders (CSO) scheme is the most radical departure made by the British penal system since the intro-duction of probation and borstal at the turn of the century. It gets away both from institutional containment and from a unidimensional approach to supervision in the community. It is not *social work* as traditionally understood but its successful absorption by the probation service, working hand-in-hand with the community, has demonstrated the inherent flexibility of a social work service, and accurately reflects the influence of social work values.

7. The social worker is responsible for organising and running day care provisions for those who have been or who otherwise might now be in a psychiatric hospital

Joint funding between the health and social services and the stimulus of central government grants through urban aid have led to the establishment of many day centres such as the one in Warrington described by Cosgrove (1983). It is available on a drop-in basis, and is characterised by informality; it relies heavily on voluntary help, and the open-door policy and the friendly atmosphere have made it acceptable to people who are psychiatrically damaged. They play games, prepare meals, participate in group meetings, and have a full educational and activity programme. The social worker reports great improvement in many of those who attend despite the lack of any formal treatment plans.

8. *The social worker – perhaps in a voluntary agency, but also in local authorities – provides a long-term support service to families in severe straits. Sometimes the commitment extends over several years*

The *Family Service Unit* is the agency traditionally associated with this kind of long-term work; it is common for a unit to work with a family for four or five years, and there will often be examples of cases which have remained open through two or three generations. The social worker may see the family at least weekly, varying the emphasis from time to time. The mother might come into the unit with her children, get material help, be taught – and often taught again and again – how to budget on a limited income. Relationships are close – often on Christian name terms – and the social worker might be a godparent, best man and mourner at one time or another. But, though close, the worker will always have a long-term strategy, and will hope, one day, to withdraw.

9. *The social worker acts as an advocate in support of a client whose tenure of a council house may be in jeopardy*

Fletcher (1978) reports an instance in Hackney, London, where a deserted mother with two children and heavy debts thought herself virtually certain to be evicted from her high-rise council flat for non-payment of rent. A social worker from the National Council for One Parent Families agreed to represent her before the panel of councillors which was to decide the issue. At the panel meeting, the client was overwhelmed and rendered quite speechless by the formality of the occasion, but the presence of the social worker as representative made it possible for a compromise agreement to be worked out and for the client to remain in possession of her flat.

10. *The social worker coordinates the range of services made available by the local authority to make life easier for a severely disabled person*

The most pressing needs of the disabled are not normally for company – though a survey of disabled housewives has shown how desperately depressed many of them are – but for improved living conditions, adequate financial support and better mobility. One problem is the scale of the demand: even the most modest estimate puts the number of disabled who 'suffer disadvantage and restriction of activity' at well over a million, and although disability and old age go together, there are said to be around 400 000 disabled people under the age of 65 in England alone. The last decade has seen a surge of social services concern for this client group, but the pattern of social work activity that is both appropriate and adequate has never been properly spelt out. It needs to be.

11. The social worker arranges for an old person to be given accommodation when the time comes that independence is no longer feasible
Nothing so characterises the existence of an in-group as the use of jargon terms that, to the uninitiated, are utterly meaningless. Such a term is 'Part III', the key phrase that refers to a section in the 1948 National Assistance Act, and that is used as a label for the kind of accommodation that is provided for those in need – mainly the elderly. A major gatekeeping function of social workers is to decide when a named lady or gentleman is 'ready for' Part III accommodation. Criteria vary in different authorities, but the time of admission is said to be getting later as the years go by and the pressure on scarce bed-space becomes greater. One Director of Social Services has said that he keeps a careful watch on the average life span of residents in Part III accommodation; if it starts to rise he quickly sends out a departmental memo indicating the need for a more cautious admissions policy.

12. The social worker is responsible for arranging and superintending a pauper's burial
'Who will bury the dead?' Nothing is quite so sad as the total isolation of a corpse without friends or relatives to see to the final rites. Rees (1978) has a nice story of the former welfare officer in a Scottish social work department who volunteers to fulfil the department's statutory responsibility for public burial of the destitute. 'I do most of the funerals in this area. That's another thing that nobody seems keen to do. Simply because I have done them before I still get them. My colleagues are always saying, "I'll come with you the next funeral you do", but I'm still waiting.'

13. The hospital social worker provides stillbirth counselling for young parents
The bereaved mother is visited in the ward as soon as possible and again at home shortly after her discharge. 'It has been found that the first six weeks after stillbirth can be a period of great isolation and sadness, when feelings of inadequacy and failure are not always

appreciated even by family and friends' (Atkins 1981). The social worker's role is therefore to allow the clients to bring their feelings out into the open. A third and final contact is made after six months.

Social work practice – and its critics

Whatever the reason, a large number of people – especially in neighbouring occupational groups like the police, medicine and teaching – often fail to appreciate either the breadth or the subtlety of social work practice. Criticisms can still be heard of the allegedly undue influence of Freudian thinking, and of the social worker's consequent obsession with 'potty-training in infancy'; magistrates will attack the probation officer for adopting what they perceive as an unduly sympathetic stance towards a violent criminal or a confirmed recidivist; and the media and the general public alternately fault the social worker for either doing too much ('spoon-feeding the undeserving') or too little (failing to prevent hypothermia in the old or child abuse in families).

In fact, as the panning-shot just used demonstrates, the elements in contemporary social work are not overwhelmingly concerned with *treatment* in a quasi-medical or psychotherapeutic sense. There is a strong emphasis on counselling and verbal support, but also a clear recognition of the responsibilities that society invests in the social worker to operate on its behalf in a preventative or restrictive fashion. A major task is to enable the citizen to retain his independence in the community for as long as possible, and to superintend his movement into or out of institutional care in a way that serves both the client's and the community's long-term interests. It is a central tenet of social work that no-one should feel demeaned or abused as a consequence of statutory intervention, and that psychological independence should be encouraged.

The practice of social work takes place almost wholly as a result of *either* statutory legislation *or* policy decisions taken by politicians in central or local government. The functions of the social worker and the focus of his work are not self-selected, but are politically sanctioned and authorised by the agency which employs him. To point that out may beg as many questions as it answers, but it does at least indicate the source of social work's legitimacy, and emphasises that social workers are not, and can never be, a law unto themselves.

The idea of social work as *maintenance* has drawn the wrath of critics on the political left. Leonard (1976) pinpoints the origins of this criticism: 'Marx saw the governmental machinery of the state and the organisations related to it as performing one crucial function above all others, namely maintaining the rule of the dominant class over the subordinate classes'. 'Maintenance' then is a dirty word. What is the virtue of maintenance if it merely perpetuates poverty, degradation and discrimination? And from that rhetorical question it is but a short step to the assertion that social work, so defined, must be a sham, a defender of privilege, and social workers the lackeys of capitalism.

It is true that a working contact with many of the social services' clients strongly reinforces the feeling that Disraeli's two nations' survive; that, despite undoubted material improvements in most sectors of society, there are still the rich and the poor, the powerful and powerless, the establishment and the nobodies. But must such a realisation lead to the conclusion that social work, as currently practised, is in error?

Some socialist critics of social work, outside the profession, seek its destruction. Others, inside, or more usually on the fringes, argue for a radical model of practice, one which will align the worker with the client *against* the state and the forces of oppression. The problem with this position, attractive though it undoubtedly is to those with a romantic tendency to believe in the coming of the millenium, is straightforward: can a social worker employed by the state continually denounce the objectives of his own department, and can he freely engage in political confrontation with a view to undermining the foundations of social and economic power?

Such an approach might be employed once or twice, provided it is done discreetly, but beyond that it seems improbable that the strategy can be pursued successfully other than on a short-term basis in a society ripe for revolution. There is nothing logically impossible about social workers, along with other groups, pursuing radical ends with a view to overthrowing the present balance of power. They might even choose to do so *as a result of* what they have seen and experienced in the course of their social work duties. But for them to claim that what they are then doing *is* social work seems of doubtful validity. Social work, as it has emerged in the twentieth century, undoubtedly depends for its existence on its acceptability to the political regime within which it is practised (and significantly social work exists as an occupational activity in nations of many varied political hues). It demands of the majority of its practitioners that they are prepared to tolerate, with a greater or lesser degree of enthusiasm, the political complexion of the state which employs them.

Inevitably this tips the balance of attitudes towards a consensus model of practice, though it certainly does not preclude the conviction that societies evolve and improve as a result of conflicts within them and that the social worker's perspective can and must contribute to desirable changes in policy and practice. It does, however, tend to reflect the view that all societies have imperfections, that the business of social work is necessarily concerned with ameliorating the pains of these imperfections, and, furthermore, that without underestimating the importance of structural reforms and corporate planning, the individualist approach of traditional social work is both necessary and sufficient to justify the existence of the profession. If social workers were not around to perform the functions outlined in these pages, any urban industrial society would find itself having to rectify the omission whether its political complexion were capitalist or socialist.

Criticisms of social work are not, of course, confined to the political left. But those normally expressed by right-wingers are more difficult to pin down. Conservative critics do not usually postulate a preferred alternative; they simply argue that social workers are undesirable and unnecessary appendages to a society which has gone soft at the edges. The right-wing starts from the complacent assumption that society would be better if the principles of self-help, free competition and law-and-order were linked to the primacy of the work ethic and the self-sufficiency of normal family life to produce a smooth-running society in which the natural instincts of men and women would ensure justice for all and altruistic support for the helpless. The social worker is disliked because his very existence questions the legitimacy of this idealised view of life in a civilised society. Ironically it is the social worker's emphasis on individualism which is despised by the radical left and which leads him to undermine the corporate model of family and community life beloved by the right. The social worker sees the anguish of the poor, shares the pain of a mother coping with a Downs Syndrome child, experiences at close range the degradation of the dole queue, realises that the offender is never all bad and so recognises the naivety of ideological attempts to manage human affairs wholly at arms-length and only according to economic theories.

Most critics of *The Essential Social Worker* in its first edition branded it as being either right-wing or, at best, centrist in its orientation. Certainly it is not a socialist text as others with a strong appeal to idealist students purport to be (Beaumont and Walker, Corrigan and Leonard, Simpkin). Nor would I be so naive as to lay claim to ideological neutrality. *The Essential Social Worker* pays particular attention to accounts of practice and to the political context within which they take place. Social work in a capitalist society or a mixed economy is both theoretically problematic and yet an empirically self-evident phenomenon. The reasons for its existence, its relationship to state finance and legislation, and where it fits into contemporary patterns of power and privilege – are all fascinating questions of political philosophy that deserve more study than they have so far received. This text is faced with the unenviable task (as are all social work teachers) of setting down guidelines for good practice in the full knowledge that, on the face of it, there is no clear consensus of opinion about aims or objectives in social work. Hence, in the course of presenting arguments about the nature of professional competence and how to prepare for it, I am compelled to indicate the framework within which I believe contemporary social workers are expected to operate. Socialist theories in our field have been significantly better at providing structural critiques than offering empirically testable alternative guidelines for practice. In this book, we start by accepting *a priori* the statutory base and the administrative structure of social work (given that each are the product of democratic decision-making), and attempt to relate both to the traditions of social work literature, the personal motivations of staff, and the known interests of client-groups. The end-product is noticeably less exhilarating than any marxist critique would be; in compensation, it hopefully offers some clues to the embryonic social worker about the whys and wherefores of the paid job to which he has made a commitment. It is my belief that social work practice under different political regimes is very much less variable than is often assumed by those who criticise its manifestation under any one – though the precise form in which it exists in the United Kingdom clearly reflects the strongly social democratic influences of the past 90 years, tinged as they are with the continuing power of capitalism and an ideological commitment to the idea of personal freedom however defined.

There are three particular settings for which the contents of *The Essential Social Worker* are not designed. Two are socio-political; one is methodological.

1. Advocates of revolutionary socialism (or indeed, their near neighbours, the advocates of revolutionary fascism) envisage a society in which social work would be rendered anachronistic. I do not believe in the achievability of such a model. Social work reflects the imperfections of political and economic structures as they have always

been, and as I suspect they will always remain.

2.   Those who seek *laisser-faire* privatisation on a grand scale foresee a society in which free market forces will govern all aspects of supply and demand. Such a view of the world is not only incompatible with social work in any form, it is explicitly and ruthlessly hostile to the caring perspective that is its *raison d'être*.

3.   On a rather different scale, this text is also irrelevant to the world of private counselling outside the public sector. Whether or not the counselling relationship is fee-paying, it nevertheless has the form of a closed encounter in which the counsellor's commitment to the client is total. Although there are some similarities to elements within social work, and the term 'counselling' has long been held to refer to a central part of the social worker's activity, private counselling is different *in kind* from social work because of its independence of any statutory responsibilities which, as will be argued throughout this text, should not be seen as an unfortunate attachment to social work but as a central element within it.

Social workers – and therefore social work students too – are unlikely to be comfortable in their work if they aspire to revolutionary socialism, to a *laisser-faire* society in which all forms of state welfare intervention are proscribed, or to a counselling role in which the client–worker relationship exists independently of the agency by whom the worker is employed. Failure in the past to clarify the nature of these exclusions has led to difficulty in practice, in training and in management. In particular, it has become important to recognise that objective clarification, efficient administration, controlled discretionary budgeting and quality control are all elements as important in a public service operation as they are in commerce or industry, and that an emphasis on their achievement is not in any sense indicative of malign reactionary intent.

Despite the unease of politicians on both right and left, and with the resigned acceptance rather than the enthusiastic support of the general public, the social services have grown apace and the social worker has emerged as a key figure in the everyday life of most Western nations (see Tables 1.1, 1.2, and 1.3).

The maintenance function will be described and discussed at length in Chapter 3, and, later, the various elements and objectives of social work will emerge.

Let us reject at the outset, however, the idea that maintenance implies a passive or reactive role for social work, a mere mechanistic response to misfortune and despair. The key to understanding its potential sophistication is to remember always that the client is a human being with a mind and a will of his own. The social worker is in the business of maintenance because we know that the client imaginatively served in this way will always respond creatively in his own right. The caring, the counselling, the facilitating, the gatekeeping, the controlling, the preventative strategy all are designed to serve equally the interests of the state and the client. When those interests conflict, it becomes a matter for law and justice or politics. The social worker starts and ends with the assumption that synchronisation and synthesis are possible – even in an imperfect world.

Tables showing the growth of the personal social services

Table 1.1   *Trends in public expenditure in real terms, 1963–83*

	1963–68 %	1968–73 %	1973–78 %	1978–83 %	Expenditure 1983 (£m)
National health service	+33	+24	+25	+21	16 016
Defence	+ 5	– 1	+ 4	+24	15 904
Education	+35	+33	+ 3	+ 6	15 583
Housing	+55	+40	+ 8	–25	6 665
Police	+35	+32	+18	+30	3 063
Personal social services	+50	+142	+38	+21	3 028

Sources: *National Income and Expenditure* Central Statistical Office, HMSO, annually; *Monthly Digest of Statistics*, October 1984, HMSO; *Economic Trends*, Annual Supplement, 1984 edition, HMSO, 1983.

The table shows that although personal social services is a relatively low spender when compared with the monster budgets of the health service, defence and education, it has shown the greatest proportionate growth in the period under review: expenditure in real terms in 1983 was five times that of 1963. No other item had grown to anything like the same extent. Rises in the costs of the health service and the police have been steady, but education and housing have failed to maintain the momentum of the 1960s; defence has received a considerable boost since the election of the Conservative Government in 1979, but until then had been held almost at zero growth.

Table 1.2   *Personal social services expenditure as a proportion of total local authority expenditure*

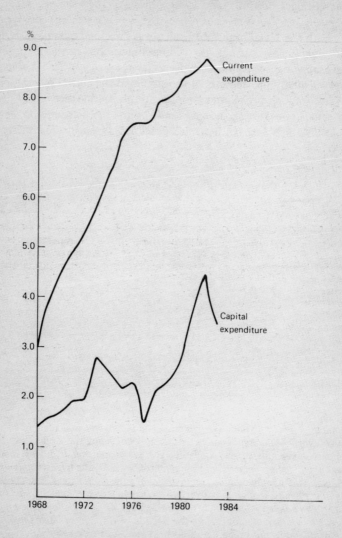

Sources: *National Income and Expenditure*, 1979 ed., CSO, HMSO, Tables 8.1 and 8.2, pp 58–61; *UK National Accounts*, 1984 ed., CSO, HMSO, Tables 8.2 and 8.3, pp 63–64.

Table 1.3   *Manpower in statutory social work offices 1973–83*

	1973	1978	1983
Social services departments in England: total numbers employed (or whole-time equivalents)	151 163	192 160	206 500*
Social services fieldwork staff employed in England and Wales	12 684	22 986	25 415
Number of probation officers in post (full-time) in England and Wales	4 449	5 184	5 821

*Provisional figure

Sources: Statistics issued by the DHSS, the Home Office, the Chartered Institute of Public Finance and Accountancy and the Central Statistical Office.

Throughout this period, there has been a steady growth in manpower, markedly among fieldwork staff between 1973 and 1978 when it grew by 81 per cent. That rate has slowed down, but the number of fieldwork staff has nevertheless doubled during the decade. The growth in the number of social services staff overall (+36 per cent in 10 years) and in the number of probation officers (+31 per cent) has been less dramatic, but nonetheless substantial.

2 Clients Point the Way: Eight Lessons to Learn

It is only in the last 20 years that the client's voice has come to be heard with any persistence in the social work literature. The publication of Mayer and Timms's *The Client Speaks* in 1970 was a major landmark in this respect and it has been followed by a steady stream of papers, books and articles presenting the point of view of those on the receiving end of welfare interventions of various kinds. 'Although the appraisals made by clients are not the only considerations in shaping services, effective service requires us to know something about the responses and reactions of those we seek to help', is the way Sainsbury justifies the accumulation of research effort in this area (1975). The client may not always be right in the judgments he makes about social work but what he has to say is relevant and his conclusions – where they seem to make sense in the context of social policy – should be taken into account when planning future practice.

Research into client opinion is one of the few fields in which sufficient empirical work has been done for firm conclusions to have become possible. Despite methodological problems and the fact that clients constitute a highly heterogeneous group of people who may be expected to want different things from social workers, it is easier now than it was a few years ago to spell out the lessons that we can learn from what the clients tell us.

Lesson 1: Improve the pathways to social work service

There are four ways in which the pathways to service might be improved. First, there is a clear need to increase the public's awareness of the existence of social service agencies. Time and again research studies recall how much difficulty clients experienced in discovering where they should go to meet a particular need – how to set about applying to adopt a child, for example, and how many different options might be open to the would-be applicant. Social work offices should be prominently located (perhaps decentralised into residential areas), their facilities should be advertised, and deliberate efforts should be made to educate the public about how social workers can help them. Some studies point out that those clients who were personally acquainted with a social worker had an unfair advantage over other clients. If a service exists, *all* members of the public have an equal right to know about it and to have easy access to its facilities.

A second point is linked to the first. We know that virtually every visitor to a social services or probation office feels some stigma in being there. (Even I as a member of the profession, when visiting a student on placement in a social work office, experience a slight feeling of being put-down when the face behind the grille tells me, not always politely, to take a seat. What have *I* done that I should be frequenting such a waiting-room? And I look round uneasily at my companions, knowing that they are looking round uneasily at me). We also know that it is exceedingly difficult to counteract stigma. But attempts should nevertheless be made to do so – partly, perhaps, by a process of public education, and partly by emphasising the universal availability of social services facilities and the public's right to them. Most social work offices receive regular referrals from a limited number of sources: doctors, councillors, the court, solicitors. The evidence from client-perspectives research shows that such referrers often display considerable ignorance of the social worker's role and convey either no idea or wrong ideas to the client of what is likely to befall them when they arrive. Particular efforts should be made to educate the sources of most referrals and so avoid the serious misunderstandings which can damage a social work relationship before it has begun.

Finally, a problem emerges with casual referrals who appear to be less likely to receive a full service than those sent to the social worker by significant others – councillors, magistrates, psychiatrists, and so on. All referrals should be treated equally. Those who have been referred inappropriately should be told so, irrespective of the status of the person who sent them, while those who have come in under their own steam should be assured of just as full a response as any sent by doctors or social work colleagues.

Underlying these four points lie two imperatives: first, it is essential for social work to establish and defend professional standards in the pursuit of publicly recognised objectives; and second, it is important for the client in particular to grasp the nature of social work, because research has shown that an absence of understanding can reduce the quality of help offered to him, can lead to reduced client satisfaction, and thence to higher drop-out rates (Burck, 1978).

Lesson 2: Handle the intake process with imagination, sensitivity and tact. Put clients at their ease

As in all public service agencies, a pervasive problem is that each new arrival represents a familiar, even a routine process for the worker, while for the client the occasion is probably unique. Many new clients have described how much grim determination they needed before they could bring themselves to cross the agency threshold. If, having done so, they are greeted with a casual, cavalier or downright hostile attitude, they are likely to turn tail and run. Not only are the clients in a strange, even alien setting; most of them have intensely emotional reasons for being there – hence the need for even more sensitivity and tact than is required of a dentist's receptionist or a building society counter clerk.

The importance of the intake process to the client is evidenced by the fact that, long after the social worker has forgotten it, the client can recount every detail of what happened. And the conclusions to be drawn from the literature are, first that the receptionist should treat every newcomer equally seriously, secondly that as a matter of principle the agency should attempt to provide *some* positive response to every initial request, and thirdly that if a referral to another agency is unavoidable, it should be made helpfully and, whenever possible, a personal introduction arranged.

Rees and Wallace (1982), in their review of client perception research studies, confirm the sense of stigma felt by many who come for social work help and, as well as emphasising the importance of an unhurried approach, a friendly reception and a non-judgmental response to all applicants for help, they say that it is especially important for intake staff to learn the art of enabling the client to ask for help. 'The ability and willingness of the worker to anticipate and articulate what help is required has been described favourably by clients.' If the social worker does accurately anticipate the request, it relieves the client of discomfort and embarrassment, and serves to convince him that the social worker and the agency are truly caring.

A particular fear expressed by some clients concerns the agency's reputation for authority and power and, although (as lesson 6 acknowledges) this is not wholly unrealistic, it can sometimes induce unnecessary apprehension. Lishman (1978) has an excellent example of this when she confesses how surprised she was to learn, long after the event, of the intensity of one mother's feelings during the intake interview at a child guidance clinic. 'I was frightened', said the client, 'I thought they would say I was a bad mother and take him away from me. When they took him away from me (to see a psychiatrist while she stayed with the social worker) I wondered where he was going. I did not ask.' Lishman was the social worker and she admits to having been quite insensitive to this woman's feelings, and there is evidence in other studies that such discrepancies are not uncommon. Certainly many clients appear to view social workers as potential takers-away of their child, and such unspoken fears will inevitably have an effect on conversation and the relationship.

At intake the public sector social worker must always be sensitive to the fears and anxieties that the client might have of his perceived role.

Lesson 3: Be concerned with the client as a person. Handle the personal in a professional manner. That is the heart of social work

Client-perspective studies have greatly helped in the task of defining professionalism in social work. It is clear that the *true professional* is not someone who is cool, detached, career-minded and disinterested, but is the worker who can display friendliness (not necessarily friendship in the conventional sense), understanding, and a warmth of manner which convinces the client of his active interest in and concern for the client's plight. And clients are remarkably sophisticated in being able to recognise that such professionalism is part and parcel of the social worker's formal occupation. 'With lawyers it's mainly a professional job for them, they don't take a personal interest in it. They wouldn't show any feelings and not really any interest. The social worker didn't behave as though it was a job, even though it was.' (Rees, 1978)

The establishment of such a professional relationship gives the social worker the power to exercise considerable influence over the client – to set limits, to give firm advice. There is clearly an element of acting in this, but the performance emerges as crucial to good social work in the eyes of the client. Professionalism is the projection of a concerned interest in the client's welfare.

Rees and Wallace (1982) identify some positive and negative factors which can be defined as good or bad professional practice:

It often pleases a client when social workers take an interest in them outside the perceived scope of contact. For example, asking clients about their families, taking an interest in their hobbies and activities, visiting outside official working hours – such actions do much to convince people that the social worker's interest is genuine.

He or she is not just 'doing a job'. This reinforces the clients' perception of the social worker as a 'friend' rather than a 'professional'.

It is important to the client that the social worker does not appear bored, and that he or she listens attentively to what the client has to say. Things like the social worker staring out of the window while the client is talking, keeping the client waiting, failing to apologise if the interview is interrupted by a phone call, breaking appointments at the last minute – all these have caused some distress to people expecting a more personal approach. When such things occur, social workers confirm the expectations of some clients that social workers are, in fact, no different from other officials.

Lesson 4: Identify the client's expectations and relate these to the agency's obligations and resources. Be active. Be alert. Be helpful. And don't string the client along

Client-focused research has demonstrated frequent instances of misunderstanding between client and worker – what Mayer and Timms dub the 'clash in perspective' – and these must be avoided or overcome if an effective working partnership is to be established. Mayer and Timms quote the case of the market-stall holder who, because of illness and unemployment, could not afford to buy stock for his stall. He and his wife were advised to go for help to the Family Welfare Association (FWA) and several interviews took place. The clients' only idea was to receive financial aid at a time of desperate need, and the stall holder's wife was particularly resentful that the social worker's focus seemed to imply that their marriage was in difficulties. She said that she asked questions about 'what our marriage was like, were we happy together, were the children contented and things like that. It had nothing to do with what we wanted. It was financial help not any other help.' Eventually the FWA did give the couple a grant, but the client's wife said that 'she would let her children starve before seeking professional help again'.

So numerous are such examples in the literature that one might be forgiven for thinking that what have been called 'pervasive disagreements' are an inherent part of the social work process. They arise partly because of the client's frequent misunderstanding of the social work role, or his misconception of agency resources, but also because of the failure of many social workers to recognise that the responsibility for providing clarification is undoubtedly their's. Having carefully and sympathetically allowed the client to state his business (providing sufficient time for difficulties of communication), the social worker must accurately assess and honestly explain whether or not the agency can respond. He must tell the client how, to what extent, and for how long help can be given – and on what conditions, if any. If the agency is not in a position to respond, this should be quickly made clear, at the same time providing advice on possible access to other sources, if there are any. If there are not, the social worker may nevertheless feel justified in asking whether there is any other way in which the agency might help. But the client should never be led to expect more than is available. The research literature is full of examples of clients who felt they were 'strung along' by well-meaning social workers and then let down when the reality was eventually made known to them.

When the client's needs or expectations have been identified, there is clear evidence that an active response by the social worker is greatly valued. 'By "doing things" or attempting to do things for clients, social workers confirm their concern and willingness to help. Clients frequently regard worker activity as being denotive of genuine concern.' (Rees and Wallace, 1982) Clients often stress their material problems and are glad of tangible assistance; many tend to measure both their troubles and potential solutions in concrete rather than abstract terms. Of course, social work has to aim at achieving a balance, not to the total exclusion of counselling or general support roles; nevertheless the recipients of social work service remember appreciatively when they received practical help that was both immediate and relevant to their needs.

Both Sainsbury (1975) and McGrath (1979) emphasise the successful way in which two very different types of social work agency established a good reputation for themselves and simultaneously laid the foundations for sometimes less tangible, long-term work by making an immediate response to specific practical problems at intake. The effort needed was often not enormous, but the pay-off in terms of the relationship established between worker and client was significant. Practical help is important, but the less easily acknowledged problems of human behaviour and relationships may also have to be tackled if a proper service is to be given. 'Just talking' is often of value in its own right.

Lesson 5: Be a good counsellor
One of the reasons why client studies have tended to emphasise the

value of tangible help, is because counselling skills – like good acting or writing – tend not to be noticed when they are present; it is only in their absence that you realise something is wrong. Warmth, informality, genuineness and non-judgmental sympathy are traditionally associated with effective practice, and there are adverse comments in the research literature on social workers who failed to reach acceptable standards in these respects.

Lesson 6: Remember that the social work role puts you in a position of power and privilege. You cannot escape or deny it. And you must be honest and open about your agency's responsibilities
Many social workers, especially those with a strong commitment to an egalitarian society, find it difficult to reconcile themselves to the power and authority which are implicit in almost all their working roles. But the message from clients is that any attempt to deny the reality of their position is confusing and results in inefficient practice.

In child care, mental health and probation, the client may well be apprehensive and fearful of whether the social worker is going to respond in a way that will be perceived as punitive; in other spheres – adoption, fostering, requests for material aid – the client knows that the social worker can give or withhold favours or facilities. It is the social worker who holds the initiative, and only when this is acknowledged can it be used sensitively and to good effect.

Sometimes the client's fears are based on fantasies about social worker power, and the worker must do everything possible to counteract unnecessary apprehension by honestly spelling out the aims, responsibilities and functions of the agency. He should give reassurance where possible, but never mislead the client into a false sense of security if he knows that critical and possibly unwelcome or painful decisions may have to be taken.

The fact of the social worker's authority carries with it two obligations: first, it is his job to give structure to the working relationship, to direct and make positive use of verbal exchanges, to focus on appropriately restricted issues, always to explain procedures, and to be absolutely certain that if further appointments are thought to be needed, the client is aware of the fact and knows that the social worker remains available. The second obligation is the traditional one accorded to the privileged person in a service relationship: always to use his influence on behalf of the client where it is pertinent and feasible to do so.

Most clients seem to appreciate the social worker who accepts his superior position and uses it unambiguously and to their advantage – even though the end-product will often be exceedingly modest.

Lesson 7: Use your knowledge and experience for the benefit of the client. Keep it up-to-date. Use the working group to supplement it
Rees and Wallace (1982) identify three elements looked for by clients:

1. They like social workers to have sufficient experience of life and the world to be effectively unshockable. Violence, deviant behaviour, degradation and psychological fantasies are often a part of many clients' lives, and it is no help to them if the social worker gazes open-mouthed at their personal revelations, adopts a condemnatory attitude towards apparently outrageous behaviour, or is salaciously inquisitive without an obviously helpful intent.
2. They like social workers who have self-evidently had the opportunity to learn about the clients' problems through their own life experiences. Clients criticise excessive youthfulness, naivety or a sheltered background in the worker; they are sceptical of how much help they can expect from someone who is childless or unmarried if their problems concern complex family dynamics; and, in some situations, clients definitely prefer a worker of their own sex.
3. They like workers who have specialised knowledge in respect of a client group – the disabled, the mentally handicapped and so on. A worker who is a jack of all trades and a master of none is not viewed with equanimity.

During the years of rapid growth in the social services (which lasted until the early 1980s) there existed a large number of young and inexperienced workers together with an organised trend away from specialisation which led briefly to a period of poor performance and low public esteem. This stage is now passed, and agencies can take greater care to ensure the availability of appropriately qualified and experienced staff wherever and whenever they are needed.

The social worker cannot help his age or sex, and all professionals have to begin their careers sometime! Nevertheless, the worker has a responsibility to have at his fingertips detailed, accurate and up-to-date knowledge about the law, welfare rights and local community facilities, and to be willing to turn for help to others in the agency if questions arise with which he feels inadequately qualified to cope.

It is not necessary for every worker to be a walking encyclopaedia, or experienced in every conceivable facet of client need, but he should always know where to find further information, and who to turn to for greater expertise.

Lesson 8: Always be trustworthy. Always be reliable

Clients frequently express appreciation of the moral goodness of social workers. They are not, in this, passing judgment on the worker's private life, but are referring to their experience of the worker's performance. Openness and honesty are seen as assets in social work. And any worker who lets a client down after building him up to expect something better is rarely forgiven.

The need for honesty is even greater in situations where the exercise of unwanted or unpleasant authority is called for. The parents of children in care are often hostile towards social workers, but there is evidence that, at least in retrospect, they are willing to give credit to those workers who confronted them with the reality of their child's – and their own – situation.

Conclusion

Social work has not emerged entirely unscathed from grass-roots criticism, but neither are the comments wholly negative. There are many expressions of appreciation and of pleasure in almost all the client-perspective studies. Even those concerned with wholly authoritarian settings, or those concentrating on unsuccessful cases, record interviews with clients who remembered individual workers with affection and respect.

There are quite clearly two component parts to the practice of good social work, as postulated by the client perspective research studies. First, the quality of the relationship established is a prerequisite of success: conversation must be easy; there must be friendly concern, commitment and trustworthiness; and the client must be able to feel confidence in the professional knowledge and ability of the worker. Second, the relationship must produce results. The worker must demonstrate an ability to provide help of a kind appropriate to the felt needs of the client within the restrictions imposed by society. The help should normally have a strongly practical (not necessarily material) component for at least part of the time, and must be offered in a way that does not undermine the carefully constructed 'professional friendship'.

It can be concluded that one of these qualities without the other is either not useful or is not social work, so far as the client is concerned.

3 Towards a Theory of Maintenance

There are a great many elements that contribute towards maintaining and developing a society and its people. Agriculture, industry, trade and commerce provide the wherewithal for material survival; defence policies and policing protect it; education lays the foundations for future growth; the health services ensure physical well-being; and so on. To an increasing extent – in both capitalist and socialist countries – the state plays a major part in pursuing policies which harness human and natural energies to meet social, political and personal needs.

An assumption in all societies is that, beyond statutory provision and within the framework of the wider social and economic community, individuals and families will maintain themselves, exist in relative self-sufficiency, and derive personal satisfactions from the way they make use of opportunities that are presumed to exist. The fact that these opportunities may be unequally accessible is a source of continuing political controversy in all nations, but the underlying assumption about the ultimate primacy of the human unit living his or her own life to the best of his or her ability is common to all communities.

Of course, it has always been recognised that some citizens will need to be looked after by others – hence the central role of the family throughout history. Social work has emerged in the twentieth century, and has developed as a major complementary force to compensate for deficiencies in the level of support that families can provide, to encourage them to do better, to protect vulnerable individuals against exploitation, and ultimately to provide total support for social isolates whose 'natural' support systems have collapsed or disappeared.

In future chapters, we shall examine and acknowledge the legitimacy of a number of roles that have, at different times, been accorded to social work, but it is the central theme of this book that they are all subsumed under a general theory of *maintenance*. Social workers are the maintenance mechanics oiling the interpersonal wheels of the community. They do so at the end of the spectrum where dysfunctioning has either reached chronic or epidemic proportions or where its effects are spilling over into the lives of vulnerable people.

They may use a variety of strategies, directive and non-directive, but their underlying aims are to maintain the independence of adults, to protect the short- and long-term interests of children, and to contribute towards the creation of a community climate in which all citizens can maximise their potential for personal development.

If social workers act as social control agents, they do so because, for some purposes, it is necessary to maintain stability in the social setting, the better to enable the client to thrive. If social workers operate therapeutically, they do so not to bring about magical change as though their clients were putty in the worker's hands, but to enable the client ultimately to assume a normal role of self-development, once freed of the encumbrances, restrictions or handicaps which prevent normal functioning.

The maintenance strategy is two-pronged – or rather it is concerned with the interface between the individual and society. On the one hand, social workers are employed by the state to curb some of the excesses of deviant behaviour; hence, the part they play in preventing non-accidental injury, in supervising convicted criminals, in arranging for the compulsory admission of mentally disturbed patients to hospital and in recommending the reception of delinquent children into care. All of these acts are intended to contribute to a smoother-running society, to *maintain* it.

But social workers are also concerned with ameliorating the living conditions of those who are finding it difficult to cope without help. Their agencies' objectives lead them to make attempts to improve the quality of life of conflicting married couples, out-of-work teenagers, handicapped housewives, terminally sick hospital patients. Social workers in such instances are striving, first, to hold the line, to prevent deterioration in performance, to combat the client's feeling that life can only get worse, and indeed, to do such work in the environment that will reverse any strong-running momentum that might make decline inevitable. Next, by their continuing contributions, they hope to reach the point where the client's own capacity for self-help begins to re-emerge, and where growth and improvement – and therefore *change* – become feasible. These are all acts of *maintenance*. Motor mechanics hope to produce improvements in the running performance of vehicles after a routine service; they aim to get the car back on the road after a breakdown. For most people, most of the time, the human way of life ensures self-maintenance; but for a minority, either because of defects at birth, deprivation during childhood, the onset of sickness or old age, the experience of an accident, the shock of bereavement or job-loss, or the ill-effects of political, economic or social planning or discrimination, self-sufficiency runs out, and the need for a maintenance mechanic becomes apparent. This need pinpoints the heart of the social worker's role.

The social worker is contributing towards the maintenance of society by exercising some control over deviant members and allocating scarce resources according to policies laid down by the state but implemented on an individualised basis. He is maintaining members *in* society by exercising control, by allocating resources, and by the provision of a wide range of supportive strategies designed to maximise self-respect and develop the abilities of individuals to survive and thrive under their own steam. These two approaches not only overlap, but, although they can be distinguished conceptually, are often difficult to disentangle in practice. For example, work with a problem family can involve pressure to get a man to work and careful surveillance to guard against child abuse while simultaneously there are warm friendly relationships between the worker and his clients. Part of the uniqueness of the social worker's role lies in his ability to handle simultaneously aspects of behaviour and relationship which, in the eyes of the naive, appear to be both incompatible and conflicting.

There is one other essentially controversial aspect of the maintenance role of the social worker, and that arises from the fact that the very idea of maintenance implies, indeed demands, a broad acceptance of the existing political and economic regime, whether that regime be marxist, capitalist or something in-between. We shall return to this issue in the last chapter because it lies at the heart of many contemporary debates in social work theory. But it is important to acknowledge at this stage that the idea of social work as maintenance is rooted in a reality-based view of contemporary existence for worker and client. There may be *some* problems in social work that do not have social or political or economic foundations, but it is easy to see that even such physically-based conditions as ageing, sickness, handicap and subnormality might present fewer difficulties in an idyllic socialist or Christian society in which competition were not the keystone to fortune and the weak were not pushed to the wall. The kinds of problems which come to the social worker's attention are a product of a political system, just as surely as is the method he uses for buying his house, the style of investment used to secure his pension rights, and the form of education available to his children. In other words, social work as maintenance is neither more nor less political in its complexion than are other aspects of everyday life or other forms of occupational activity. In any society, there are bound to be yearnings for radical or revolutionary reform, but such feelings are not *in themselves* to be identified with social work. Political agitators or conflict theorists may regret this; they may think that the greater exposure of social workers to poverty and degradation should lead them to be activists in the front line of rebellion; and there may well be circumstances in one society or another which ultimately persuade social workers that their role as the maintenance mechanics of that society is no longer defensible or sustainable. But, unless or until that happens, it is a fundamental precept of the idea that social work is socially sanctioned (that is to say, created by, paid by and allowed to operate under the aegis of the existing regime) that its employees, *as social workers*, acknowledge a broad acceptance of the legitimacy of the government. They may do this by consent within a democracy or they may do it under duress in a dictatorship – but the effect of their so doing is much the same in either case. The social worker may disagree with the government as a voter; he may campaign against it as a citizen; he may rise in revolt against it as an insurrectionist or freedom fighter – and, in each of these roles, he may find himself, in the polling booth, on the platform or at the barricades, arm-in-arm with erstwhile clients. The social worker may do all of these things, but, in doing them, I cling to the view that he is not practising social work.

However, although explicit political action is not in itself social work, an essential step towards the improvement of the social worker's maintenance role is for him to exert an influence on decision-making processes within his own authority and to negotiate improved conditions and additional resources to the extent that they impinge upon the welfare of his clients. Such maintenance functions might occasionally be carried out by the social worker as an individual, but they are more likely to be effective if they are carried out through the corporate strength of the department as a whole. It thus becomes essential for the social services or probation departments to ensure free lines of communication between grass-roots practitioners and influentially-placed administrators. The role of client pressure groups and professional organisations is also significant in this area, although the temptation for the professional associations to campaign primarily for their own members' interests rather than those of the clients appears to be difficult to curb or resist.

The role of the social worker in society can be represented quite simply in diagrammatic form, as in Figure 3.1. The social worker is concerned with maintaining each individual and society as a whole,

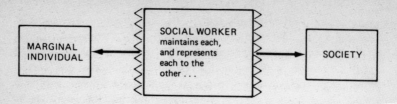

Figure 3.1   The role of the social worker in society

and with negotiating the interdependent relationship *between* each individual and society: it is a policy of reconciliation. The social worker frequently finds himself defending or at least explaining the laws of the land to a client who has offended against them or feels himself to have suffered from them; and the fact that the social worker's position in society is relative is illustrated every time the law changes or by observation of the different patterns of social work in different countries and within different legal systems. But the social worker also finds himself defending or explaining the behaviour or the plight of a client in the face of social pressure and public criticism. He has to reconcile marginal individuals to their social position, while simultaneously helping them to improve it; and he has to reconcile society to the existence of marginal groups while simultaneously working to secure improved conditions for them. It is this two-way process that makes social work a unique occupation, and goes a long way to explaining why, at different times, it comes under fire from both directions, but why it survives and generally retains the respect of both sides.

The existence and survival of social work is dependent, then, on two conditions: first, its practitioners, implicitly or explicitly accepting a consensus view of the state, must retain broad respect for the political and economic viability of their society and for its underlying political philosophy; and second, the state itself, as represented in particular in the governing class (whatever its philosophical foundations) must retain a broad commitment to a fair, just and humanitarian society, in which the rights of each individual, and especially of each most vulnerable citizen, are given due consideration. Whenever one or other, or both, of these prerequisites is missing, the consequences for social work will be far-reaching. On the one hand, social workers themselves will be divided, with some setting up in rebellion against a repressive state, and others aligning themselves with the oppressors of the individual, and so denying their basic social work identity. On the other hand, the state will begin to attack its social work services because of the way in which the social worker draws society's attention to the rights and the needs of oppressed minorities. An attack on social work is of necessity an attack on the vulnerable and to that extent, social work, like law, is a sensitive barometer of the social climate in a free society and of its concern for the deprived. The social worker, as an apostle of latter-day gradualism, emerges as a key figure in contemporary social evolution.

Maintenance and general care

In 1967, Peter Nokes, drawing on Max Weber, showed how the *general care* role in the welfare professions (as elsewhere in medical care, penal administration and school teaching) is undervalued and under-rewarded. He pointed out that the Walter Mitty ideals of being a doctor, a scientist, a concert pianist or an air pilot are an accurate reflection of where free ambition leads because of the attraction of such *virtuoso* roles. They have glamour; they enable the practitioner to demonstrate skills and to reveal distinctive know-how; they carry effective autonomy; they produce observable and measurable outcomes; they are characterised by being concerned with limited objectives, clearly specified; and they usually involve a degree of social distance which is institutionalised by occupational structures. It follows that any occupation which tends to be the reverse of these things carries low status. Nokes's analysis enables us to understand instantly why social work has been so anxious to emphasise its *change* perspective. Such an identity would not only take it in a quasi-medical direction (with the expectation of high status by association), it would give the social worker relative status vis-a-vis *other* general care staff – ancillaries, prison officers, nurses, home helps and their organisers, social security counter clerks. It is an essential part of my argument that the social worker's emphasis on a change perspective is not only unjustified and misleading (because of the relatively marginal nature of change as a virtuoso-type activity in social work), it is and has been counterproductive for the client. An insistence that *maintenance* is the true role for social work has the immediate effect of placing the profession back in the mainstream of welfare practice, of justifying equality of function between the various participants, and, above all, of establishing a springboard from which the general care role in society might come to be recognised as the crucial activity that it undoubtedly is. Social work may well have succeeded too well in espousing a decision-making, therapeutic role and turning its back on general care. Its achievement has meant that the possibility of upgrading care in the wake of social work's strengthened base has been lost because of the profession's determination to separate itself from those beneath it and to encapsulate its differentials in salary scales which merely reflect traditional patterns of social and economic discrimination.

Nokes concludes, gloomily, that 'general care roles are not generally admired, nor understood, nor do they attract theoretical interest'. But such a conclusion should not be regarded as inevitable, and it is more likely to be reversed if the social work caring task is recognised for what it is: a large-scale maintenance business, involving a variety of different occupational groups all with equally important contributions to make.

Underlying the problem are two aspects that, in themselves, need to be tackled. The first is the crude distinction that is drawn between maintenance and change – a distinction that we argue is wholly false for good maintenance work, in which, for example, the domestic staff in residential care can and do play an important part, will itself induce change. The second is the traditional sex, or sexist, distinction in which the virtuoso performer is thought of as the male, and the general carer as the female. Even if it were thought that there are personality characteristics in the sexes which produce such differences (a point obviously contentious in itself), there is no reason why the roles should have such different statuses. Indeed, again, it is more important to achieve recognition of the equal value of the two roles than merely to open up the virtuoso role to women, for that would not, in itself, do anything to upgrade the general care role, which is fundamental to the idea of maintenance.

Society's failure to recognise the legitimacy and the centrality of the general caring role has led not only to false trails in search of stages upon which virtuoso performances might be given, but directly to the reduced status of work with the elderly, the disabled and the mentally handicapped – groups for whom maintenance is obviously crucial.

All social work research has demonstrated the central position of caring in practice. Critical gatekeeping decisions and the occasional therapeutic group may attract public attention, but for almost all the clients of probation and the social services, and especially in residential care, it is the day-in-day-out routine that truly identifies the nature of social work.

If client change occurs, it will come only slowly, and often as the result of a long programme of selected inputs: social work is about removing obstacles, providing facilities, giving extensive verbal support, freeing the client's mind from restraining fears, opening up new perspectives, fighting for improved conditions, encouraging self-development, resisting decline in body and mind for as long as possible, and counteracting negative pressures whencesoever they may come. Such processes are an integral part of a caring approach, and have been employed time and again by ordinary social workers who have thereby earned the gratitude of the client. The yearning for an instantly observable breakthrough, a miracle cure, a revolution in attitude or behaviour is understandable but almost always illusory; perhaps it is important for social workers to believe that one day they will achieve it, just as every journalist yearns for a Watergate scandal and every pop group for a place in musical history. It may be necessary for personal motivation, but it is not necessary for good social work.

The objective of social work is maintenance, and if that were now to be accepted, a whole new programme of teaching, research and experimental development could be embarked upon to improve the quality of everyday performance. Let us consider now three areas which illustrate the argument.

1. The provision of active support for families

Family casework is the most traditional of all forms of social work, and it still plays a dominant part in both training and practice. It is obviously of critical importance in child care, but support for the family also often enters into the programme of work in probation and is a major contribution towards the provision of welfare facilities for the elderly and handicapped. There is some controversy over the right of the social worker to adopt a family focus in all cases. In probation, for example, there is occasional resistance from families to any active intervention by the officer on the grounds that the court order only gives him the right of access to the offender himself, and although limited visits are sanctioned, undue intrusiveness is not. Sometimes, during the entire period of a probation order, the personalities of parents or wife will remain quite shadowy.

Routine visiting to the elderly-at-risk is a major task facing any social services department, and it is a responsibility now generally delegated to ancillary staff – a policy which has largely re-established the pre-1971 model of operating an old peoples' welfare service. Goldberg (1978) has questioned the efficacy of professional surveillance of this kind, arguing that even quarterly visits (a frequency which would be regarded in many departments as unachievable) cannot really be expected to guard successfully against mishaps and misfortune. Much better, it is suggested, to establish neighbourhood groups, with volunteers playing a part, to keep a weekly or even daily eye on the really vulnerable elderly.

One field in which work with the family has been identified as being particularly crucial is that of the mentally handicapped. Moroney (1976) has argued that the presence of a mentally handicapped child is likely to affect family life quite seriously: it can lead to social isolation, reduce the chances of holidays or recreational activities, affect career opportunities, and precipitate serious housing and financial problems. Above all, it imposes a day-to-day strain that frequently reaches crisis proportions. Many studies have suggested that the kind of help currently given by social workers is insufficient to meet the needs of these families, and Moroney speculates that part of the problem may be that social workers have often been trained only to operate according to a clinical model, in which they concentrate on treatment and the reversal of problems. But the families of the handicapped (like those of the elderly) need a preventative and developmental focus.

> Many of the families who care for the handicapped are not faced with acute crises, rather they are normal families who are under pressure from long-term, chronic management problems. They require support and need to feel that someone is interested in them. They want someone to take the time to listen and to provide them with useful information. Finally they need relief and practical help.

A research survey in Avon (Butler *et al.*, 1977) revealed that a majority of the families of handicapped children had complaints about their local social services departments and social workers: there was not enough contact, the social workers were too young or too inexperienced, the system was too slow to respond to expressed needs, the workers had insufficient knowledge about available benefits or services, and the personnel changed too often. 'Social workers?', responded one mother, 'Awful! She hardly got over the doorstep and she said can you keep that child quiet. She was in it from self-glory.' Only 46 per cent of those reporting a major problem looking after a handicapped child at home said they had received any help at all.

What, then, should be the standards aspired to by social workers in the provision of support services for the families of mentally handicapped children?

1. Routine surveillance of a detached and occasional kind is not sufficient. Where there is real stress (and this also applies to other client groups, such as physically handicapped housewives and families in severely deprived circumstances), there exists a need for regular, reliable and warmly committed support of the kind pioneered by the Family Service Units. If the local authority departments can no longer provide this, then they certainly have a responsibility to devise strategies whereby it might be developed – either by voluntary societies, community volunteers or an organised system of network support. Without some such facility, community care for families in need is falling far short of the ideal.
2. Social workers must be knowledgeable about available facilities and services. If *they* do not have expert knowledge, it is difficult to know who should have it. They must develop their skills as the providers of useful information.
3. Youthfulness need be no disadvantage and it is certainly not a sin, but both training courses and departments have a responsibility to ensure that social workers have enough sensitivity and skill to be able to do a useful job with clients whose experience of the world often far outstrips that of a typical new graduate recruit to the social services.
4. Ways must be found to overcome the situation that prevails in some departments where work with the mentally handicapped is placed low on the list of priorities. Even where this is a justifiable administrative procedure in the face of political and economic pressures from other client-group areas, any spillover into staff attitudes must be avoided.
5. Interdisciplinary contacts with medicine and education should be developed, and social workers should become skilled at encouraging and enabling parents to learn the arts of structured teaching for their children. 'Quite substantial advances are being made by the application of systematic educational and behavioural methods, demonstrating that the abilities of mentally handicapped people have been greatly underestimated and that even the most profoundly handicapped are capable of learning in very small steps' (Mittler, 1979).
6. Parents must be drawn into partnership with the professionals.
7. Emergency residential care should be available when needed.
8. Social work involvement is essential shortly after the birth of a mentally handicapped child and before and after school leaving. Close liaison should also be provided with the special schools.

There is no client group which so clearly illustrates the contemporary dilemma of differentially allocating responsibility between society and the individual or the family. We expect those with problems – handicapped children, delinquent children, alcoholic members, the sick elderly – to carry the burden for as long as possible, and although the involvement of social workers and others in the provision of help for such families is partly a humanitarian commitment, it is partly (perhaps mainly) an economically sensitive strategy to *maintain* the family in the business of community care in the full knowledge that, should it break down, the costs to the state of residential provision will be significantly greater. Even so, as we have argued, the evidence suggests that the quality and extent of active support for burdened families is in need of radical improvement if practice is to conform to the normal expectations of a social work model.

Presland and Roberts (1983) have suggested ways in which a community and group work approach can be used with the families of mentally handicapped children. Operating over a four-year period, not according to a predetermined plan but in response to opportunities as they arose, they created a climate in which the parents of moderately handicapped children began to work together for their mutual benefit. They surveyed parents' opinions, increased the regularity of supportive visits to families, created an efficient maintenance network of parents, volunteers and professionals and set up a dialogue between the client group and the department which ensured a more responsive strategy.

On the face of it, parents' groups, summer playschemes, coffee mornings and encouragement to self-help are modest enough gains, but in a situation where they did not exist their introduction is a major step forward, and Presland and Roberts demonstrate the challenge to social work's flexibility in emphasising the critical importance of taking the lead in such initiatives and in maintaining them once begun. 'Even if problems cannot be removed perhaps we can help parents to feel that there are ways of adapting to situations – that might bring some comfort.'

2. The provision of fostercare

'We have reached the conclusion that almost every child, however handicapped, would be better equipped to face the adult world if growing up in a family rather than an institution.' This assertion by a council fostering organiser (Eaton, 1979) accurately reflects the majority view in the social services today, although there is a minority view – which received some support from the children who contributed to the influential client-perspectives pamphlet, *Who Cares?* (Page and Clark, 1977) – that a secure and stable base in a children's home is preferable to a fostering placement in which the child is unhappy, discriminated against, or unable to settle.

Fostering is our society's prime strategy for the provision of maintenance for children placed in the care of the council and there are significant signs that parallel steps are being taken to develop similar programmes for the elderly, the handicapped and those discharged from psychiatric hospitals. The system at its most modest, provides shelter, accommodation and food. Additionally it should give a warm and sensitive social environment in which the child can live as normal a life as possible. At its best, foster care gives a stimulus to development and growth, a framework within which disturbed and disruptive attitudes and behaviour can be, first, contained, and then countered in a fully therapeutic process.

The organisation of foster care is a large-scale business, and many departments have moved towards the appointment of specialist personnel. The backbone of a first-class fostering service is partly organisational and partly dependent on professional practice skills. The two qualities cannot be divorced from each other: good organisation is quite simply impossible without a practice component – it would then not be *good* organisation – and there would be nothing to practise on unless foster parents were identified and maintained.

Key components in the process can be described:

1. Publicity and recruitment are essential in order to find potential foster parents. Increasingly adventurous techniques are employed in a field where it is now accepted that marketing strategies are relevant. Radio, television and newspaper advertising and the exploitation of editorial opportunities are now commonly used, where a decade ago such an aggressive style was often deemed inappropriate.
2. Potential foster parents must be trained and prepared. From a situation where training and preparation were almost non-existent, most departments now recognise that they have a responsibility in this respect. The goals of one training course are listed as: providing basic knowledge; sensitising participants to situations which may occur; developing participants' self-awareness; helping them

understand the role of the agency and principles of good child care practice; developing a group identity with other foster parents and stimulating further learning. (Crowley, p. 29)

3. The aim should be to provide support for all foster parents, before, during and at the end of each placement. Foster families need to be maintained, just as they are contributing to the maintenance of children at risk.

4. Increasingly, foster parents themselves are being involved in the fostering process much more actively – through groups, newsletters, and so on.

The most exciting developments in recent years have been in the recruitment of professional foster parents who receive sums of money significantly greater than the modest allowances normally payable, and who in return accept children who would generally be considered unsuitable for fostering. The scheme was pioneered by Nancy Hazel (1980) and the Kent Social Services Department, following Hazel's recognition that some European countries had developed much more radical fostering policies than Britain's. In Sweden, for example, more than 80 per cent of children in care were fostered, compared with 40 per cent in England and Wales. Sweden used specialists rather than generic practitioners and the foster parent was given considerable autonomy and responsibility. (Hazel, 1976)

The Kent experiment was launched in 1975 and is widely regarded to have been a success. Recruitment was no problem; salaries for foster parents were generous, but the scheme still cost less than half the money needed to provide equivalent placements in community homes. There were four principles underlying the project – again all drawn from Swedish experience:

(a) *normalisation*: ensuring that any child separated from his parents leads a normal life in a family and community rather than in an institution;

(b) *localisation*: any child has the right to remain in his region of origin;

(c) *voluntariness*: the child and his family should always agree with the decisions except in situations which are either urgent or dangerous;

(d) *the right to participation*: the child and his family should participate in an active fashion in all the decisions which concern them.

Foster parents in the Kent project met fornightly and gained greatly from mutual support. Any applicant for fostering joined a group for two or three months and was assessed by the group – including themselves. Said Hazel, 'We lay down no guidelines for foster families. Nobody really knows how to assess them. Groups seem to be the best way of selection, and people discover for themselves whether they are suitable.' Children were referred by Kent's social workers; families and children were then seen by one of the project workers who emphasised that the foster care system was primarily working to reunite the original family, not to provide a substitute family. When a matching had been made, contracts were drawn up between the various parties involved – the child, his natural family, his foster family and the project workers – and the goals of the placement were established. The tasks to be undertaken were written down together with a forecast of the time needed. Hazel claimed that her project was providing more than storage in foster care – it was a form of treatment prompting optimism about its effectiveness (Knight, 1976).

A case example. Mary, aged 16, was in an adolescent psychiatric unit. She'd been in a variety of institutions since her early childhood and was said to be violent and uncontrollable. Her psychiatrist said she was schizophrenic and her behaviour had been 'stabilised' in the unit with drugs. Referred to the project, she was placed happily in a foster home and managed to hold down a part-time job. Mary complained that the drugs, which the psychiatrist had said would have to be continued, had unpleasant side-effects and made her feel worse. A second psychiatric opinion agreed that an effort could be made to wean Mary off drugs. This was successfully done over four weeks, and 'She is now back to normal, a happy, though not very bright, adolescent girl, far more alert and far more human,' says Nancy Hazel. She can be very rude, especially to her natural parents who opposed the ending of drug treatment, but she is never violent. After a year's fostering, Mary had changed so much that 'you wouldn't believe such a transformation possible' (Knight, 1976)

The success of the project demonstrates the critical difference between storage (or warehousing) and maintenance. The maintenance approach, though modest in its objectives, and always prompting pleasant surprise at such achievements as Mary's is positive, planned, and consciously strategic. It never implies resignation to failure, but always expresses a belief in the capacity of human beings to grow, given the right conditions and adequate and appropriate facilities.

3. Maintaining the elderly

The elderly are the largest single client group confronting social workers. Their numbers are rising all the time, both in proportion to other client groups and in absolute terms. Given their numerical importance, our knowledge about the services they need is exceedingly patchy, although the last ten years have seen a growing number of significant developments in practice.

The two prime areas for social work activity with the elderly are in the community and in residential care. The focus of community care is heavily geared to the provision of services which will preclude the necessity for residential admission. For example, for many elderly, the 'solution is to remain in their own home in an area familiar to them' for as long as possible, and social workers can facilitate this 'by ensuring that adequate day care services, home helps, meals on wheels, financial advice, counselling, support and adaptations are available' (Fellows and Marshall, 1979).

Although there are significant variations between authorities, the range of services available to old people is now considerable and adds up to a major programme of community maintenance. Day centres and luncheon clubs have made extensive use of voluntary help and community support: the local press is often extremely helpful in an area which is probably less stigmatised than most spheres of social work. Boarding out or fostering schemes have been tried, and Kent Social Services Department has reported an especially important initiative in its Community Care Project (Challis and Davies, 1980; Challis, Davies and Holman, 1980).

Recognising the need to strengthen the contribution of social work to the welfare of the elderly, a strategy has been drawn up in Kent intended to give field social workers more discretionary powers in their attempt to maintain old people in their homes for longer than has previously been possible. The policy hinges on money – both spending it and saving it. The aim is to improve the range of services available and so to postpone or even avoid admission to residential care where previously it would have been thought necessary. Each worker is given a budget per client with which they are able to buy-in services; this enables maximum individualisation of response to meet personal needs. The client is herself involved in decisions about the services required and the various helpers are recruited either by advertising, word of mouth or personal contact. Most of them are remunerated for each task performed, although the payments are at a level likely to be of symbolic rather than economic value. The programme lays heavy responsibility on the social worker who makes the assessment and then coordinates and develops the programme. Challis, Davies and Holman comment that

> the work draws on a number of aspects of social work: on elements of a casework model in achieving a successful assessment and on groupwork and community work principles in recruiting and sustaining local helpers in their caring role. It particularly draws upon specific knowledge of the needs of the client group in question and the available resources, formal and informal, for caring within the local community.

It is the aim of the Kent project to undercut the cost of equivalent residential care, and it claims to be doing so, but Armitage (1979) has warned that there is a point beyond which community care is *more* expensive than residential care: she estimates it to be when the community commitment to a client is in excess of six or seven hours service per day.

Conclusion

The critics of the theory of maintenance consistently misconstrue its intention. The model is neither static, nor pessimistic, nor limited in its potential for good. It can – indeed must – incorporate a commitment to raise the minimum standards of provision and performance.

There is a problem of attitude that is nicely illustrated by three quotations from Birmingham social workers (Black *et al.*, p. 163):

> I would say a social worker is a person who tries to help someone else with a problem they can't deal with themselves. And because as social workers you're given resources you can pass them on. You're a relieving service, not always a solving service.

> I'm trying to get people to cope as best they can with the situation they're in and get the most out of that situation.

> I see social work in very simplistic terms as supporting people and trying to change their environment . . . I accept that sometimes all I can do is to help them cope within the environment they've got even if it's a lousy environment.

These three accounts of work in hand certainly reflect a commitment to maintenance, but they also, in varying degrees, convey a mood of disillusionment or dissatisfaction with the role, or at least a sense of the social worker needing to defend its shortcomings. It may be that such an approach is not sufficient, and Black discusses the hazards of agencies trying to embark on more innovative and developmental work. But it *is* the core of the discipline, and all else follows from it.

Perhaps the word *maintenance* is at fault, with its connotations of work done on motorcars or washing machines or other inanimate objects. For no machine is like any human being. The whole point of providing maintenance in the human arena is that, once given, its recipient can always respond actively as a unique pro-active personality and can grow, change, develop, and interact. Human nature is such that it confounds any limited perspective.

The theory of maintenance is preferable to a central theory of change, because it better and more accurately reflects the true nature of the relationship between the client, the worker and the agency. If change occurs, it will do so because of the will of the client – not because of the magical effect of social work. To speak only of therapy is both to exaggerate the powers of the social worker, to overestimate the plasticity of the client's personality, and to risk denigrating the wide range of maintenance functions which, taken as a whole, properly characterise the nature of the profession.

The impact of an erstwhile if erroneous medical model in social work dies hard. Social work is not about curing, and failure to recognise that can lead to absurdities, such as the situation in which a department decides that it can no longer provide a support service for the families of elderly people in which all hope of a cure or improvement is said to be medically unachievable. Those are *precisely* the kind of families in which social work support is critically needed.

This chapter has provided three examples of mainstream practice which undeniably demonstrate the maintenance emphasis in social work: the provision of support for families, foster care and the care of the elderly. Corby (1982) has pinpointed the high degree to which social workers practise a form of maintenance with long-term clients, but he found that neither their training nor their theoretical assumptions had fully prepared them for the role. He says that practitioners need to be able to discriminate more clearly between maintaining or monitoring situations and intervening more actively, and he concludes that the social workers he studied both undervalued the maintenance role and lacked the techniques for intervention.

It is the argument of this book that such shortcomings reflect a chronic loss of confidence in the field of practice. It is not so much that one needs to *discriminate* between maintenance and intervention, as to recognise that maintenance is the goal, and an interventive strategy may often be the way of achieving it. In other words, social workers must be careful not to confuse maintenance with benign or passive neglect; the whole point of their occupation is that they should adopt an active stance when confronted with the needs, the fears, the vulnerability of their clients. There is a middle course between 'solving the problems of the world – or at least of the client and his family' – and 'doing nothing': it is a commitment to maintenance.

The theory of maintenance is neither simple nor yet as well developed as it deserves to be. In the next three chapters, I shall argue that it contains within it but supersumes elements of statutory and agency responsibility, a commitment to pursue change strategies, and the use of skills in pro-actively involving the worker in the community. Self-evidently and additionally it presumes a degree of personal and agency support for the client at risk. Because of the organic basis of human nature and society, the successful pursuit of a strategy which has as its goal the maintenance of society and its members will *necessarily* produce growth and a dynamic response. But this can only be so to the fullest degree in a climate which values consensus, not conflict – and to that extent social work and the maintenance model are not ideologically revolutionary.

Of course, there are many outstanding issues. How, for example, do you encourage independence in the client without being callous? How do you avoid inducing degrees of over-dependence which might waste scarce social work resources? And, especially in residential work, how do you prevent a premature decline into client passivity? How do you provide care while still allowing the stimulus of risk-taking behaviour in residents?

Such questions are to do with the psychology, the sociology and even the economics of maintenance, but they can only begin to be tackled once the model itself is agreed. The model may appear to be modest in its objectives, but in reality its acceptance would both legitimise much of contemporary social work and be a major step towards a more truly ambitious goal: the conscious and planned provision of general care facilities as a high priority for a compassionate society. We have moved more or less steadily in that direction for more than a century in the United Kingdom and social work's eager assumption now of a maintenance role would lead, not only to the political recognition of the importance of caring, but also to new and more positive approaches to applied social research and to far-reaching developments in the design of social work training and the structure of the profession.

4 The Achievement of Change

Nothing better characterises the disjunction between textbook idealism in social work and the real world of everyday practice than the concept of *change*. From the rent-collecting days of Octavia Hill through years of therapeutic commitment by the Freudians and post-Freudians, to the yearnings for conscientisation and social revolution: there have always been teachers anxious to imbue would-be social workers with an evangelical fervour to reform the client. The poor have to be educated, the children to be saved; egos have to be strengthened, insight achieved; criminal tendencies must be excised, marital conflict resolved; communities must be developed, residents led into battle; the deprived must be brought to full consciousness (education again), the depressed given renewed vigour to face the world.

And students have responded with a will. They want to see people change just as a gardener revels in the cycle of growth from the planting of the sweet pea seed in the spring to the cutting of the sweetly scented blooms in the summer, just as a parent glows with pride as the child's developing skills become manifest – in football, mathematics or music, and just as the sculptor experiences the satisfaction of seeing an artistic shape emerge from a slab of stone or a trunk of wood. Social workers are human, and they live in a society which praises achievement more than it values service; little wonder, then, that the temptation to regard the client as a seed to be cultivated, as a child to be encouraged and shepherded, as material to be shaped is too strong for many to resist. And it might, therefore, be thought unfortunate that much of the social work literature has consistently encouraged the social worker's potential delusions of influence by tending to concentrate on aspects of practice which confirm their currency. Casework texts have sought case examples which illustrate therapeutic effectiveness; advocates of radical practice choose clients who conform to their political interpretation of family conflict; and behaviourists concentrate on those more specific aberrations of human behaviour that lend themselves to a learning theory analysis. But empirical studies of social work practice have shown that such interpretations are at best half- or quarter-truths in any local authority or probation setting: in addition to the important client perspective accounts, detailed investigations of probation practice (Davies, 1974, Boswell, 1985) and of local authority social work (Goldberg, 1977 and 1978; Stevenson and Parsloe, 1978, Black *et al.*, 1983) have served to place the concept of change in perspective, and to show that too many writers on social work have made the unforgiveable error of confusing 'is' with 'ought': they have been so concerned to develop a model of instrumental intervention as they think it *ought* to be that they have paid insufficient attention to the real-life context of professional social work – how it *is*.

This is not to say that changes never occur – either in clients or in communities. 'Change is inevitable, change is constant', said Benjamin Disraeli; and the clients of the social services are no different from the rest of us: they experience stress, they grow older and more experienced, they have good and bad luck, they learn to avoid trouble or they plunge ever deeper into it; they have rows, they kiss and make up; they have fantasies and they see reality with brutal accuracy; they make love, or feel frustration; they become absorbed into a new social group, they lose their job or their husband or their children or their budgerigar. All of these daily events, involving as they do complex patterns of human and psycho-social interaction, produce change – for better or worse, and sometimes in the opposite direction to that which common sense might envisage.

Nor is it to say that social workers never do anything to bring about change. For example, the social worker becomes, to a greater or lesser extent, an integral part of the client's own social system – that conglomeration of people and groups whose interactions with him constitute his whole social life: his employer, his foreman and workmates, his friends, the police, the doctors and nurses in a hospital, his family, his landlord, the lodger, his pet dog, and so on – and as a participant in the environment, the social worker may well play an influential role in the client's decline or growth. Indeed there is one sense in which the social worker can and does have an enormous impact on the client: by effecting, or at least being a party to, his removal from home to an institution – an assessment centre, a mental hospital, a borstal, an old peoples' home. That, perhaps, is not what the textbooks normally have in mind when they write about the social worker's achievement of 'change', – but we know from the literature that those *are* the changes often most strongly associated with social work in the client's mind.

Many of those who come within the orbit of the social services inhabit such a 'turbulent field' of disruption and confusion that the addition of a social worker to it is no more than a further irritant in an already chronic existence. The social worker couldn't make it worse, because it couldn't *be* worse. But the research evidence suggests that there is little chance of the social worker making it better either; even the physical removal of the chronic client to a sheltered setting – which may well be the only feasible strategy – might fail because of the tortured state of the client's mind and the self-defeating, masochistic nature of his personal relationships.

Finally, of course, and, it might be said, contrariwise, there is evidence – limited evidence, but nonetheless evidence – that most (perhaps all) social workers do play a positive part in the lives of some clients by effecting beneficial change: some of the poor have been educated, some children have been saved; some egoes have been strengthened, some insight given; some marriages have improved with counselling, while other partners have been helped to face up to the inevitability of separation or divorce; some communities have responded to the leadership of a community worker; some of the oppressed have found new hope in spirited radical leadership; and some in the throes of depression have been helped to relish the dawning of a new day once again. But what is important is to recognise three facts. First, such *effects* are not the sole *raison d'être* of social work; they are an integral part of the maintenance objective, but only a part, and their significance should not be overestimated. Secondly, the changes achieved are not necessarily either permanent or complete, nor are they sometimes as effective as the client or his family would choose. Thirdly, although the social worker may facilitate change, the will and the determination to bring it about are the client's.

Changes do not normally come about as the direct result of a magical specific called 'social work'. They occur in response to a wide range of possible variables reflecting either the agency or the worker, or more commonly both together. The goals of practice are primarily determined by agency policy and the social worker's contribution is to work towards the achievement of those goals. In most circumstances, he could not make that contribution unless it were sanctioned by his employers. Thus any changes that occur in the client are agency-facilitated and possibly agency-determined. On the other hand, the personal style and professional skill of the worker are major components in goal-achievement. His approach to the job, his relationship with the client, are known to be key factors in securing a positive response and bringing about change. Nevertheless it is erroneous to think of the social worker as having more skills in social engineering than other similar occupational groups: trade union negotiators, school teachers, insurance agents, clergymen all need to achieve excellence in the use of interpersonal relations if they are to be good at their jobs. The social worker differs from them primarily in the identity of his work-base, and it is his work-base – the agency – which, through him, effects changes in the clientele and their circumstances.

What we see then is that the social worker is a professional agent of change only as one part of his maintenance role. Man is not so malleable nor his social circumstances so amenable to change as to be radically reformed by the mere intervention of a social worker, one who is, moreover, similarly dealing with anything from 10 to 100 other people or problems at the same time. Such changes as the social worker can prompt are best considered as contributing to the maintenance of the client and society – for maintenance in a living system, like man, implies continual evolution. Change in social work cannot be miraculous, instant, or magical, and the individual social worker is but a modest participant in a large number of interacting networks involving different clients. Within these, there are models of practice which are thought to be capable of influencing to some degree the attitudes and behaviour of clients and others, and there are models of practice which have been shown to have an impact on social groups and their intrinsic interactions. Although care must be taken never to regard any one of these aspects of practice as *the whole of social work*, they do nevertheless make an important contribution to it.

Ten strategies for achieving change

The achievement of change can be attempted in a variety of ways, and in the remainder of this chapter I will outline a selection of those strategies regarded as feasible in practice and thought to be effective to some degree – although in many cases their effectiveness is not proven and in some it is subject to serious empirical doubt. The first two strategies are basic to almost all community-based social work: counselling and environmental intervention. The remaining eight are a sample of others currently thought to be of some importance: they are by no means mutually exclusive, and some overlap significantly with others, but they are sufficiently separate to be regarded as different strategies.

1. Counselling

There are libraries of books devoted to counselling and there are numerous schools of thought, many of them led by charismatic figures like Carl Rogers. The traditional body of social work knowledge labelled 'casework' is primarily concerned with counselling activities, and almost all studies of social work in practice reveal the dominance of the one-to-one interview. Both Davies (1974) and Browne (1978), however, show that in statutory social work, counselling rarely takes a 'classical' or 'in-depth' form. It tends to be brief, often superficial, and geared either to routine maintenance or to the provision of practical help or guidance. Nevertheless both research studies also demonstrate that most social workers (at least, those engaged in medium- and long-term work) do use a variety of counselling techniques with *some* clients much of the time. Formal counselling is not a preponderant aspect of their working week, but it is a recurring part of regular practice.

There are many hundreds of possible examples of counselling as a medium for change, and, out of them, I will quote just three:

The Denver response to baby battering   Variously termed child abuse, non-accidental injury or baby battering, the phenomenon presents special problems to social workers brought in when a child is thought to be 'at risk'. In the United Kingdom, pioneering work has been centred, not surprisingly, on the National Society for the Prevention of Cruelty to Children. But the NSPCC was itself influenced by a clinic in Denver, Colorado, which trail-blazed a therapeutic response to child abuse, under the leadership of Dr C. H. Kempe.

The Denver unit emphasises the importance of *caring and intimacy* in its programme of therapeutic work with the parents of an abused child. A team of professional therapists and lay workers use a strategy of providing 'a corrective, nurturing experience' with the aim of encouraging the parents to seek their satisfaction from other adults rather than being child-dominated. In the first instance, the children must be removed from home, and efforts made to reduce any financial or other stress on the family. Ideally the therapists then work intensively with both partners. Immense time and energy are needed, and it is usual for the client to become heavily dependent on the therapist – so much so that the therapeutic role has to be played by a lay worker who can become a 'parent aide' with the task of 'befriending and mothering' each abusive parent. The aim is not to give insight, but to provide intensive support with a view to improving basic child rearing practices. 'The team observed that the majority of parents responded positively over time in the sense of being able to perceive and treat their children more realistically and less punitively.' (Jones and Jones, 1974)

The Midlands experiment in prisoner counselling   In British prisons, probation officers are available to provide a welfare service as needed, but they do not normally offer a long-term counselling facility. In 1969, in two prisons in the Midlands it was decided to experiment with the provision of regular interviews for prisoners for six months prior to discharge. Casework techniques were to be employed but no further restrictions on the theoretical approach were imposed. Most men had between 12 and 15 interviews and each one usually lasted for about 40 minutes – although some were considerably longer. The facility was appreciated by the men, and those who had received the counselling service were significantly less likely to be reconvicted during the two-year period following release. 'The findings indicate that as a result of their greater contact with welfare officers, the attitudes and behaviour of the experimental group differed significantly from the control group.' (Shaw, 1974) Unfortunately it was not possible to pinpoint the true reasons for this result – it could have been due to the content of the counselling sessions, or to the fact that these men simply received more attention from concerned people. Nevertheless the experiment is an important one and perhaps suggests that social work might be important for the way in which it can be used to counteract the damaging effects of imprisonment *per se*. The casework sessions in which the men were treated as people may have been important for improving their morale and so leaving them better prepared to cope with the stresses of society after they left prison.

A foster-care prevention programme in New York State   Almost all state welfare organisations would, other things being equal, prefer not to have to remove children from the care of their own parents, and one experiment in New York State was committed to the objective of trying to keep children at home for as long as possible rather than admitting them to foster care. In order to pursue the experiment money was made available to provide a 'more intensive service to families than is ordinarily available'. A wide range of provisions were on tap but the researchers concluded that counselling made by far the greatest contribution to progress in the sample. It was the workers' view that, however important the other services, they could not have been provided and would not have been of value, without the counselling relationship. The most important topics discussed between social workers and clients were:

1. parental functioning
2. parental behaviour or emotional adjustment,
3. the child's functioning in the family, and
4. the child's behaviour or emotional adjustment.

The experiment was a success and it is claimed that the provision of intensive counselling facilities significantly reduced the number of children who were taken into foster care, and so achieved substantial economies for the states (Jones, Neuman and Shyne, 1976).

The time has passed when it was always assumed that counselling had to be non-directive to qualify for the designation. Jones, Neuman and Shyne note that in the foster care prevention programme, one of the two dominant roles fulfilled by the social worker was to give advice, guidance and direction. And Sainsbury (1975), in his study of Family Service Units, notes that social workers did not hesitate to employ firmness when it seemed to be appropriate: 'Direct instruction and strongly worded advice were employed (for example) to get the house cleaned up, to prevent the abandoning of children, to get the rent or other debts paid and to get a man back to work.' But he emphasises that the ability of the social worker to be directive depends very much on his having established good working relationships with the client-family, and it is now widely accepted that Truax *et al.* (1967 and 1968) have successfully identified the major characteristics required in a counsellor if he is to work successfully with a client and help bring about improvements in the client's life-setting. The counsellor must have:

(a) *authenticity:* the conveying of genuineness, of being himself, as distinct from adopting a role in his dealings with clients;
(b) *non-possessive warmth:* the attitude of caring, conveyed by a friendly and concerned approach to the client;
(c) *accurate empathy:* the capacity to feel with those who seek help, so that the client feels understood; and
(d) *persuasiveness:* the giving of strong social reinforcements in a chosen direction.

There are, of course, a great many unresolved problems and issues concerned with counselling. Can the four identified qualities be taught and learnt? And how is it that the demand for and the provision of counselling facilities grows despite the accumulation of empirical doubts about its efficacy? For although I have quoted three fairly positive examples from the literature, the body of evidence overall is much more sceptical: it seems doubtful whether the counsellor is justified in regarding himself as a reliable agent of change under all circumstances.

2. Environmental intervention

In addition to conversing with clients in interviews, a great deal of a social worker's daily routine involves him in environmental intervention: phoning the job centre or the gas board, visiting a youth club, placating a neighbour, negotiating a grant, meeting a headmaster, discussing treatment with a psychiatrist, arranging a place in a day centre – all with the hope of making some kind of impact on the environment for the client's benefit. It is inconceivable that such functions should ever cease, but the extent to which, under normal conditions, they produce measurable changes in behaviour or circumstances should not be exaggerated. Two studies in the Home Office's probation research series emphasise the need for caution.

In the first (Davies, 1974) a retrospective study of routine casework practice found that environmental intervention – for example, helping the client to get a job, finding accommodation for him, mediating in family conflict – tended to take place in response to pressure from the probationer rather than as a planned treatment strategy, and rarely led to any long-term improvement. The author comments on a paradox that continually recurred in the study and that is illustrated by the problem of accommodation:

> Accommodation is a basic need for young men under supervision. Where those young men have sufficient ability to satisfy that need on their own account, the probation officer is only too glad to let them do so, although he will happily give them verbal support or advice if they appear to require it. Where the probationer shows signs of personal or social inadequacy, however, or where his general environmental condition is exceptionally bad, the officer can seldom enable the probationer to settle himself in medium or long-term accommodation; the whole sample (of 463 men) contains no more than six cases in which the probation officer recorded a positive achievement in placing his client in accommodation and in keeping him there for as long as six months.

Later, a specially designed experiment, IMPACT (Folkard, 1974 and 1976) created the conditions for intensive efforts to be made on behalf of clients in their environment, by reducing caseloads and requiring officers to concentrate on practical needs. The results were wholly negative so far as reconviction rates were concerned: the increased environmental support strategies did not have the effect of reducing the chances of these probationers re-appearing in court.

One major criticism of IMPACT is that the increase in the intensity of environmental intervention provided for was really quite slight, and that its negative results should not deter the social work services from pursuing developments in the use of groups, sheltered workshops, day centres and specialised accommodation over a lengthy period of time. If the aim is to produce more of a continuum of community care in order to avoid the extreme step of institutionalisation, then the rather haphazard and cursory approach to environmental intervention that has traditionally characterised social work will need to be improved.

For there to be any chance at all of change being effected, two prerequisites must be satisfied: there must be additional resources to which the social worker can turn in order to intervene successfully in what is inevitably a complex and turbulent environment; and the client's full cooperation and involvement must be secured if the strategy is to work. In other words, positive contributions must be expected, not just from the social worker, but out of the wider environment and from the client himself.

As we shall see in Chapter 6, the introduction of a 'Patch' philosophy in social work encourages practitioners to adapt their one-to-one counselling skills for use in the wider community, and to develop the use of networks of associates for the benefit of the client. Although Hadley (1984) is careful not to claim too much in the way of environmental gains, there is no doubt that such a strategic approach offers more scope than traditional reliance on the supposedly charismatic influence of the solitary social worker. Cooper and Stacy (1981) illustrate the point by describing how, in Normanton, 18 wardens for the elderly were allocated to patches of about 1,200 population.

They are responsible for organising care for any needy old or handicapped person in their patch and also to encourage the informal networks to help in this process. This should provide an effective early warning system as well as an encouragement of community care at street level. Already the scheme is showing that wardens are offering a contact point to people who would never normally consider they needed help and who have been struggling with serious difficulties.

In this way, the concepts of maintenance, change and prevention merge into one another – something that seems inevitable in the complex field of environmental intervention.

3. The use of structure and sanctions

The planned use of structure in social work depends on the practitioner's confidence in the validity and viability of his own performance. More, perhaps, than with any other aspect of practice, this confidence comes with training and experience, and fulfils the client's expectation that the social worker 'knows what he is doing'. Often, for example, in the simple business of helping the client to cope with everyday problems, the social worker who is prepared to sit down with him and, putting pen to paper, work out a sensible strategy for tackling them can hope to bring about modest changes in the client's ability to manage his own affairs.

Some aspects of agency practice involve more structure than others, and some clients are more likely than others to have the threat of sanctions held over them. Perhaps the most clearly structured innovation in recent years has been the community service scheme for offenders which is administered by the probation service. Empirical research studies have not been able to prove that community service orders reduce crime rates, but most of the parties involved in it – probation officers, work supervisors and the clients themselves – are enthusiastic about its value in society. 'There is much a community service order can do to rehabilitate the persistent offender – to create for him a situation in which a more accurate measurement of his potential as a member of society may be made. In the process, cure may occur, but that is a spin-off and not the primary aim.' (West, 1976) Community service can develop sensitivity to self and to others, teach the client to undertake tasks and complete them, and demonstrate that authority can be consistent and insistent without being destructive or cynical.

The critical components in community service orders as social work are:

1. The orders are explicit contracts, binding on both parties. 'Offenders know precisely what their obligations are, how long they

will last, and the nature of the work they must undertake.'

2. They are legal penalties with a punitive component, but a rehabilitative aim. The use of control and authority are an integral part of the process, but primarily, suggests West, because the social worker can thereby emphasise the centrality of the 'work currency' for the functioning, status and value of the adult male. Thus 'the community itself, rather than any mediating social worker, can *rehabilitate* the offender, re-invest him with dignity and put him on a proper footing in society'.

3. Because of the explicitness of the contractual and punitive component, there has been a greater tendency for probation officers to return offenders to the court on breaches of community service orders than is the case with probation orders. Research (Lawson, 1978) has shown that breaches of probation are both rare and inconsistent, and, although there may be occasions to justify leniency, all the evidence in child care and behavioural psychology would lead to the conclusion that a social work which threatens sanctions and then never resorts to them is unlikely to gain the respect of those it is trying to help. It is significant that most residential child care workers learn to recognise the value of consistency and structure, if life is to be tolerable for both residents and staff, and if the experience is to be beneficial for children whose earlier lives were themselves all too often characterised by threats and discipline unevenly and illogically distributed.

A different kind of structured setting has been developed by the Kent Probation Service in the Medway Centre, where, in the face of vigorous opposition from within social work, a range of projects has been established offering disciplined alternatives to custody and imprisonment and explicitly designed to 'prevent crimes involving gain and violence'. The Probation Control Unit is a radical development intended to provide a community-based option for adult offenders who would otherwise be sentenced to imprisonment. It requires 15 weeks of intensive contact of up to 48 hours a week, followed by post-unit supervision continuing for the remainder of the probation order. The Criminal Justice Act 1982 confirmed the appropriateness of building such a restrictive, semi-punitive requirement into the probation order. Attendance in the Unit involves a night-time curfew, weekly home-checks, evening activities and (if the probationer is unemployed) attendance at a Day Training Centre.

4. Behavioural methods

No social work approach falls so unequivocally into a chapter on 'achieving change' as behaviour modification. Derived from, and still closely linked with, the work of psychologists, behavioural methods have enjoyed varying degrees of popularity in social work over the years, and the 1980s see them occupying a leading position. This, as Sheldon (1981) has said, is not just because 'they are attractively tough-sounding at a time when this is in vogue, but because they are based on a steady accumulation of knowledge, derived not from armchair theorising but from solid research and rigorously conducted practical experiments.'

Behavioural methods involve the application of learning principles to specific behaviours with a view to reducing or eradicating problem behaviours and encouraging or reinforcing desirable behaviours. Clinical psychologists, of course, also use such techniques, but the lure of them to social workers is understandable both because of client need and because of the virtual impossibility of referring all such problems to specialist professionals.

They have been used in two main settings: mental health and child care. For example, Holbrook (1978) describes the technique as it was applied to a 9-year-old child displaying severe behavioural problems. As described by his mother, a typical day would begin something like this:

> There would be problems over breakfast because Christopher was faddy about food and eating a very restricted diet; most of the time he would eat only pancakes. He refused to use cutlery and his parents tolerated his using his hands to handle food in order to avoid arguments. There would be a tantrum over his going to school, and he would shout, kick and often have to be carried out of the house.

At school he was quiet but not progressing; he had no friends, and sometimes stole small objects. He tended to pull his hair out and the resultant bald patches 'made him look strange'. As a result of his behaviour, family life had virtually broken down.

Christopher was first admitted to hospital and then returned home. Behavioural methods were used in both settings, with his parents playing a key role on his return home. Casework techniques were employed simultaneously but three important behaviours were tackled behaviourally: the temper tantrums were controlled by 'time out' techniques (that is, by depriving him of pleasurable activities with absolute consistency); the use of cutlery was enforced by removing his plate, without scolding or fuss, the moment he reverted to the use of hands; the hair pulling was reduced by shortening his hair style. The treatment, though exceedingly costly in the use of staff-time, was regarded as highly successful.

Behavioural methods emphasise the importance of structuring a therapeutic approach, of concentrating on achievable elements within it, and of proceeding logically step-by-step towards clearly identified goals. The methods are particularly suited to work with phobics, and they have been employed with patients suffering from a stutter and other speech defects. Aversion therapy with alcoholics, drug addicts and sex offenders is a major area of work, although it is generally carried out under psychiatric direction rather than by social workers on their own initiative.

Behaviourism has been used in residential settings to good effect, but there are often organisational problems because of the need for a consistent approach towards the resident in order to ensure success, and that means involving *all* staff. Brown (1978) says that behavioural methods enable staff to concentrate on eliminating undesirable behaviours and developing new skills, often by the use of a 'token economy' in which good behaviour is reinforced by tangible rewards. Barlow (1978) is clear about the advantages of such an approach in his youth treatment centre at Glenthorne: it enables the staff to achieve a framework of care, control and consistency; it focuses on the present rather than the past; it offers some hope to young people whose past has been chaotic and traumatic and to staff who have to try and pick up the pieces.

Moreover, Barlow argues, far from being alien to a social work philosophy, a behavioural approach concentrates on small improvements, rather than changing the whole person. And it offers some protection for the child's rights: 'Any behaviour under question has to be scrutinised and the reasons for our intervention justified in very precise terms.'

Vevers (1981) has described how disruptive behaviour in a children's nursery was reduced by rigorously imposing a system of 'time out' and rewards on a single child, and Harris (1981) has recounted ways in which goals can be set for the residents of mentally handicapped hostels with a view to improving behaviour:

1. The client should participate in setting the goals;
2. The client's strengths and needs should be listed;

3. Goals should be reached by a series of small steps;
4. It should be made clear who is doing what, and when.

The advantages of this approach were said to be fourfold: client's skills did improve; clients benefited because they were given constructive personal attention; staff communication improved; the method related to the business of ordinary day-to-day living, and thus made sense.

There remain some vigorous opponents of behaviourism as a contributory discipline to social work, but its advocates in recent years have adopted a pragmatic, non-doctrinaire approach which has helped to strengthen its position. Its emphasis on objective clarification, evaluation, role clarity and a structured style of working which makes sense to the client are so obviously preferable to the vague virtues of 'doing good by stealth' that its contribution is certainly likely to grow. Sheldon puts the case in admirably balanced terms:

> In advocating that social workers should take behaviour modification more seriously, I am not arguing that they should be blinkered by it. Social workers cannot be just therapists – whatever their persuasion. An ability to work together on community projects, a knowledge of welfare rights, and certain personal qualities are among the many other skills and attributes necessary. However, when social workers do find themselves involved in counselling work, or making plans to change someone's behaviour, then there is very considerable evidence in favour of an approach based on behavioural principles.

5. Social skills training

Social skills training is a direct spin-off from behavioural methods: it uses similar underlying theories and requires the same specificity in goal-setting, contract agreement and consistency. It is concerned not so much with restricting undesirable behaviours as with overcoming deficiencies and enabling the client to survive, and even thrive, in his everyday environment. Given the fact that many studies have shown how frequently social and personal inadequacy are core elements in the problems presented by the social worker's clients, it is not surprising that practitioners have been enthusiastic about the possibilities of this approach.

Three examples drawn from the social work literature describe the use of social skills training with a group of sex offenders, with a depressed woman and in a hostel for the mentally ill:

1. Burgess *et al.* (1980) set up a skills training group for six sex offenders held in close confinement (for their own protection) in prison. They were all seen as anxious and inadequate men: 'The basic criterion [for admission to the training group] was social incompetence. Those who appeared overly submissive, who spoke quietly and diffidently, whose posture was withdrawn, who either stared or avoided eye contact, or had difficulty conversing, were given priority.' The skills training programme 'focused on five "micro" components of social behaviours: eye contact, voice, use of hands, posture and facial expression, and on incorporating these into the situational dimension of the social skills.' Three therapists engaged in structured role plays and modelling in an attempt to improve client performance. The kind of situations tackled in this and similar programmes with other offenders have included:

   (a) how to handle job interviews (including the development of scripts for coping with the inevitable and awkward questions of how to account for missing stamps on an insurance card);
   (b) how to handle aggression without temper-loss;
   (c) how to ask for help from a probation officer;
   (d) how to talk to an unhelpful landlady;
   (e) how to relate to an unknown person of the opposite sex;
   (f) how to resist pressure to engage in crime;
   (g) how to claim your rights at the Supplementary Benefits Office.

   In their study, Burgess *et al.* claim that worker assessments made before and after the programme showed improvements in specific behaviours, but no information was available on whether these were maintained or generalised into other areas of everyday life.

2. Cree *et al.* (1979) describe a skills programme designed for a 22-year-old woman, Heather, with a psychiatric history and current depression. During the joint worker-client assessment, Heather identified as particular difficulties her lack of social relationships and her loss of interest in recreational activities. It was agreed that she and the worker would concentrate on improving her conversational skills as a first step. Exercises were employed to develop both listening and speaking skills, and interviews were so structured by the social worker that the client was required to take

the initiative, so using the occasion to practise the art of conversation. Progress was rapid after initial difficulties, and Heather was then directed to begin to employ the same arts with friends. 'She recounted with delight the first time she found herself alone with a relative stranger when visiting a friend and, although terrified, sustained a ten minute conversation while her friend made coffee.'

3. Scott (1982) recounts how he and a colleague set up a social skills group in a hostel for people who had all been diagnosed schizophrenic and who had spent a year or more of their lives in a mental hospital. He claims that the method seemed particularly suitable for them, since chronic schizophrenic clients probably show the most extreme deficiencies in social skills and he argues that, in order to make them acceptable to the community, they need to be adequately prepared in communication skills.

The project consisted of nine sessions which included relaxation and trust exercises, but focused chiefly on practising how to initiate a conversation and keep it going. Evaluation of the exercise led to the conclusion that the more intelligent members of the group improved markedly in non-verbal and attending skills, but that complex verbal skills proved elusive. Scott says that, although they provided some assertion training (that is to say, 'being firm when someone has done wrong to you'), the workers felt that the programme would have benefited from more.

Skills training can be carried out in a number of different ways, but Scott's project illustrates a good range of approaches and demonstrates the need for planning and structure.

Index cards summarising the contents of each session were given to group members about an hour beforehand, partly to allay fears. The leader started each session by *modelling* a particular social skill, then indicating how it was in keeping with what was on the index card; then the modelling was *repeated*. One of the group would *role-play* the same scene. *Feedback* was provided on the client's role-play, being as *specific* as possible: for example, 'The questions you asked really showed that you were interested in what she said.'

Feedback included *praise* wherever possible, and poor performance was followed by *constructive advice*: for example, 'How about looking at her during the conversation next time?' Following the feedback, the client *re-enacted* the scene once more.

Homework was given, requiring the client to practise the lesson in real life. They were expected to make a commitment for the coming week: for example, 'I will initiate a conversation with two strangers.' The next session began with a *review* of homework. Later, attempts were made to achieve *transfer* of the learning to the real world by taking the clients out or simulating external reality.

In any spell of social skills training, considerable encouragement, repetition and reinforcement will usually be needed if the new improved behaviours are to become permanent and transferable to different situations. Cree *et al.* are probably being optimistic when they say that the method, which in their case was based on weekly meetings over a period of a year, is little different from normal work in its demands on time and commitment. Indeed one characteristic of all structured change strategies is that they almost certainly require investments of energy and involvement which are unusual in contemporary practice. If they get the results that are sometimes claimed for them, however, the time might be considered well-spent.

6. Task achievement

Task achievement methods again concentrate on specificity of aim, contractual agreements between worker and client, and a concentration on achievable goals. The main difference from the social skills training model is that it does not involve the social worker in a training role (although the two approaches are of course entirely compatible with each other and may be used in tandem).

Goldberg (1977a) has reported on a small project in Buckinghamshire Social Services Department where a task-centred approach was tested. Clients were invited and helped to carry out problem-alleviating tasks within agreed time limits. Particular attention was paid to clients' *own* conceptions of their problems, and the method had five phases:

1. Problem exploration, in which the client's problems were identified and placed in rank order.
2. Agreement on the target problem.
3. Agreement on action: What was to be done to alleviate the problem? How were the tasks to be formulated? Agreement was reached on how much time the social worker would devote to working with the client on task achievement.
4. The social worker directed techniques and strategies towards bringing about the achievement of the task by the client. No precise

method was specified. Imagination, spontaneity and creativity were required, but the precise focus had to be maintained, and this could lead to a relatively directive approach.

5. Because time limits were set, the time for termination was known throughout. In the last interview, a review of the problem was carried out, and an evaluation made of the effectiveness of the client's efforts.

In the Buckinghamshire study, 23 fully task-centred cases were identified, and tasks were either substantially or completely achieved in 15 cases. Goldberg reports enthusiasm for the method among social workers, although it was found to be applicable in only about one-third of agency referrals. The workers 'felt strongly that the model enhances respect for the client, stresses the client's equality, and helps to demystify social work by clarifying the social worker's role.'

> *Case example:* Mrs I., middle-aged divorcee, was referred by the GP suffering from hypertension and back pains. She admitted to having financial worries. The allowance she received from her ex-husband was too low, but because he was a chronic invalid she felt unable to press for more. Her son paid her only a small sum for bed and breakfast, and she supplemented her income by many hours of dressmaking, for which she charged very little. The task agreed was 'to find ways of improving her general financial position while the social worker would try to meet some specific debts'.
>   First, Mrs I. was to ask her son for an increased contribution; he willingly agreed. Secondly, the social worker was to seek a grant from a voluntary agency; this was successfully accomplished. Thirdly, Mrs I. was to seek advice on realistic charges for her work; by the fifth interview she had the information, and raised her prices accordingly. The financial strains were eased, and her health improved. In review, Mrs I. was clear that the partialising process had been invaluable and expressed appreciation of the social worker's understanding role.
>   (Abridged from Goldberg, 1977a)

A successfully administered experimental study in Southampton found that a task-centred social work approach could be employed with just over half of a sample of parasuicide clients in a hospital-based department. In controlled comparisons, it was found that the task-centred treatment had positive effects on clients' social and interpersonal problems and led to a reduced dependency on psychiatric services; it was also found that the clients were significantly more satisfied with the service they had received, compared with the 'normal' service. However, on the critical and central question of whether the task-centred approach reduced the likelihood of further suicide attempts, the researcher reported wholly negative findings: there was no difference between the experimental and control groups. (Gibbons, 1981)

Gibbons, however, is quick to emphasise that the experiment should not be regarded as a reason for abandoning task-centred methods. It strongly suggests, she says, 'that social work intervention can produce encouraging improvement in clients' immediate social situations and morale and is much appreciated by them. "Effective" social work achieves modest (from a social policy perspective) but important (from an individual perspective) objectives.' The important thing is to be clear about one's objectives.

7. Self-help groups

Self-help groups are notoriously vulnerable. The typical group is started by one or two energetic, charismatic figures and collapses when they withdraw, exhausted, or move away for work or family reasons. (Crine, 1982)

Such is the reaction of many social workers to the idea of self-help groups; others recoil from the untidiness and amateurishness of vulnerable clients struggling to further their own interests without direction from the welfare professionals. Nevertheless it is now generally recognised that self-help groups are not only therapeutically valuable, but represent an important element in the community orientation of social work.

Probably the most common examples of self-help groups have been found in the probation service with prisoners' wives groups, and in local authorities with foster parent groups. In each case, it is normal for the social worker to take the initiative and bring together a number of potentially interested members. Often the groups are primarily talking shops and, although mutually supportive discussion *is* a form of self-help, it has usually proved difficult to encourage them to aspire to more ambitious objectives. Other examples are to be found in community action with social workers being instrumental in encouraging and enabling a variety of self-help initiatives. In South-East London, a 'Patch' team in Lewisham has seen a housing estate in Honor Oak take on a wide range of self-help functions with social work encouragement: mothers and toddlers groups, womens groups, pensioners clubs, and a community transport scheme.

At first sight there is a logical inconsistency in any *self*-help group being prompted or initiated by a professional social worker. Levy (1976) has defined self-help groups in five ways: their *purpose* is to provide help and support for members; their *origin* rests with the group members themselves and not with some external agency; the *source of help* is to be found in the members' own efforts, skills, knowledge and concern (where professionals do participate, they do so at the pleasure of the group, and only in an ancillary role); the group's *composition* is of members who share a common core of life experiences and problems; the group will be *controlled* by its members, although they may seek professional guidance.

Such a definition would preclude the social worker from launching self-help groups, and the need for caution is further emphasised by the fact that many of those who turn to self-help often claim to have had unhelpful or unpleasant experiences of social work. Alcoholics Anonymous has claimed that its approach is superior to 'the overtone of parental disapproval and discipline' that it senses in professional helpers, and one of the best British examples of a successful self-help group, Chiswick Women's Aid, says that it came into existence *because of* the failure of social workers to satisfactorily meet the needs of battered women.

Glassner and Freedman (1979) pinpointed the difficulty when they say that 'professionals find it difficult to be "peers", rather than "experts", unless they fit into the focus of the group (as when an alcoholic physician joins AA)'. It is perhaps significant that the founder of Chiswick Women's Aid, Erin Pizzey, though not herself a battered wife, has said that she was powerfully influenced by her vivid childhood memories of the atmosphere of violence which pervaded her own home.

To insist on such a clear-cut separation is, however, too restrictive. The social worker needs to employ a high degree of professional sensitivity: where self-help groups already exist, clients can be told about them and encouraged to attend, and, despite Levy's restrictive definition, professional encouragement to a group starting up, if handled with sensitivity and humility, is often of immense value and greatly appreciated. 'She gave us the confidence to believe we could do it,' commented the members of a parents self-help group about a social worker. And in another instance: 'She gave us moral support at a time of crisis, although she never came to our meetings.' (Brimelow and

Wilson, 1982) Social workers can offer practical resources, information and advice, and they can give groups credibility to help them to cope with opposition from departmental officials.

On the other hand, if the social worker assumes and retains a leading role in the group, then it will be prevented from being or becoming a true self-help group, and its members will be thrust into a dependent role of an inappropriate and perhaps unwanted kind. Brimelow and Wilson (1982) argue that the attitude of the worker is crucial. Those social workers most successful in maintaining the 'sensitive balance between offering constructive support and taking over the group' believed in the intrinsic value of self-help and in the capacity of members to organise their own affairs. Workers expressed this in different ways: 'It's important for people to do things for themselves'; 'A bunch of clients together may be much more effective than a professional'; 'They are the experts about their own problems'.

> The effective workers saw their role as complementary to group members, and described the relationship as one of partnership, in which worker and members had different roles. Even if they played a significant role in starting a group, they saw their role as facilitators, helping to bring people together and provide back-up support. (Brimelow and Wilson, 1982, pp. 12–13)

Do self-help groups work? It depends, of course, on what one means by 'work'. To any one who has observed them in operation, there can be little doubt that they are a key element in the maintenance and improvement of morale and the will to survive. Whether they are therapeutic in a narrower sense is, as always, more problematic. It is generally accepted that the best-known of them, Alcoholics Anonymous, has been more successful in its approach than has any other strategy for the cure of alcoholism. Whether this is due to the 'selfness' of the help or to the rigorous and ruthless use of shaming techniques and group discipline is, however, not clear.

8. Social advocacy

Strategies of change in social work might sometimes need to be directed, not at the client, but at dysfunctional elements in the client's environment. In her study of an intake unit, Corney (1981) found that the majority of clients coming to a social services department for the first time wanted some form of advocacy from the worker. More often than not this would involve contacts with local authority departments, but the DHSS and voluntary agencies were also involved.

Advocacy in social work can be either personal or structural: that is, it can either focus on the needs of a particular client or it can take up cudgels on behalf of an entire community. In either case, the assumption is that the social worker has skills and qualities or access to resources that are likely to tip the balance in the favour of those whose interests would otherwise be overlooked or overriden. Kahn (1972) has identified the qualities that make for a good advocate in social work: he is likely to be a natural leader with a strong personality and expertise in his subject; he will be knowledgeable and have his facts right; he will be politically adept, knowing which are the appropriate leverage points to bring about change; he will be known for his professional integrity; and he will be capable of presenting his client's case forcefully and efficiently. Kahn found that workers needing to have constant recourse to team meetings or to consult with colleagues did not make good advocates: the practitioners of sound advocacy programmes were found to be more self-reliant and autonomous than other social workers.

How might a social worker be drawn into advocacy? Many instances are likely to involve accommodation crises or financial problems: the worker acts on behalf of a harassed mother in a face-to-face confrontation with a housing manager or landlord wanting to evict her and her family for non-payment of rent; or he speaks up for an ex-prisoner whose boss is threatening to sack him because he has found out about his convictions. In each of these cases, the social worker's intervention, if successful, will have a significant impact on the client's welfare – at least in the short term.

Structural advocacy is probably less common in routine social work, but most practitioners are likely to engage in it at some stage of their careers, and many will see it as a major aspect of their agency role. The social worker – probably operating within a group, and drawing on supplementary help, perhaps from students – might carry out a survey in his local community and, using the results obtained, set out to persuade the relevant authority, for example, to provide more play space for youngsters, to improve the quality of its housing stock, or to run a better transport system. Another social worker, because of his intimate knowledge of client-group deprivations, might make an organised and persistent attempt to persuade national charities like MIND or Age Concern to establish or sponsor improved local facilities.

There is some controversy over the extent to which structural advocacy is a legitimate activity for all social workers and any kind of advocacy can undoubtedly lead to delicate situations because of the statutory social worker's position as an employee of a politically managed local authority. However, although the nature of the boundary between social work and politics will always be imprecise, it is certain that an advocacy role for the social worker will remain valid.

9. Developmental perspectives in social work

The developmental perspective involves exposing the client or the resident to new, perhaps challenging and even risky experiences. In intermediate treatment (IT), for example, children whose horizons have been limited can be taken on adventure trips to the sea or to the mountains; mental patients with a long history of institutional containment can be placed in domestic situations where they have to learn how to cope with the demands of cooking, budgeting and social cooperation; and old people in residential care can be encouraged to walk out to the shops, go on buses to the town and even play wheelchair sports. The assumption underlying these tactics is that all human beings have innate strengths which not only enable them to cope with limited stress, but which, when encouraged, produce responses that are in themselves beneficial and growth-producing. Although the model is closely associated with a social work philosophy of individualisation, its efficacy has never been effectively tested, and it is known to carry with it some dangers: the child on an exciting IT course in the mountains of North Wales may find the ordeal too threatening for him and so have his feelings of inadequacy confirmed, or he may return to the humdrum world of his urban home disillusioned and embittered by the glimpse of something better; the institutionalised mental patient may break down under the strain of coping with everyday life and have to be re-admitted to hospital; and there is evidence to show that old people in homes which encourage independent activities have a higher incidence of broken limbs and consequent admission to long-term stay in hospital.

The use of developmental models in social work is still at a very early stage but it offers a major field for research and experiment, with a wide range of questions to be explored. For example:

1. How can developmental perspectives be employed with different client groups?
2. When, and under what circumstances, are they inappropriate?

3. What resources are needed to facilitate them?

10. Therapeutic models in residential care

Balbernie (1966), Bettelheim (1950), Wills (1967), and Winnicott (1964) are all practitioners in residential child care who have attempted to formulate their ideas about therapeutic intervention and present them on paper. It is not enough, they say, to provide shelter in a children's home, not enough to give meals and friendship, for many of the children in care have been damaged by faulty upbringing, disturbed by anguished social and family relationships, deprived of the kinds of infantile and childhood experiences which other children can take for granted. Therefore, such children have to be *treated*, to be assessed and diagnosed and appropriate programmes outlined and provided: only thus will they be helped to mature normally.

Dockar-Drysdale (1968), writing about the Mulberry Bush School, has formulated as precise a therapeutic model as anybody. She describes different kinds of children, all of whom have experienced a break in the mother-baby unity during their first year of life and who have been unable to make up for the consequential damage. In different ways, she says, these children need to live in a residential setting which will facilitate their regression to a point where they are enabled to enjoy primary experiences of a kind which have hitherto been missing from their lives. 'There is no question of ego support' during the treatment process. The illusion of unity between therapist and child must be pursued in the same way as there is an illusion of unity between mother and child immediately following birth. Only when they have experienced this illusion will they be able to tolerate the inevitable disillusion that must follow.

Dockar-Drysdale argues that it is the job of the residential children's home to provide the illusionary experience and it must be done over and over again for each new child who arrives. The task is one which, it has been recognised, presents formidable problems of staff management, especially when the home is a part of a large social services department. The crucial need is not to lay down standardised responses to all children, but to be alert to the individualised needs of each, and then to respond consistently and without hesitation. This might involve the holding of a child's hand, the warm cosseting of another, the provision of specially requested foods, condoning theft from the larder, responding to personal requests and idiosyncracies.

Many residential settings employ therapeutic models implicitly, although they are rarely so thoroughly founded on theoretically argued principles as those employed at the Mulberry Bush. Unfortunately, the empirical evidence about their value is not strong, although the way in which they emphasise the individuality of the residents, and the organismic nature of the institution are very close to social work ideals.

Moreover, it is at least possible that any effects achieved under given therapeutic regimes may be due as much to the Truax and Carkhuff variables (genuineness, empathy and warmth + persuasiveness) as to the theoretical validity of deliberately planned programmes of intervention. This comment could apply even to the notion of a therapeutic community (in which residents/patients are as much the treaters as the treated), for it might well be that such an approach succeeds because of the way in which it produces practically effective personality characteristics in the members of the community as a whole.

Conclusion

Nothing so illustrates the confused state of knowledge in social work as a discussion of the concept of change in practice. There are at least four elements involved in such a review:

1. *Empirical evidence:* The empirical foundations of social work practice have proved exceedingly difficult to establish. While lip service has been paid to the importance of research, almost all developments of any significance in the field have been based more on pragmatism and politics than on positivism. The main contribution of research has been to introduce a sceptical note to counteract managerial or professional enthusiasms; it is a foolish man now who would speak too easily of social work's capacity to achieve radical change, no matter how the task is attempted. Reid and Hanrahan (1982) however, have said that a structured approach to therapeutic aims does have the backing of empirical support.
2. *Practice theory:* Social workers draw on their knowledge of the psychological and social sciences and their experience of similar situations in the past to decide how to act in specific circumstances. They may not always be able to locate the theoretical origins of their actions, but that they do exist is quite clear (Curnock and Hardiker, 1979).
3. *Conventional wisdom:* Very little is known about conventional

wisdom in social work – the practice of 'doing things' because that's the way they've always been done – but the suspicion is strong that its effects are powerful. We know, for example, that conventional wisdom varies significantly from one agency, one office, one home to another, and that, although leadership is obviously a factor, the traditions often outlive each generation of participants (Takagi, 1969).

4. *Fond expectations and personal ideals:* The motivations of social workers are important – whether they are, as Pearson (1973) has suggested, salving their consciences in a materialistic society, or rendering themselves capable of surviving the inevitable stress of living in residential settings. Social work has always had its idealists, its visionaries, its prophets and its believers in the millenium: salvation might come through psychoanalysis, revolution or organisational efficiency – but that it *will* come is not by some people doubted.

Whichever framework is adopted – and it might be a combination of any or all of them – there is frequently an underlying assumption that change is a legitimate, even a necessary, objective. The yearning for change is a long-lasting element in man's psyche: the desire for miracles to reverse the inexorable onset of illness and the decline of human faculties, the longing for beneficent influences to counteract evil forces, and the feeling that because life is a rearguard action against death, the ability to 'change' people is a welcome proof of one's own superhuman strengths. Social work is operating in this most emotive of human areas and the temptation to proffer solutions and elixirs is always great.

It is impossible to deny the occasional legitimacy of a change-objective, though to embrace it too enthusiastically must be to invite disappointment and disillusionment. Conventional wisdom is unlikely to offer much reliable guidance. Idealism might inspire a response, and if the goals are relatively modest, lead on occasions to success; it may also be a necessary morale-booster in some spheres of social work. Practice wisdom is probably more at ease with modest expectations, and despite the setbacks and the shortcomings of research to date, the scientific optimist in me has to conclude that only empirical study and theory development can ultimately hope to improve the performance of social work in respect of achieving change.

However conventional wisdom and fond expectations can only be discarded, if at all, when empirical research does two things: it must demonstrate the inappropriateness of current practice; and it must suggest – and justify – a viable alternative. Unfortunately, to date, research studies, while drawing a number of conclusions in the first area, have been notoriously weak in the second. Behavioural psychology has contributed a little in highly specialised areas, but sociology – which has been active in undermining present practice (especially in casework and counselling and in all attempts at achieving change) – has been exceedingly disappointing in its prescriptions. The problem for sociology is that its subject matter – the framework of society – is highly complex, unpredictable and yet conservative. Hence strategies of change are necessarily structural/political, and the place of the social worker in them either problematic or irrelevant. Two of sociology's proffered solutions – radical non-intervention and the resort to revolution – are antagonistic to social work *per se*, while a third – the use of networks and community intervention – is relatively undeveloped. It has not been subjected to the same kind of analytical investigation that has been applied to casework over 40 years, and given the vagueness of many change objectives in the community, empirical evidence would almost certainly be hard to come by.

Significantly it is a social scientist whose entire career has focused on social work who has produced some of the most stimulating research material in the field. Thorpe (1982) has clearly demonstrated that intermediate treatment (IT), intended to be both therapeutic and benevolent in its effects, has more often than not been neither. After its introduction, he argues, the commitment of young delinquents to institutions soared – the very opposite of what was intended. Although the launch of IT was well-intentioned, it led to an immense growth in the target-group for intervention and to a phenomenon of penological drift – offenders being 'sucked into' the institutional system simply because they had become more visible to the critical decision-makers. From there, the future would hold for many of them only a life of crime and punishment, as a direct result of the therapists' preventative intervention.

However, Thorpe, instead of detachedly leaving his critique there (as tends to happen in sociology), goes on to emphasise the importance of social work learning the lessons of his investigations. We must be much more specific about our target-group and about the problems we focus on with a view to bringing about change. Just because a child has committed a minor crime is no reason for subjecting him to the full panoply of welfarist responses – especially if it leads to him being admitted to care on grounds which, *if he had not committed a crime*, would not have justified the making of a care order. The problem with IT, he says, is that it has been decidedly non-specific and non-problem-focused.

To the extent that maintenance is the aim of social work, then it is certainly crucial to ensure that intervention does not lead to deterioration. The achievement of change (*beneficial* change, that is) is seen as an element in the maintenance strategy; but it is only one element and is not a precondition for the profession's existence. Other elements include the provision of effective support, the exercise of responsibility and pro-active intervention in the community. And a full recognition of the range of activities, strategies and emphases in social work facilitates a more sophisticated and valid understanding of what the discipline is all about.

5 The Fulfilment of Responsibility

The trainee manager, school teacher, trade union official and surgeon quickly learn and accept that, both by virtue of their paid position and by their confidence in the use of acquired skills, they are each in positions of responsibility. If one of their number seeks to deny this role, if he is confused about its legitimacy, ambivalent about the appropriateness of taking decisions, acting firmly and asserting his ascribed authority, he is unlikely to be a good manager, teacher, workers' leader or surgeon. No firm wants a manager who vacillates; neither school nor children want or respect a teacher who cannot keep order; and a trade union does not want an official who fails to fight for its members' interests.

All this is clear. Why then have social workers traditionally been so reluctant to recognise the responsibilities which society has placed on *their* shoulders? For that it is so cannot be denied: a training officer in a social services department, for example, says that new employees 'fail to recognise the power which their organisation generally has over individuals who seek help from it, and the authority which help-seekers invest in them. ... They have considerable difficulty in acknowledging the relative power they hold when interviewing as part of their job'. (Redford and Goodenough, 1979) It has to be admitted that the literature of recent years has not helped, although Foren and Bailey's *Authority in Social Casework* remains eminently sensible in much of what it says:

Social caseworkers, especially those in the so-called authority settings like probation, are often surprised by the extent to which other people expect them to be authoritarian.

Clients ... will usually perceive the worker as possessing authority of different kinds.

A relationship in which one person occupies a relatively dominant position (which is how we defined a casework interview) must necessarily involve the exercise of personal influence of one kind or another.

Magistrates and judges ... regard their probation officers ... as down-to-earth, sensible people who are able to accept the necessity for authority and discipline.

Insofar as the child care [social worker] possesses the knowledge and skill which is common to all trained professional case-workers, he will also enjoy the authority which this confers – an authority which derives not only from the agency he represents but from the profession of which he is a member.

Why is it that these carefully balanced and moderate messages have fallen on so many deaf ears? Partly, perhaps, because the Seebohm reforms quickly gave the text a dated appearance, by virtue of its references to child care officers, almoners, and so on. But much more, I think, because it had the misfortune to be published in 1968, year of mini-revolutions presaging a decade in which notions of authority and control became inextricably entangled with the idea that Western society was not only class-ridden but repressively so, with the result that many students and social workers were caught up in a melée of incipient conflict. The exertion of authority, let alone control (the word *coercion* was preferred), would mean the radical social worker being untrue to his fundamental aims – the liberation of the poor and the overthrow of privilege. The revolutionary trend, encouraged by the writings of critical sociologists, fuelled by the organisational chaos of the new local government bureaucracies, and given added fervour by the youthfulness of new recruits to social work, ran its course for nearly 10 years. And although a semblance of order has now returned, the damage done to the profession's reputation was considerable, and the task of laying new foundations for post-Seebohm practice was, as a result, far longer delayed than it should have been. Hence the depressing conclusion drawn by Stevenson (1978) at the end of her mammoth investigation into the work of social services departments: 'The best endeavours of many individuals to provide good services to those in need are ... undermined' by, among other factors, 'an overriding lack of clarity about objectives and roles, about the proper functions of the personal social services and of social work in particular'.

Thankfully, the pressure of public opinion has compelled the profession to recognise that, as Howe (1979) has pointed out, social work *can* have no existence independently of the agencies in which it operates. And without any doubt, the two largest employers of social workers in the United Kingdom – the local authorities and probation committees – while recognising and valuing the special contribution of social work as a compassionate and humanising force, nevertheless expect it to operate according to guidelines, some of them laid down by statute, others by administrative decision. Within these boundaries, social workers carry heavy responsibility, and it is the purpose of this chapter to describe briefly the many different ways in which they are expected to fulfil it.

Oversight and containment

'Now, John, I'm going to place you under the supervision of Mrs Bakewell. You'll have to go and see her, and you must do as she tells you. I'm sure she'll help you if she can, and we don't expect to see you back in this court again. Is that clear?' With words like these, many a probation or supervision order begins, and the new client goes off with his social worker to find out what is expected of him.

Social workers in all agencies are deputed to supervise, to oversee, to keep an eye on a wide variety of clients, young and old, delinquent and distressed, recidivist and 'at risk'. The hope is that the worker can *contain* the situation or, if it deteriorates, take action that will prevent further trouble. A great deal of residential care is similarly concerned with containment, with 'holding the line'. We will consider three examples.

Supervising clients in the community

Offenders constitute one major group supervised by social workers in the community. In 1983 over 95,000 convicted persons in England and Wales were made subject to a variety of supervision orders by the courts, and so passed on to the caseload of a social work agency (see Table 5.1). Forty per cent of them were adults placed on probation for anything from six months to three years. By far the biggest group were given two-year orders, although there is a gradual trend towards shorter periods on probation. Sixteen per cent were juvenile offenders (that is, aged between 10 and 16 inclusive) and they, like the adults, had mostly been convicted of theft, handling or burglary; two-thirds of these juveniles were supervised by probation officers, the rest – mainly younger children – by local authority social workers. About eighty per cent of probation orders either ran their full course or were discharged early for good progress, and there is evidence that the older the client the greater the chance of successfully completing supervision.

Table 5.1   Court orders on convicted persons which required supervision by a social worker (1983)

	Number	%
Adults placed on probation	37 950	40
Juveniles placed under supervision following criminal proceedings	14 930	16
Suspended sentence supervision orders	1 850	2
Community service orders	35 100	37
Money payment supervision orders	5 800 (est)	6
Total	95 630	

Source: Probation statistics, England and Wales 1983, Home Office, London, October 1984

Community service orders were introduced in 1975, but with over 20 800 on the probation service's caseload at the end of June 1983, and the number rising steadily, it is already clear that they represent the most radical and far-reaching penal innovation of recent years. The scheme involves unique liaison between the probation service and other organisations in the community who provide the work setting in which referred offenders must do up to 240 hours' service. It has no explicit therapeutic component and has been welcomed by both liberal and conservative wings of the social policy spectrum: by the former because it is a viable and positive alternative to imprisonment, and by the latter because it is seen as a real punishment on tariff principles rather than the soft option that probation is often seen as by hard-line critics.

Apart from those 'sentenced to social work' by the courts, there is one other large group of offenders under supervision: those who have been released from penal institutions, including prisoners on parole. In 1983, there were about 50 000 after-care clients on the probation service's caseload: at one extreme were a small number of murderers who had come out on parole and would inevitably be treated with circumspection by a probation officer alive to the political sensitivities of his supervisory responsibility – the entire policy of releasing serious offenders on licence is perpetually poised on a knife-edge of public acquiescence, and any suspicion that the social worker is oblivious to continuing crimes or misdemeanours is always likely to put the policy in jeopardy. At the other extreme were the large number of petty recidivists, of whom it has been said that at least a half ought not to have been in prison at all. They come to the after-care office for immediate help, but their problems of homelessness, unemployment, alcoholism and ill-health are often so chronic that the social worker's contribution is self-evidently inadequate.

Occasionally voices are raised against the use of social workers in surveillance (see especially Harris, 1977) but, as Bottoms and McWilliams (1979) say, the probation officer is 'inescapably an officer of the law', and so too is the local authority social worker so far as the supervision of juvenile offenders is concerned. If they were to deny the appropriateness of their responsibility for such offenders and withdraw from a surveillance role, a new service would have to be created instantly. Moreover the use of social workers to perform this function has undoubtedly had the important effect of slowly, if hesitantly, instilling a humane voice into the penal system. The state of prisons in most countries shows that there is still a long way to go before they are truly civilised, but there is little doubt that the probation officer has been and remains a moderating factor in institutions known to be especially resistant to outside influences.

Offenders are not the only clients whom social workers supervise in the community: ex-mental patients, the physically handicapped and the elderly can also be subject to oversight, not of course in lieu of punishment, but rather to protect their own interests or to detect warning signals of impending trouble. Goldberg (1978), examining the supervisory role of local authority social workers, notes that their visits to the elderly under the review system are generally rare and superficial. She expresses scepticism about the probable effectiveness of such a pattern of surveillance, and argues that it would probably be better either to replace it or supplement it with a system of community networks, in which volunteers and neighbours were formally deputed to keep an eye on old people thought likely to be at risk.

Monitoring children at risk

Although there have been other alleged scandals of child abuse or neglect which have led to inquiries and published reports, it remains the misfortune of East Sussex Social Services Department that the case of Maria Colwell should have been the headline-hitting *cause célèbre* in the emergent phenomenon of non-accidental injury. For most of her life, Maria had been fostered by her aunt and uncle, and for five years had been in the care of the county council. In October 1971, she went to live with her mother and stepfather, the Kepples, whom she had been visiting for some time. The care order was revoked and a supervision order made; while this arrangement was in force, William

Kepple, Maria's stepfather killed her, an offence for which he was convicted, first of murder, and then, on appeal, of manslaughter. The Secretary of State for Health and Social Services set up a public inquiry which reported in September 1974, and which, more than any other single event, highlighted the developing pattern of complex and generally unsympathetic relationships between social work and the public. Shearer (1979) has graphically depicted the pain, the bewilderment and the continuing air of injured innocence that social workers have expressed whenever the events of 1973–4 are recollected. 'It was bizarre', remembers Jeanne Wall (an area director in East Sussex at the time): 'It was so beyond one's experience to be a sort of pawn or puppet, pushed and pulled. It felt so totally unreasonable, so totally unjust ... It [the inquiry] was so unprofessional – Olive Stevenson apart – and so sensational which was beyond our experience, because until that time nothing had been more private than social work.'

'Nothing had been more private than social work.' A telling phrase: a phrase that illustrates the traditional temptation to ignore the public context and communal responsibility of social work; a phrase that contradicts the Timms's reasonable assertion (1977) that social work is performed under social auspicies; a phrase that evokes the real feelings of people who were caught up in something that had taken them totally by surprise and that they did not know how to handle. Above all, it is a phrase that marks a watershed in the history of social work – before it, social workers really could believe in the private nature of their activities, after it, they would have to get used to media exposure, to the need for public explanations of their actions, and to the idea that, never again, would society be prepared to assume that the social worker's good intentions would always and necessarily be translated into good deeds. Of course the abuse hurled at the profession in general, and at the East Sussex Department in particular, was exaggerated. The fact that the social worker concerned had to have physical protection as she went in and out of the hearing was outrageous. And, of course, the Colwell case could have happened anywhere in the country, to any social worker. But the strength of feeling provoked by it, and the strong undercurrent of hostility towards social work could not be and still cannot be ignored.

Parton (1979) has argued that social workers were the victims of political prejudice and moral panic, but, although media manipulation certainly contributed to a mood of scapegoating, the social work profession of that time had rather laid itself open to public criticism and ridicule by the way in which many of its practitioners and some of its leaders seemed to claim too much for it: it would repair and strengthen family life, combat juvenile delinquency, ameliorate the conditions of the handicapped, improve on the record of the NSPCC and reduce the incidence of child cruelty. And here, in the case of Maria Colwell, the social worker's fallibility was cruelly exposed.

It became painfully apparent that the Colwell Inquiry was ultimately concerned with the nature of the relationship between the social worker and society, and social work and the state. Indeed, it now seems clear that it marked a watershed in pinpointing the accountability of social services departments in areas of public concern. The public declared its interest in the matter of child safety, and social workers were compelled to accept that their decision-making processes had to become more formalised, more rigorously recorded, and more open to investigation and assessment by political superiors.

In the wake of Colwell, we have had to tackle two separate but equally critical issues with regard to the monitoring of children at risk. The first is this: can the social worker operate a surveillance service efficient enough to satisfy the public's desire to reduce the incidence of child abuse? For society and its representatives are here undoubtedly demanding a *policing* function: for example, when a 13-month-old child died of hypothermia after being found by ambulancemen on a urine-soaked mattress covered in sores and suffering from gangrene, the judge commented that the social worker had called 51 times 'but didn't go to the right part of the house', (*Guardian* news report, 2 February 1980). Social workers have always strongly resisted the role that is implicit in such comments. Hughes (1976) puts it like this: social workers are uneasy and anxious about 'the much more formalised response that is now demanded' in cases of non-accidental injury – suspected or actual. And underlying the unease is the fact that, 'when non-accidental injury is suspected there can follow a radical change in one's role-relationship with one's client/patient; what was seen as a helping, supportive role may now be perceived as punitive and authoritarian. In extreme cases the client/patient may feel that his trust has been betrayed and may react accordingly.' The slowly accumulating evidence, however, seems to point to the conclusion that social workers are either going to have to adapt themselves and their role to fulfil a policing role of this kind or they will have to make way to allow some other service to do so – a service which will not, presumably, be influenced by the humanist philosophy which underpins contemporary social work.

The Beryl Day Risk Model

1   In what way(s) is this child at risk?
   Injury from parent
   Inadequate physical care
   Frequent leaving alone
   Poor housing
   Homelessness
   Failure to thrive
   Poor educational facilities
   Emotional abuse due to unrealistic demands of parents
   Emotional abuse due to parental incapacity
   Lack of adequate emotional response and care
   Increased traffic hazards

2   Which of these risks fall within the child protective functions of the social worker's role – defined in terms of legal requirements, agency function and community expectation?
   In the event of a positive identification, two things follow:
   (a) The child becomes the client whose needs take priority over all else.
   b) 'The worker becomes involved in making a full investigation of all the factors involved in the risk. The worker needs to become proficient in both direct and open-ended questioning to elicit facts, as well as skilled in understanding the feelings which surround the facts. He also needs skill in assessing the whole situation...'

3   Is it a *now* risk, a *cumulative* risk or a *potential* risk?
   Now risk is characterised by:
   Serious neglect;
   Loss of parent with no obvious substitute;
   Leaving alone which amounts to abandonment;
   Homelessness;
   Serious violent or self-destructive acting-out behaviour;
   Complete emotional and/or physical rejection;
   Cumulative risk is characterised by:
   Failure to thrive (unless life threatened);
   Violence between parents ('yo-yo' children);
   Failure to provide for physical necessities;
   Leaving alone;
   Neither parent able to relate adequately to child;
   Chronic disorder and neglect;

Scapegoating;
Delinquency;
Child very withdrawn;
School non-attendance;
Accident prone.
Potential risk is characterised by:
Mental illness in parents;
Parent committed offence against another child;
Parent showing signs of 'classic battering syndrome' but
as yet no physical attack on child;
Frequent complaints from neighbours or extended family
but no evidence;
Parent prone to episodic violence in other areas of life;
Accident or crisis prone family;
Child home on trial;
High level of stress.

Now risks indicate that some kind of immediate action is necessary. *Cumulative* risks require skills of diagnosis, assessment and treatment, and represent the bulk of the child protection cases in any caseload. They cause worry and concern, and 'are open to such a variety of decisions that the issues tend to become clouded resulting in action being taken which, with hindsight, has exacerbated rather than reduced the risks.' *Potential* risks are the most difficult to assess. They need careful and frequent reassessment and detailed understanding of what constitute the trigger points in each case.

Adapted from Beryl Day, 'Unmasking child abuse', *Community Care*, 16 March 1977, pp. 18–20.

The second issue is related to the first and is this: having satisfactorily determined that a child is 'at risk', how can a preventative policy best be pursued? In extreme cases of neglect or easily perceived cruelty, the initial response is fairly straightforward: the child is taken before a juvenile court, a care order is made, and an alternative placement found. But most reported cases are by no means as simple, and only a minority are ever reported by social workers to the magistrates because of the problem of presenting sufficient admissible evidence to prove a case. 'Moral certainty' is not enough. The foundations of monitoring lie in the case conferences that departments now call in order formally to identify 'risk' cases (see Hallett and Stevenson, 1979) and in the 'Risk Registers' that are kept by local authorities. But because of public awareness of the incidence of non-accidental injury and because of professional sensitivity to the need for caution, such registers almost always contain a large number of names where the risk is relatively slight. The fact is that, as with all human behaviour, we are simply not – and never will be – in a position to predict with absolute certainty whether and when a violent act is going to be perpetrated in private on an innocent child. No amount of social work monitoring is going to be able to claim 100 per cent preventative success if the child is living at home.

Why then do social workers not play safe and engage in much more child removal, even when the risk is marginal? One answer is given by the spokesman for a social services department defending its decision to allow a 15-year-old schoolgirl mother to live with her lover, a few weeks before the couple's baby daughter was murdered by the father. He said that social workers were often forced to take a gamble with children who might be subject to battering. 'We get 40 child abuse allegations every month and if we play completely safe and put every one of these children into care then our homes would be overflowing. We try to keep families together and in doing that take inevitable risks.' (*Guardian* news report, 19 January 1980)

If removal to care were the policy desired by the community, then the community would have to invest enormous additional sums of money in residential child care. But even if that were to be politically and economically feasible, we still have to confront another dilemma: it is the experience of social workers everywhere that the removal of a child from its own family setting is very often not the better alternative that is widely assumed. If first-class, stable foster care were available to all who needed it, then hooray! – the child at risk could indeed be offered an attractive, long-term alternative. But a more common pattern is for the child to be admitted into an assessment centre, possibly separated from his brothers and sisters, and placed in a home or with foster parents who might or might not give him a stable base for growth and development. In other words the choice facing the social worker is not usually between an appalling home setting and an idyllic alternative, but is between two imperfect and uncertain options:

which of them will do the least damage to the child in the short, medium and long term?

Because the social worker knows, from his experience, that *sometimes* – other things being equal – the preferred option must be to leave the child with his parents, to work with them intensively, supportively and encouragingly while still keeping a storm watch out for future violence ... because of this we come back, full circle, to the first issue. Can the social worker fulfil the policing role firmly, even aggressively, if he also has to gain the family's confidence, and to convey the personal warmth and genuineness implicit in his professional role? The answer is that it *has* to be done; and the evidence from earlier models of child care and probation suggests that it is by no means impossible to achieve – provided the social worker is crystal-clear about the nature of his job and the duality of his roles. Furthermore, there is evidence from client-perspective studies that clients prefer openness, and are neither deceived nor impressed by the social worker who appears to want to deny the importance of such functions as the prevention of child abuse.

Containment in residential care

All social workers who find themselves employed in residential care quickly discover that they cannot deny the reality of the power-element in their relationships with residents. Let me give just three examples.

First, it has been shown convincingly that residential hostels can and do succeed in containing the criminal behaviour of some people (Sinclair, 1971) – especially those, who, before they came as residents, lived in relatively stressful circumstances in the community. It has also been shown that when they return home, they revert to their patterns of misbehaving. But the important fact is that *while in care* the hostel is influential. Moreover Sinclair was able to demonstrate that the most beneficial hostels were those in which there was a firm but emotionally warm warden in charge and a wife who supported her husband's leadership. Thus the achievement of containment did depend on the *kind* of regime operating. Given that it has been extremely difficult to prove any kind of social work effect on criminal behaviour, such a finding is both an encouragement to professional development and a significant indication of the power of residential care.

Second, social workers in residential settings all discover that they have to evolve a pattern for exerting authority in appropriate situations. They are the guardians of corporate peace, and many a fieldworker, accustomed to a non-directive style appropriate to the casework interview, has come unstuck when trying to transpose it into residential work. Tutt (1979) illustrates some of the stark alternatives facing the residential social worker:

> 'If a child attacks you because he is angry with you as the authority figure that removed him from home, how are you to deal with that behaviour? Do you strike back, a natural, but illegal response? Do you go through the ritualistic procedure of corporal punishment? Do you try to get him locked up? How do these reactions equate? Are six strokes of the cane equivalent to half-an-hour in a separation room, or a stopped weekend at home?'

Third, a continuing debate among those involved in residential care concerns the extent to which containment is not enough. The problem is how, in a relatively, sometimes totally, closed institution, initiative, development and creativity can be encouraged. The issue concerns all residential settings, but it has been explored best by Miller and Gwynne (1972) in relation to homes for the chronically sick and disabled. They contrast two models of care: the warehousing model and the horticultural model. The warehousing model, in its best manifestations, is based on a humanitarian commitment to caring, but requires the inmate to remain dependent and depersonalised. 'The "good" inmate is one who accepts the staff's diagnosis of his needs and the treatment they prescribe and administer.' The horticultural model, on the other hand tends to have a social work rather than a nursing identity, and is based on liberal ideas of growth: independence is encouraged, opportunities for activity are provided, and the residents are encouraged to 'do things'. Miller and Gwynne admit that they began their study with a strong commitment to a horticultural approach, but their research persuaded them that both models could fall short of the ideal, and their conclusions revert to the idea of individualising choice in residential care. Residents should be free to take advantage of developmental opportunities, but they should also be free to opt for a dependency role. 'Thus the declining multiple sclerotic may feel just as deprived in the horticultural climate as the lively youngster with polio in a warehousing culture that is geared to brain-damaged "vegetables".'

Miller and Gwynne emphasise the importance of recognising the reality of the purpose of terminal care homes. Their task is to cater 'for the socially dead during the interval between social death and physical death.' Such a recognition may clarify the position conceptually, but it does little to help the staff whose responsibility for defining the regime is considerable, and for whom, in such settings, medium-term objectives may not exist: 'the only outputs are dead patients.' This dilemma, though starkly posed in Miller and Gwynne's study, is by no means unique to the chronically sick. It has its parallel in mental health and handicap, in work with alcoholics, addicts and hardened recidivists, and in 'ordinary' homes for the elderly. In all these settings, the post-workhouse philosophy of practice is still in the process of emerging, and the responsibility for determining its direction is principally in the hands of residential care staff.

Considered recommendations

The responsibility that social workers bear is rarely absolute. In writing reports, for example, they are required to assess the circumstances surrounding designated persons – clients, potential clients or target groups – and, having done so, they are normally expected to make recommendations for action. The decision-makers – doctors, magistrates, judges, committees – then consider the recommendation and make a judgment, sometimes bearing in mind factors which it was not the business of the social worker to take into account; for example, a judge might be influenced by the need to pass a sentence which incorporates an element of general deterrence. If the social worker is familiar to the decision-makers, and if there is trust between them, it is often possible for quite radical recommendations to be acted on, and there is clear evidence that social workers are, without doubt, influential in this respect.

Social enquiry reports in criminal cases

Every year the probation service prepares about 250 000 reports on offenders appearing before the courts; about half are concerned with adults appearing in the local magistrates courts, the remainder are either on juveniles or for the Crown Courts. In addition, local authority social workers prepare court reports, mainly on children aged under 14.

The prime purpose of a social enquiry report in criminal cases is to convey relevant information about a convicted person to decision-makers who have the difficult task of deciding what penalty he should pay. The social worker's contribution is a reflection of the twentieth century's emphasis on *individualised sentencing* in which society's penal response is matched more to the needs of the offender than to the nature and seriousness of the crime. This has followed in the wake of research evidence that many manifestations of criminal behaviour appear to be correlated with psychological and social variables. However, although most commentators still accept this as being at least partly true, they also see that the correlation has been oversimplified in the past: it is now recognised that there are many offenders who commit crimes despite having plenty of money, friends and personal competence. Tax evasion, shoplifting, theft from one's employers, commercial dishonesty, family violence: it is known that there is a vast 'hidden figure' of crime which never comes before the courts, and which, in a statistical sense, may even be deemed to be relatively normal behaviour. Some people have suggested that such sociological evidence might invalidate the part that social workers play in the sentencing process, but it is still possible to make an essentially pragmatic response: a great many offenders at the time of sentence do appear to be in personal difficulties which are not likely to be helped by any other service; others are manifestly inadequate persons – that is often how and why they got caught – and they too need help; yet others appear to respond to the traditional opportunity of being given a chance to 'prove themselves'. Thus, although there might well be a case for conceptually separating the justice and the welfare approaches to offenders, the essentially humanitarian role of the social worker advising the sentencer and being available to the sentenced offender is one that must be retained, because of the way it softens the harsh edges of the law. If there are still deficiencies in the penal system (as undoubtedly there are and always will be), they derive not from the role of the social worker, but from the limited community alternatives to imprisonment and from the illiberal regimes in prisons themselves.

When the social worker receives a request for a social enquiry report, Perry (1975) says there are four things for him to do immediately:

1. Check the details of the offence;
2. Get hold of the subject's complete criminal record;
3. Look in his own agency's records – but read previous papers carefully and with an open mind;
4. Make an appointment with the subject.

The report should cover the circumstances of the offence, and a summarised account of the offender's psychosocial circumstances. It should always be shown to the defendant and should be written in language that he can understand. Horsley (1984), in a disturbing research study has shown that probation officers more often than not use words and grammar that demand a far higher IQ than average. One officer, instead of saying 'He can tell right from wrong', put down: 'He can differentiate between the correct course of action and the inherent wrongness of his offences.' Such writing may be clever but is not good social work. As much information as possible should be checked, and the report should be kept as brisk and as brief as possible. The recommendation, reflecting the social worker's assessment of the offender's needs, his judgment on the balance of risks, and his appraisal of the availability of resources (Curnock and Hardiker, 1979), should relate to the contents of the report, should follow logically from it, and should be an accurate and honest conclusion in the light of all the evidence.

There is disagreement over whether the social worker ought, at all times, to be an advocate on behalf of the client. Perry says he should be impartial; Bottoms and McWilliams (1979) say that the probation officer should never recommend a prison sentence – his job is to divert offenders from custody. The conclusion is again a pragmatic one: there is no doubt that social workers *do* act as advocates, but their ability to do so successfully almost certainly depends on them being accepted as at least relatively impartial. Mott (1977), for example, concludes that, in one juvenile court, probation officers prevailed upon magistrates to change their intended sentences in 23 per cent of all cases. If it were thought that the social worker always defended his client's position, invariably proposed a soft option without reference to the offence committed, distorted the evidence accordingly, and consistently challenged the court on every decision, a totally different working relationship between the social worker and the bench would exist. It might conceivably be a better system, but the evidence is not unambiguous. For the moment, the assumption is that social workers and magistrates operate within a setting in which there is a broad consensus about penal policy: each influences the other, and both are expected to bear in mind public opinion, and the practicalities of penal system management. It is a system in which the balancing-skill of the reconciliatory social worker is tested to the utmost, but in which the cumulative effects of his influence are considerable.

Reports regarding the care of children
Apart from reports prepared on children who have broken the law,

social workers also have to assess family circumstances in a variety of other legally defined situations. Local authority workers, for example, write reports on children of all ages who are the subject of care proceedings. These may lead either to the making of a supervision order or to a care order in which the local authority assumes full parental rights. Because the social services department normally initiates such proceedings and presents the report justifying them, both the responsibility and the power vested in the social worker are very great. It is, perhaps, not surprising that it is in this area, that client hostility to the social worker is at its peak. The mother of a child taken into care knows that, although the court sets the seal on it, it is the social worker's report that effectively makes the decision both possible and inevitable.

Despite suggestions that the responsibility for all child care enquiries should be transferred to Seebohm departments, the role of the probation service in England and Wales has, in recent years, grown rather than diminished. As well as remaining primarily responsible for the middle-teen years (which constitute the prime age-group for detected crime), probation officers, acting in their capacity as social workers of the courts, have assumed greater influence in domestic proceedings. The rise in the incidence of divorce has led to a steady increase in the number of enquiries concerning questions of custody and access to children following the break-up of a marriage. A probation officer, often one who specialises in the subject or is even attached to a specialist team, will need to interview the children in the case (if they are old enough to be involved), both parties to the divorce, and any other relevant persons – grandparents who may be called on to care for the children, potential step-parents who may themselves be involved in the court hearing as co-respondents, and other relatives. The recommendations in such cases (of which there were nearly 16 000 in 1983) are normally unambiguously made, although the balance of reasoning that leads up to them is rarely straightforward. Divorce court enquiries involve the probation officer in an arbitration role, in which there is no room for faintheartedness. The clients may be rich or poor; lawyers will be actively involved on both sides and ready to challenge evidence that seems to go against the interests of their client; and, at the end of the day, there usually has to be a winner and a loser, with the probation officer necessarily being identified with the decision. There is no research to show what proportion of probation officers' recommendations are accepted, but the suspicion is that the majority are.

Adoption enquiries

There are two quite different kinds of adoption enquiry: one is concerned with the matching of a child with prospective parents; the other, the kind considered here, is concerned with the request that the adoption order should be made absolute in court.

Whenever an adoption order is requested by the adoptive parents, the court has to appoint a guardian *ad litem* whose job it is to safeguard the interests of the child before the court and to investigate all circumstances relevant to the proposed adoption. The guardian – who is usually a local authority social worker, but may also be a probation officer – has to verify statements made by the applicants, assess the psychosocial setting, and finally make a recommendation to the court.

Often the recommendation will be straightforward, but not always. For example:

> Mrs Bailey and her husband had been married for five years. Living with them was Mrs Bailey's ten-year-old son by her first marriage, Alexander. Alex continued to have contacts with his father, Mr Kristianson, and his paternal grandparents who lived in Denmark. Mr and Mrs Bailey wanted to obtain a step-parent adoption for Alex in order to ensure that, in the event of Mrs Bailey's death, Alex's future with Mr Bailey would be assured. The social worker, however, judged that the Baileys had not been properly advised as to the legal implications of an adoption order, and concluded that the interests of Alex could best be served by varying the custody arrangements attached to the divorce order. This recommendation was made because of the social worker's conclusion that the continued interest and concern for Alex's paternal grandparents and natural father were important to him and should not be disrupted. His absolute right of access to them should be protected. Of particular interest in this case was the fact that the social worker made the recommendation despite the acquiescence in the request for adoption by both child and the natural father. In other words, the social worker claimed, by virtue of his experience and expertise, the right to judge what would be preferable in the long term, irrespective of the present feelings of all the parties most intimately involved. The recommendation was accepted by the court.

The guardian *ad litem*, then, has considerable power in determining whether or not adoptions should go ahead, and, partly because of this, as Rowe (1966) puts it: 'His work demands a high degree of professionalism in every sense of that word.' She lists the qualities needed in a competent guardian *ad litem*:

1. detailed knowledge of the adoption law;
2. objectivity;
3. a genuine understanding of human needs, motives and anxieties;
4. casework skills of a high order;
5. a profound understanding of adoption as a road to the happiness and fulfilment of family life for some parents and for some children.

Abortion counselling

The Abortion Act 1967 created a whole field for social work activity: counselling potential applicants for abortion. Independent agencies like the Pregnancy Advisory Service have provided a simple counselling facility in which the worker would have no power of decision-making, although Hildebrand (1977) illustrates how an interview could lead to a change of mind in the applicant:

> Mrs I. was a happily married woman of 38; she already had three children all of whom were already at school or working. She wanted termination for financial reasons because another baby would mean less time and material comfort for the remainder of the family. After discussing her real feelings about having a baby as opposed to those the counsellor felt she was projecting on to members of her family, it became evident that it was basically embarrassment at this unplanned pregnancy at her age plus fears that it might be self-indulgent to have another child which had brought her for termination. After further discussion with Mr I. and the counsellor, it became clear to Mrs I. that her husband was prepared to support her through another pregnancy and had only agreed to termination because it appeared to be what she wanted. Mrs I. left smiling. No application for termination was made.

But abortion counselling also takes place in hospital social work departments, and here it is likely to be influenced by the well-documented variations in the exercise of medical discretion in response to abortion requests. In some hospitals the role of the social worker is similar to that in the private agency: to provide a counselling service as a constructive exercise aimed at offering emotional support and practical help and hopefully enabling the client to cope more effectively with the consequences of her decision, whether it is to lose or to keep the baby. But in other hospitals, as well as fulfilling a traditional counselling role, the medical social worker can be asked by the consultant gynaecologist to prepare a report on applicants for abortion, to provide a detailed social history and to express an opinion about the appropriateness or not of a termination (Cheetham and Learner, 1972). Where this happens, it is obvious that the social worker is making a significant contribution to the decision-making process, but Cheetham (1980), who closely observed the developing pattern of practice after the passing of the Abortion Act, comments that the role of medical social workers has always been fairly limited numerically: 'In the early '70s they saw only about 6 per cent of women who had abortions in NHS hospitals and about 19 per cent of those who were refused.' Since then, Cheetham believes, the part played by social workers has diminished considerably as doctors have become more experienced in implementing, and more reconciled to, the Act.

Pre-release reports

In mental health, in the penal system and in residential child care, social workers play some part in deciding whether a particular patient, prisoner or resident is to be allowed home or into specialised accommodation in the community. With regard to parole, Morris and Beverly (1975) suggest that the influence of the prison welfare officer and the probation officer is not very great. In the two prisons that they studied, welfare officers made no recommendation in 21 per cent and 48 per cent of the cases respectively, and a home circumstances report was found to have been not always available to the Local Review Committee. The most influential recommendation appeared to come from the Assistant Governor; where he gave a firm opinion, the Local Review Committee was very likely to follow it; where he was uncertain or expressed equivocal views, the likelihood was that the committee would not recommend parole.

This pattern remains valid, but the probation officer is most likely to influence the decision-making machinery, not by a simple assertion that the man would be better off out of prison, but by taking active steps to facilitate release. In cases where homelessness is likely to be a problem, for example, the probation officer can often tip the balance of probability by making sophisticated arrangements for supportive accommodation to be available on discharge.

In psychiatric hospitals, the decision to discharge is ultimately in the hands of the medical profession, but in many hospitals the recommendation of a social worker – as of other ancillary personnel – can influence that decision and especially its timing. In residential child care, however, decisions to return children to their homes are generally made by social work personnel – although increasingly machinery has been established for this to be done at a managerial level following the receipt of reports from the residential head of home and the relevant field worker. Some authorities, in the wake of adverse media publicity, have instituted procedures for such decisions to be confirmed by committee members rather than professional staff, but this would still be done on the basis of social work reports containing recommendations and the arguments supporting them.

Resource allocation

Social services is now a major spending department in the local authority, and almost the whole of its money goes, directly or indirectly, on the provision of facilities for selected clients. A part of the selection process is determined by legislation, but significant influence is exerted both by management and social worker – and the social worker, of course, is normally the person responsible for conveying the results of decisions to all clients. Thus, both in appearance and in reality, the allocation of resources is another area in which the social worker can wield substantial power.

Admission to service

We shall see in chapter 7 that the admissions, reception and intake systems in social work can all act as rationing devices. Clients can be deterred from even setting foot in an agency by its inaccessibility, its unattractiveness or by inconvenient or restrictive opening hours. Hostile receptionists and unhelpful telephonists can be effective deterrents to a hesitant enquirer, and both can be encouraged in their behaviour by social workers feeling the need to keep the clients at arms length. In the intake system, a curt response by the social worker or a departmental policy of priorities which excludes some applicants from all service can be an additional means of administering scarce resources.

The converse of all this is a generous, non-restrictive 'open-door' policy, in which the availability of a service is given maximum publicity, new clients are always welcomed, and the organisational structure is constantly adapted in order to respond more efficiently to changing patterns of demand. This was the intention of the Seebohm Committee (1968):

We can and should encourage those who need help to seek

it...Information must be simpler and more widely available (and research into need should become a permanent feature of the new service). One single department ... is an essential first step in making services more easily accessible. The organisational structure of these services should not deter those in need and they should be available to all. There need be no uncertainty about where to turn for help nor any ambiguity about where responsibility for providing assistance lies.

In two respects these hopes have proved rather naive. First, they ignored the intensity of demand especially in the more deprived areas of present-day society: there is almost certainly *no* limit to the facilities that *could* be provided in the absence of formally agreed and clearly defined criteria for service. Secondly, to an extent that was not envisaged by Seebohm, many of the most pressing problems presented to the social services departments (as to other social work agencies) are often derived from poverty and the inadequacies of accommodation – matters which, in the long term, are not within the social worker's sphere of responsibility. Hence, the need for social workers to refer on a surprisingly large number of applicants for help – the very tactic that Seebohm had hoped to discourage.

The allocation of community resources

The bald analysis of how the availability of resources gives social workers power has been most clearly articulated by Handler (1973):

The social worker has command over goods and services that people need and want. Thus, there is no problem in recruiting clients to the agency. The creation of power arises out of this command over scarce resources. It is a power relationship because the clients need the resources and the agency has discretion as to how the resources are to be distributed. Many clients are extremely dependent and more than willing to accept administrative conditions as the price of receiving benefits. (Adapted)

Handler's analysis has been extremely influential on the social work climate, and I shall return to it shortly. But before I do, we need to consider which are the resources (apart from admission to residential care) that the social worker may dispense.

For the disabled, all departments have available a range of aids and adaptations. Hill (1978) reports that there are varying degrees of central control over their allocation, with occupational therapists often playing a more influential part in the decision-making process than social workers. Expensive house adaptations are always centrally controlled, and the procedures for effecting them often ponderous and slow. Free telephones can be provided for those thought to need them but, because of the cost involved, it is common for councillors to play a part in the decision-making.

For the elderly, the main resources available are home helps, meals-on-wheels, and day-care. In all cases, the overall provision is effected by the administration, and central directives to restrict meals-on-wheels to no more than three a week per person or home help to a maximum of two hours a week per person, for example, are policy decisions not at the discretion of fieldwork staff. But, within these boundaries, the allocation or withholding of service is usually either determined by the area team or strongly influenced by it.

The social worker often has access to a second-hand clothes or furniture store, or alternatively can use departmental authority to allow the client to buy necessities under voucher schemes. And his influence can be employed to secure access to residential facilities: the arrangement of either emergency provision in overnight hostels or bedsit space with 'known' landladies, or, most critical and valuable of all, string-pulling influence on the local housing department in an effort to secure accommodation for a homeless family. Most social workers are well aware that, in the majority of cases, the effort will be futile, but, in extreme circumstances, 'it might be worth a try', and it has been known to work.

In one London borough the process of negotiating with the housing department on behalf of clients has been formalised by introducing a system of housing assessments: if a client is seen to be in *prima facie* need of accommodation, the social worker completes a detailed report on family composition and current circumstances, passes it up through the hierarchy via the team leader, area officer, to the assistant director who, if he is in agreement with the assessment, passes it on to the Housing Department, with a firm recommendation that a sympathetic response be made.

The provision of cash

Social workers have always given money to some clients on some occasions – not infrequently out of their own pockets, when faced with the hopelessness of the real down-and-out. But, undoubtedly, the simple financial transaction has also always presented difficulties – either to the worker, the client or both.

The precise manner in which money is given may assuage feelings of shame. The case of Mr Dale provides an example: 'She [the social worker] didn't make me feel embarrassed about accepting the money. It wasn't given to me and counted out in one pound notes. It was all rolled up in an envelope and put in my hand...It was done in such a way that it was like a loan.' (Mayer and Timms, 1970)

Hence the shock to social work's delicate constitution when Geoffrey Parkinson (1970), a London probation officer, trumpeted from the hill-top pages of *New Society,* 'I give them money!':

I give most of my clients money. I give it because it is the one thing they all accept joyfully; it makes them feel valuable; it breaks down, if only for a moment, their sense of isolation. It makes them believe that I may solve their problems, it buys their cooperation and their friendship which invariably they would not sell for any other price. It shows my concern in the only way they understand. I give money with all the difficulties and dangers of dependence it can produce because I feel I have precious little choice within the context of the situations my clients offer me.

Parkinson presumed that his profligacy would be most likely to come under attack from the traditional casework lobby who would see giving money as a dangerously superficial response which ignored the 'real' underlying problems presented by clients of all kinds. But in the changing shapes of the 1970s, the reaction against money-giving (and indeed against resource-provision as a whole) came from the radical left. The lead was given by Handler (1973), an American academic, who made a study of the pre-Seebohm children's departments, and came to the conclusion they they used their capacity to give financial aid (under section 1 of the Children and Young Persons Act 1963) in order to coerce client-families into cooperation and even subservience. 'The Children's Departments tried to develop two principal strategies for controlling the use of section 1 financial aid: not making known the availability of the resource, and attaching a social service or casework plan as a condition.' Handler argued that access to section 1 money gave the social workers real bargaining power: they could demand the right to 'practise casework' in exchange for giving financial aid; they could insist on specific behaviour changes – getting work or paying off debt-arrears, for example; they could refuse to pay electricity bills, knowing that the supply would be cut off; if help was being given to buy food, the social worker could say where the client should buy it.

Handler concluded that the power relationships created by such discretionary award systems are inescapable and said that many caseworkers are 'openly contemptuous and vindictive towards the poor', while others 'treat the clients as children who must be directed and told how to behave;...these ingrained tendencies of superiority are encouraged by the pressure of work.'

There is little wonder that some student social workers, accepting Handler's analysis as not only 'the truth' but 'the whole truth' have been less than enthusiastic about having to give financial aid to clients. If section 1 payments make them 'coercive', perhaps it would be better if the system were abandoned (see Parsloe, 1978). And yet, as Jackson and Valencia (1979) have shown, it is really not so simple. The section 1 provision was a rational response to the felt need of the social services for discretionary power to respond to crisis situations, and as Hill says, social workers and their clients have benefited from the facility. The money *is* used mainly to meet immediate needs for food and other household necessities, to pay debts to fuel boards where the termination of supply is threatened, to pay other debts, especially rent arrears, and to counteract homelessness. If such powers were removed, they would have to be assumed by other authorities, and, inevitably, social workers – who would retain the responsibility for protecting the vulnerable elderly, taking children into care, keeping families together – would lose the tactical manoeuvrability that section 1 powers have given them. After all, if the payment of a bill or the provision of bed and breakfast in an emergency at public expense can preclude the making of care orders, the break-up of a family and the assumption by the department of financial responsibility for looking after the children on a long-term basis, it must be worth it – although the action should obviously be seen, not as a discrete event, but as a carefully thought-out step in a programme of maintenance and development.

The reverse solution – of transferring all income maintenance functions from the national Supplementary Benefits Commission to the local authority – would be wholly unacceptable: first because of the inevitable inequalities that would follow (with generous authorities naturally picking up a majority of itinerant claimants) and secondly because it would concentrate into one set of hands the enormous discretionary powers that are currently split between two, and would render it impossible for any social worker to act in an advocacy role for the client inside the income-maintenance system.

No, the right to dispense discretionary payments is a valuable tool in the hands of social workers, and it must be retained. Departmental guidelines are gradually becoming clearer and individual workers retain control only over relatively small sums. Of course, it gives a degree of power, and of course there are bound to be anomalous variations. But social workers cannot both seek discretionary powers and then express discomfort at the attendant responsibility. Much of the unease about handling money comes from two misconceptions: first, that there is something called 'social work' which is in some mysterious way wholly distinct from, even grander than, the allocation of financial aid; and second, that it ought to be possible to draw up absolute rules that can be taught and contained in a handbook in order to avoid the awkward processes of discretionary decision-making that arise when a request for financial aid is made.

Because of these misconceptions social workers now find themselves under attack, from those who they thought were their friends and supporters, for engaging in allegedly arbitrary and coercive acts against the interests of the poor whom they thought they were helping. But the critics make the mistake of not recognising that social work is essentially a legitimate short-term function in an imperfect world and that the social worker's job is to try to minimise the imperfections – however marginally – in the here and now. Moreover, to say that dispensing money gives social workers power over their clients is not necessarily a cause for concern. Power in a human relationship is inevitable and the direction of authority in the social work relationship is clearly defined whether or not the payment of money is a part of it. Social workers, especially inexperienced ones, find it hard to come to terms with the reality of their ascribed role, but to imagine that avoiding the distribution of small sums of money will in some way expiate the sins of power and thereby lead to moral improvement in practice is naive in the extreme.

Of course, there should be campaigns for improved programmes of income maintenance; of course, there should be battles to raise the wage-levels of low-paid workers; of course the social worker's personal contacts with those who experience the degradation of poverty will lead him to lend his support to such campaigns. But there is now, and will almost certainly always be in any society, a need for crisis responses of a discretionary kind. It is an integral part of the social work agency's task to make such responses. Cash should be given on an individualised basis. It should not be used to undermine the client's civil rights or his self-respect; it should not be unfairly withheld or indiscriminately provided; special care should be taken with the provision of loans, because of our knowledge that the relationship between the money-lender and debtor is a difficult one to sustain simultaneously with the social work relationship. Although there should be departmental or agency guidelines, these should stop well short of being seen as a code book intended to cover every eventuality. Councillors and administrators should respect the right and duty of the individual social worker to exercise discretion in his cases; and, at all times, the power which the social worker undoubtedly wields should be used to maintain and extend the self-respect of the client, to avoid further deterioration in the client's circumstances, and, preferably by explicit agreement with the client, to enable and encourage him to become self-sufficient within the laws and conventions of society.

Gatekeeping

Society is full of gatekeepers. In return for money, you can gain entry to a four-star hotel, a football match or a brothel; with money and influential friends, you can join an exclusive club; with ability and effort, you can be admitted to a university; with perseverence, talent and good looks you can make it to the top in show business. But the gates to which social workers hold the key are not opened to applicants with money, influence or talent. They are not for people who are climbing up or seeking pleasure. They are retreat routes, survival strategies, and they offer risky solutions to often intractable problems.

The press and the public, made aware of the plight of the people in desperate situations, might plead: 'Why doesn't someone do something about it? Why don't the authorities move them, take them away, give them a chance?' But, as Stevenson (1976) puts it, 'Those who press for the removal of the vulnerable person are frequently ignorant of the alternative care which will be offered... But social workers are uniquely placed to see the consequences of removal in respect of children and, to a lesser extent, old people.' And the consequences are, to say the least, often uncertain.

The social worker's responsibility as a gatekeeper is therefore all the greater because of the very riskiness of the operation, and because of his commitment to a philosophy which accords the vulnerable client rights and respect.

For the onlooker, Stevenson (1976) reminds us again, it is the *removal* of a child or a vulnerable old person or a troublesome disturber of the peace that is the critical event; when the event occurs, a sigh of relief goes up. But 'for the social worker, it is only the beginning' – indeed, it is not even the beginning, for his involvement starts much earlier.

For gatekeeping, the social worker and his agency operate in five stages:

1. *Obtaining resources*. The opening of residential accommodation, the recruitment, selection and preparation of foster parents.
2. *Quality control and maintenance*. Inspection, the provision of adequate funds to maintain standards, the continuing employment of suitable staff.
3. *Preparation of the client for transfer*. Explanation, persuasion, reassurance, ventilation, bargaining.
4. *The act of transfer*. The physical process, transport, acceptance of emotion, the bringing together of the critical parties, the provision of a safety net in the event of rapid breakdown.
5. *The provision of support and supervision* – for the client, and for the new setting. Possible preparation for later moves and another gatekeeping process.

The most critical of all skills is that of being able to achieve maximum organisational efficiency while simultaneously fulfilling the normal obligations of the social worker to establish good rapport with the client and his relatives and good working relationships with other employees in the gatekeeping process. To do that to everyone's satisfaction is the mark of a very good social worker operating in a first-class agency.

We shall consider five gatekeeping processes in social work: fostering, adoption counselling, residential child care, the admission of an elderly person to Part III accommodation, and admission to psychiatric care.

Allocation to foster care

The act of fostering other peoples' children is centuries-old and the allocation of orphans to foster parents was officially authorised by the Poor Law Amendment Act of 1834. The tradition has been maintained and the first child care officers to be appointed following the 1948 Children Act were designated boarding out officers. Since then the level of enthusiasm for fostering among social work theorists has fluctuated, but the use of foster care remains a major plank in Western child care policy. Its importance is reflected in the fact that fostering practice is one of the few areas to have stimulated the DHSS to produce a detailed and extremely practical guide (1976).

The social worker's task in arranging a foster-placement involves liaising with all the various parties: the child, the natural parents, the foster parents, other child-care personnel and colleagues in his own agency. He will have to cope with negative as well as positive reactions, while at the same time acting within 'the statutory and policy constraints of the agency' and working for the 'best interests of the child'.

There are four stages in the foster-care gatekeeping process, in all of which the responsibility on the social worker's shoulders and the power that he exercises are considerable.

1. *The selection of foster parents*   The recruitment of foster parents is a complex process in itself, although the frequently-seen newspaper advertisements asking for somebody to care for '9-year-old Catherine who is in need of a loving home' may perhaps make it look deceptively straightforward. As Crompton (1979) points out, even the role of the prospective foster parent is ambiguous: is she an applicant for employment, a volunteer offering a service, or a supplicant waiting for a gift? The social worker's position is correspondingly mixed: does he represent a potential employer, the beneficiary of a service, or the donor or withholder of a favour?

The first task of the social worker, then, is to discuss the nature of fostering, and to explain that all prospective foster parents have to be carefully vetted. The vetting procedure will, 'if completed, comprise several interviews (with the applicants and their own children, if any), a medical reference or examination, personal references, a police enquiry, possibly attendance at a group, a report, recommendation and decision' (Crompton, 1979). The worker will need to know about the applicants' attitudes, feelings and family relationships, their life style, emotional strengths and weaknesses, and any experiences that they have had that are relevant to fostering. The worker's approach should be 'encouraging and relaxed', enabling the family to reveal their approach to domestic life, and so gauge the likely impact on them of any foster child and vice versa. The worker's professionalism comes from his controlled use of informality in order to get beyond the official questions and the stereotyped answers to the reality of the home climate.

The decision should normally be made as speedily as possible, and, if it is negative, the family should be told so, not unpleasantly, but clearly and without evasion. If the decision is positive, and there is to be a waiting period before the allocation of a child, care should be taken to maintain contact with the family, to explain why there is such a delay and to use the opportunity for further preparation or training – perhaps by drawing them into a foster parent group.

2. The selection of the child   The assessment of the child – either in his own home, in an assessment centre, or in a community home – will be made by one or more social workers, and in most cases, the decision to place in foster care will be a part of a continuing period of planned supervision. At one time it was thought that foster care was always, and for all children, the preferred alternative. This is now no longer the case, although the DHSS guide says that it still is or should be considered 'the first choice ... for a pre-school child'.

Apart from assessing the basic family background of the child, factors of special relevance to a fostering decision include:

(a) the reason why he is in care, and his perception of his current situation;
(b) his typical behaviour patterns, hobbies, skills and ambitions;
(c) mental and physical health;
(d) his school or work experience and performance;
(e) previous history while in care: relationships with other foster parents, residential staff and social workers;
(f) peer-group relationships, and how he is perceived by his friends and contemporaries.

3. Matching child with family   There is no certain key to matching and, in any case, the pool of prospective foster parents is rarely so large that coincidence can be achieved on a wide range of variables. Thought will inevitably be given to the preferences of foster parents for different age-groups: babies, adolescents, and so on. Handicapped children, disturbed children, and children thought likely to present discipline problems will require careful allocation. The DHSS guide extrapolates from the research literature, and identifies a number of known predictive factors, of which the following are a selection:

1. Long term foster placements have a high risk of breakdown,

especially during the first year and during adolescence. This emphasises 'the importance of social work support and supervision during these periods'.

2. Placements of children placed before the age of 12 months tend to be more successful than those involving older children.

3. Contact between the child and his natural family during a foster-placement appears to help.

4. Three positive factors in the foster family are that (a) the foster mother is an older woman, (b) she has previous experience of fostering, and (c) her own children are significantly older than the foster-child.

5. Childless foster-families seem to be particularly successful.

Of course, as with all predictive studies, the conclusions are never absolute. A foster family and a child could present all the negative factors imaginable and still produce a remarkable success story – and vice versa.

4. Placing the child   Although the selection and matching processes complete the gatekeeping tasks, the social worker's skills continue to be required with the actual placement. He must provide all the necessary information to the three main parties involved – the child, the natural parents and the foster parents; he must be ready to cope with each party's questions about the placement, and to support it in its early days. There should be adequate preparation for the child with no hint of concealment of what is happening; and wherever and whenever possible the natural parents should be involved in the placement process. Under normal circumstances, there should be preliminary meetings between the child and the foster family before final decisions are made. And clarity should be reached on whether the placement is thought likely to be short-term, long-term or is truly indeterminate.

The recent enunciation of the 'Permanency Principle' emphasises the potentially damaging effects of uncertainty in child care.

The principle of permanency planning is based on the idea of removing the child as soon as possible out of temporary substitute care, and returning him or her to the biological family as the preferred alternative, or to an adoption home as the second priority, or if necessary to another permanent alternative such as a family with legal guardianship'. This involves not only the placement of the child in a stable or permanent plan, but also the provision of services and support necessary to maintain him or her in that plan... Permanency planning aims therefore to refocus child welfare services in a way which accepts the primacy of the needs of children over the claim for inherent advantages in the relationship between the biological parent and child. It reduces the likelihood of children being lost in care. (Morris, 1984.)

Adoption counselling

The Children Act 1975 gave adopted children in England and Wales the right, on reaching the age of 18, to have a copy of their original birth certificate, thus enabling them to go in search of their origins. But the Act also makes it compulsory for any applicant to receive counselling before the information can be divulged. The intention of this clause is to ensure that the information is presented in a helpful and appropriate manner and that the adopted person has considered the effect of any enquiries that he might make both on himself and others – especially, perhaps, on his adoptive and natural parents. The counselling interview, then, is a hurdle which applicants must surmount if they want the information that is their's by right. The social worker does not have any power to grant or withhold access; a copy of the birth certificate must be given on request once the interview has been held.

A government circular has emphasised that this counselling role requires a high degree of skill and maturity in the worker, as well as experience of work with families and knowledge of adoption practice and procedure. Haimes and Timms (1984) interviewed 46 social workers who had done the job, and report some of the difficulties they face because of the lack of clarity as to the purpose of the interview. Aggressive clients who 'go about their enquiries like a bull in a china shop' particularly worry the workers who prefer to approach the interview in a more discursive fashion. In some cases, the workers act both as enablers and detectives, helping the client to track down not just his birth certificate which is his legal right, but also his natural parents in person, and to offer continuing support during any meetings that take place; in other cases, the workers act more as 'safeguarders', trying to delay giving information in order to protect the sensibilities of the natural parents, and ultimately doing no more than they are legally required to do.

As Haimes and Timms point out, the job of adoption counselling provides a nice example of the 'Who is the client?' conundrum. Is it the adoptee making the request? Or is it an invisible person – the as yet unknown natural parent?

The major weight of counselling applicants under the Act has fallen on social services departments, but only a tiny proportion of adopted people – as little as 1 or 2 per cent – have actually taken advantage of the opportunity provided by the legislation, and an even smaller proportion have said that they intended to try to meet up with their natural parents (Hall, 1980).

Commitment to and release from residential care
Social workers exercise great power over the lives of young children and teenagers. They do so by virtue of their professional and departmental responsibilities for all children placed in the care of local authorities. The making of a care order, although strongly influenced by the social worker's report and recommendation, is itself in the hands of juvenile court magistrates. But, once made, all effective powers pass to the social work service which has to decide how best to carry out its newly assumed parental duties. Hoghughi (1979) has suggested that the burden of this responsibility has led to the development of large-scale observation and assessment centres in which assessment has become largely a ritual: by its use, the social worker makes an explicit assertion of social control and insures himself against criticism by outsiders – magistrates, committee members, the press and the public.

Once the initial period of assessment – with its battery of psychological, educational and social tests and reports – is over, decisions can be made as to where the child should reside. McGrath (1979), in her study of Cheshire's care policies, reports that in March 1976 roughly two-fifths were in residential establishments, two-fifths in foster homes and one-fifth were at home under the supervision of a social worker. The evidence suggests that, although the child's parent(s) see the social worker as the all-powerful (even the wicked) fairy, the reality is somewhat different: the social worker in the field will often tend to resist care proceedings and to argue *against* residential care until the pressure of circumstances and events is undeniable; the residential worker will constantly look for the prospect of a return home or for a foster-placement; the allocation to residential care will often be made on educational grounds because of negative school reports to the court or the refusal of a head-master to accept the child; and the referral to specific facilities will often be influenced more by the availability of resources than by sophisticated matching of child to preferred treatment. McGrath illustrates at a down-to-earth level some of the resource problems: she found that social workers were especially concerned that children were being placed in community homes in which there was insufficient emphasis on counselling and a one-to-one relationship, a shortage of male personnel, and not enough staff with the skill and experience to meet the needs of disturbed or deprived children.

The risk with an assessment system, though necessary in some form to any organisation which is processing large numbers of children through a potentially harmful experience, is twofold. First, it can lay claim to spurious and pseudo-scientific skills with regard to assessing the personality and environmental circumstances of children, thus inducing a false sense of confidence about its efficacy. Its diagnostic pretensions have to be set against the actual effects of requiring children and young people to reside for a short period of time in a transit-camp setting and then to re-adapt to a further change of residential location. Secondly, even if its classificatory claims can be defended and justified, they are rendered meaningless if child allocations are always then influenced more by the availability of limited departmental resources or by variations in managerial policy than by proven diagnostic needs.

The practical snags in implementing a total treatment strategy are nowhere clearer than in residential child care, and it is the average social worker's awareness of these that can lead him into conflict with others over the question of when and whether a child should be removed from home. The critic of social work can see only the inadequacies of the present – a poor home, warring parents, a weak father, misbehaviour at school and truanting – but the social worker knows that, however sensitive the assessment process and whatever the nature of the treatment regime, the balance of advantage probably rests in most cases with the natural home. The power of the social worker, then, in arranging for the child's removal into care is a relatively arbitrary and, for the child, a potentially hazardous business. Often it is pursued more as a salvage operation than as a therapeutic endeavour, and it is governed by resource factors and departmental policy considerations as much as it is by professional skill in predicting need and risk.

Nevertheless, delaying a child's admission to care can, of course, also be dangerous, as one social worker recounted to Thoburn (1980):

Intensive support was given for two years. But things got worse.

Both children came back into care and the family is broken up. And when you look at the degree of emotional disturbance that Wayne had when he came back into care finally, it's then you look back and say, I wish we had more sophisticated tools for telling when things will just not work out. I had more confidence in their ability to cope than was justified. My initial diagnosis was wrong.

But the unpredictability of human behaviour and the complexity of social relations are such that quasi-scientific foundations for decision-making in areas like residential child care are never likely to be available. Hence we will continue to see wide variations in boarding-out policies between departments – partly because of political differences in the council and partly because of ideological differences among decision-makers. There will continue to be contrasts between nations, as for example between Sweden and the United Kingdom: whereas in Britain, a foster home breakdown leads almost invariably back to residential care with the added handicap of a 'failure' label, in Sweden breakdowns are regarded as almost inevitable foster care 'happenings' en route to survival, and every effort is made to persevere with a boarding-out strategy once it has been adopted (Hazel, 1976). And the decision to return a child home will have to be reached frequently in the face of conflicting evidence or in response to mounting pressure from the child and his family themselves. In Thoburn's study, for example, in 12 per cent of the cases where the child was returned home, this was done either because nothing better was available or because the parent was pressing strongly and, though reluctant, the social worker thought there were no good grounds on which the decision could be opposed.

Decision-making in such areas of public policy requires extreme sensitivity and skill – but it is skill derived not from any mathematical calculation of risk but from an awareness of the many elements involved, and often from the kind of intuitive knowledge that only comes with long experience and constant reflection.

There is, however, growing evidence that management policy can play a major part in reducing the extent to which residential care orders are resorted to. Essex, for example, proudly proclaims that it has reduced the number of children in care from over 2 000 to under 1 500 in four years 'and it is still declining'. The need, says Hawker (1984), is for an improved family support service and the abandonment of all voluntary routes into care. Of course some children need to be separated from their families, but most should not be. To this end, Essex has a stated child care philosophy to govern its social work practice:

1. All children have the right to a family life;
2. The department will interfere as little as possible in peoples' lives commensurate with its attempts to help people manage their own lives. The aim is to help people help themselves;
3. The department will provide discrete services as an aid to rehabilitation or maintenance, and to prevent wherever possible the disruption attendant upon the removal of people from their usual environment;
4. The department will only assume control and provide direct care when the needs or safety of the individual or others cannot otherwise be met;
5. No action will be taken without the knowledge, consent and cooperation of the consumer except where these are overridden by specific statutory duties.

The Essex approach closely reflects the lessons learnt from Thorpe's research in intermediate treatment, and they are explicitly designed to avoid at all costs the risks of social work action leading to short-, medium-, or long-term damage to the client of a kind and to a degree that would not otherwise have occurred. They are based on an assumption that, whatever the therapeutic intentions of a residential setting, its likely effects – given the stresses and strains of practical reality – are potentially dysfunctional.

Evidence from many local authorities shows that the number of children contained in residential care is declining (Table 5.2). This pattern is likely to continue through the cumulative impact of a number of different factors: demographic trends will see a major fall – down by as much as a third overall – in the number of teenage children during the next 10 years; empirical evidence about the potential damage done by the residential experience is increasingly persuasive; and, for politicians, the temptation to save costs by closing down expensive capital facilities is too much to resist. The figures in Table 5.2 reflect a steady trend in falling usage which shows no sign of being reversed. Indeed, the wide discrepancies between those authorities which have made determined efforts to reduce their reliance on residential care and those which still use it extensively would suggest significant potential for further reductions. Warwickshire, in particular, has achieved radical changes in residential care usage: only 5 per cent of its children in care are in community homes compared with Richmond's 33 per cent, and only 1 per cent of them are in community schools compared with Leed's 10 per cent (1983–84 data). The key statistic is that of boarding-out rates, and here sharp contrasts are found between authorities that are not easily explained by differences of geography, social circumstances or political complexion (though urban metropolitan boroughs do tend to have lower boarding-out rates than most):

Boarding-out rates compared

High	%	Low	%
Camden	71	Redbridge	24
Warwickshire	69	Northumberland	36
Dudley	59	Leeds	41

(All data refer to 1983–84 CIPFA Returns)

Table 5.2   Trends in residential child care, 1975–84, England and Wales

	1975–76	1983–84
Total number of children in care	96 842	76 318
Percentage distribution:		
In community homes	25%	17%
In observation and assessment centres	5%	4%
In community schools (CHEs)	7%	4%
In other residential accommodation	2%	7%
Total proportion in residence	39%	32%
Boarded-out (foster care)	33%	48%
Home under supervision	18%	18%
Others	11%	3%

Source: Chartered Institute of Public Finance and Accountancy.

Accommodating the elderly

At any one time there are about 100 000 people living in publicly-financed old peoples' homes and the demand for places is likely to remain strong until the end of the century, for although the total population of the elderly will begin to level out by 1991, the numbers of those over the age of 85 will continue to rise until 2001. Local authorities are required by law (enacted in the National Assistance Act

1948) to 'provide residential care for all persons who, by reason of age, infirmity or any other circumstance, are in need of care not otherwise available to them', and it is the social worker who has the primary task of making the assessment, which is likely to be based on Curnock and Hardiker's three concepts (1979): *need, risk,* and *resources.* If an old lady applies for admission to an old peoples' home (or if her relatives apply on her behalf), are her needs really sufficient to justify it? If a neighbour draws the plight of an old man to the department's attention, does the social worker agree that he is truly 'at risk' and is the risk great enough to justify admission to care. Even allowing for the validity of a particular request or referral, has the authority any vacancies? Are there any applicants in a worse situation who have higher priority? Or are the needs of the applicant such that the social services department's accommodation is inadequate to cope? For example, does he or she need more intensive nursing care than would be readily available in an ordinary old people's home?

Decisions on the allocation of scarce Part III places are not normally taken by isolated fieldworkers – who are often untrained social work assistants – but in a committee of social services staff, ideally involving heads of home, and representatives of management, fieldwork and hospital social work. Needs assessments are drawn up by the social worker who knows the case best, reports from doctors are considered (paying special attention to the twin curses of a residential care regime – incontinence and senile confusion), and, depending on the availability of bed-space, allocations are made. Because of the scarcity of resources, applicants may often find themselves in homes other than their preferred choice and at some distance from their familiar territory. But 'the local authority has control over whether you go and also of where you go ... The nature of the system is such that individual "choice" is a very small portion of the actual procedure of going into a home' (Wilding, 1979). Hence the department's power is very real, and social workers in different parts of the authority play a significant part in wielding it, although, sadly, often at the end of the line the power is more bureaucratic than personal, the decisions more influenced by logistics than client need.

Since 1980, a new factor has entered the situation, with the heaviest dose of privatisation yet introduced into the heartland of the personal social services. The 1980 Social Security Act was amended in November of the same year to make the DHSS financially responsible for all those elderly people needing residential care, 'if no suitable accommodation elsewhere is available and the local authorities will not provide funds, providing means test criteria are met'. This innovation, which came about with very little realisation of its implications, effectively means that any elderly person in rented accommodation and without capital will be able to rely on the DHSS to fund their admission to private care and to keep them there for as long as they wish. The result has been startling: there has been an immediate flood of private homes opening, and in many areas the number of their residents now far exceeds that in local authority homes. Consequently, social services departments have had to take on the serious responsibility of inspecting a vastly increased private sector in order to minimise the risk of maltreatment and neglect. (Bird, 1984)

Admission to psychiatric care

For 24 years, the Mental Health Act 1959 governed the process of admission to psychiatric hospital, but it came under increasing attack partly because of the way the facility for emergency admissions was abused and partly because of the ambiguous role of the social worker in the process.

As a consequence, the Mental Health Act 1983 is intended to ameliorate affairs. There is a statutory requirement for 'approved social workers' to be properly trained for the responsible task of being involved in psychiatric admissions, and strong emphasis is placed on the fact that, in order to fulfil their role, social workers are required to make a professional assessment of the case. This is intended to rectify the situation criticised by Oram (1978) in which generic social workers were at best uneasy in the situation and at worst downright incompetent – a charge that was more than confirmed in Bean's (1980) research study of the psychiatric admissions process.

The passing of the 1983 Act, however, has not seen the last of the debates within social work about the incompatibility of carrying out policies which commit mental patients to forms of institutional treatment sometimes thought to be potentially harmful, and the social worker's duty to defend the client's rights against the possibility of persecution by his family, to work with him in the community, and to move towards a more sympathetic view of mental illness as a social phenomenon.

Under the 1983 Act, it is the duty of an approved social worker to make an application for admission to hospital provided he is satisfied that it is proper to do so. BASW (British Association of Social Workers) has emphasised that this procedure should only be carried out if the relatives are unable or unwilling to do so themselves, and furthermore that the approved social worker must be strong enough not to be steam-rollered into it either by a doctor or by the local authority (Rashid and Ball, 1984). To a large extent, the sectioning process remains unchanged, though the concept of an 'approved social worker' increases the profession's legitimacy.

The system should lead to an increase in the availability of specialist expertise in social work, so that we may begin to see a situation in which the community perspective can exert a stronger influence. Certainly it is right that social workers with specialist skills in mental health should strive much more forcefully to bring about the development of community alternatives to compulsory detention, and work for the emergence of multi-disciplinary teams in which psychiatric emergencies can be handled sympathetically and efficiently.

In the eyes of the patient, however, there may remain some confusion. For the social worker is not only a party to the compulsory order, but may well be the agent by whom he is forcibly conveyed by ambulance to a place of detention. With this role remaining, it is difficult to see how the social worker can simultaneously fulfil the role of a campaigning civil rights worker and still retain credibility in the eyes of both patient and the psychiatric system of which he is inevitably a part.

Certainly the 1983 Act recognises the fallibility of the social worker and the need for patients to be protected against malpractice or incompetence. The most important innovation in the Act is the emphasis given to patient rights, and the role accorded to the Mental Health Review Tribunal to scrutinise both psychiatric and social work activity.

With the rapid growth of the counselling and developmental roles of 'competing' professions like psychiatric nursing and occupational therapy, social work's future position in the field of mental health remains unclear; for the moment, the worker's statutory involvement with the gatekeeping task remains the most visible example of social work practice in psychiatry.

Review

It is no accident that the chapter on the responsibilities borne by the social worker is by far the longest in this book. It should be clear from it that the authority of the social worker is considerable. It should also be clear that his discretionary powers are rarely straightforward: sometimes they are enacted in parliamentary legislation, though these are frequently ill-defined; sometimes they are determined by council committees or by departmental management (for example, in one fuel strike, social workers in several departments were delegated with the power to allocate coal coupons to deserving people); sometimes the powers are derived from professional judgment; but most frequently they are defined by agency function and especially by the way in which that function is limited by restricted resources – a ceiling on the number of places in residential care, for example.

In recent years there has been a steady tightening-up in local authority definitions of social worker powers. Instructions have been issued indicating which clients should have priority in the rationing of services, how to classify new referrals so far as their eligibility for admission to care is concerned, when and under what circumstances to return children-in-care home on trial, what procedures to adopt when notification is received that either a child or an old person is at serious risk of injury or neglect. Many departments have drawn up manuals in more or less permanent form, and there has been some negative reaction to this from social workers. 'We are becoming petty bureaucrats!' is the cry of pain. But the phenomenon is now both too well-advanced to dismantle and too obviously necessary to decry. Maybe this is not what some people came into social work to do. If not, it is better for them to realise it early in their careers and to depart. For there is no escape from the undeniable fact that the social worker, caught up in the affairs of the state, is necessarily a party to the state's programme of policies and practice in respect of the deprived, the deviant, the underprivileged, the needy, and the disabled.

Social work not only has to operate within that framework, it has to ensure that its practitioners fulfil statutory and agency responsibilities to the highest achievable standards of professionalism. In allocating resources, in making recommendations or reaching decisions, in exercising control, and in all gatekeeping functions, the social worker must be just, sensitive to his role of mediation between the interests of the client and the state, and concerned always to act in the way that best achieves the overriding goal of maintenance.

The crucial role of social work is to influence *the way in which* welfare policies are put into operation, *the way in which* power is wielded, and above all, *the way in which* man's humanity is protected against abuse. It is the responsibility of the social worker to challenge aspects of policy which appear to require him to act in a way that is incompatible with social work's ideals of the importance of the individual and the ultimate worth of man. Problems, however, undoubtedly arise if the social worker challenges the *status quo* in the course of his practice – that is to say, if he seeks to effect a change in policy by unilaterally refusing to operate it, and there is necessarily a limit to the frequency with which this can be done. As Hunt (1979) says with regard to the role of the social worker engaged in mental health admissions:

> The social worker is not only presented with an emotionally charged situation, he is also caught up in his own internal conflict and uncertainty about the issues. He doubts whether he would want to be admitted to a mental hospital himself; he may be unsure whether the hospital has much to offer his client; he is aware of the environmental and personal stresses on his client and suspects that they, rather than his client, need treatment. He also has a deeply held commitment to the basic right of the adult individual to make decisions about the way he will order his life.

At the same time, the client is clearly disturbed, and 'tension is escalated by the fearful social worker, and the likelihood of a clumsily executed emergency admission is increased.' Now, it is clearly the right of every social worker to refuse to participate in any single process against his conscience. But on purely pragmatic grounds, it seems doubtful whether social work *per se* could survive a situation in which large numbers of professional staff were refusing to operate a range of functions across the board. In other words there is a difference of degree between conscientious objection selectively employed and a total unwillingness to recognise the legitimacy of the role of social work in a statutory setting, and it would be only sensible for employing authorities to ensure that the staff they appoint to social work posts are conscientiously able to reconcile their professional commitment and their humanitarian ideals with the realities of the political economy within which they will be expected to operate – whatever ideological complexion it might have.

What happens, it may then be asked, if and when the social worker in a statutory agency becomes satisfied that the deprivation, the deviance, the disabilities and the lack of privilege in the people with whom he is required to work are all either caused by, or are seriously aggravated by, the state's own approach to social policy, or, even worse, are an integral and inevitable consequence of its political philosophy? Can the social worker continue to operate *as a social worker* with such views? Of course, again, each will respond to the question individually. But my view is unambiguous. If the worker's critique of the state is ideologically rounded and total, then his role as social worker *for* that state can only be pursued clandestinely, dishonestly. For it is a crucial aspect of the model of social work presented in this book that the worker is engaged not *solely* for the benefit of the client as an individual (such a commitment, it should be clear already, is logically unattainable) but for the benefit of achieving a reconciliation between the client and the society of which he is a part. In given societies, there may well be a case for political and revolutionary overthrow, but such activity is not and cannot be, in my view, synonymous with social work.

On the other hand, it is not a consequence of this position that the social worker should not engage in policy debates and in attempts to change and to improve the climate for practice. But again, though essential to progress in a democracy, such campaigns are not *of themselves* social work. They are paralleled by teachers campaigning for comprehensivisation, textile manufacturers campaigning for import restrictions, and doctors campaigning for improved research facilities or a ban on cigarette advertising. Policy campaigns are an essential component of any area of contemporary practice: hence the need for reforms in the field of mental health, penal policy, the provision of support facilities for disabled housewives, and so on – but at the same time, practice has to continue in each of these areas, and according to current conventions and legislation. Anything less than this, and the whole body of social work practice would be wholly idiosyncratic, answering the needs neither of society nor the client but only, perhaps, of the worker. And although some social workers may think that they know best, the powers which they wield are potentially so far-reaching that they must be and must remain subject to publicly defined and culturally sanctioned limits. The mere fact that social workers claim that their aim is always to 'do good' is no guarantee that they will never, if left to their own devices, do harm.

6 Pro-active Involvement in the Community

Active involvement in the life of the community is now acknowledged to be a crucial element in the achievement of social work's primary objective of maintenance. Although, as we shall see in this chapter, there have been major developments towards this goal in recent years, the idea itself is not a new one. Some probation officers and social workers have always seen themselves as community managers or social care planners, but the duties involved have tended to be regarded as extra-mural, providing something of a bonus for the client and offering a contribution to social welfare above and beyond the call of duty. That is not the case now, and many social work posts require the practitioner to engage in community activities which are a world apart from the roles of office interviewing, home visiting and maintaining telephone contact with other agencies.

There are two major questions concerning social work's involvement in the community. The first is this: should social workers operating in the community turn their backs on a client-focus? Should they, in other words, be community workers pure and simple, without reference to the client-group for which their agency exists? The profession is nearly unanimous that the answer to this is clearly negative. Social workers are not general-purpose community operators, but are recruited to serve the needs of particular groups, and any community strategy must not lose sight of that fact.

The second question concerns how best to involve oneself in the community – especially bearing in mind the limited time and resources of any social worker and the scale and complexity of any community, for the social worker, as Figure 6.1 illustrates, is necessarily on the outer fringes of his client's network.

For some time now, increasing thought has been given in the social work literature – and in practice, too, of course, – to the implications of networks. Will the probation officer's influence always be negated by a delinquent peer-group? What is the effect of the husband on a woman's depression? How is a marriage affected by the demands of a spina bifida child? Can a mentally handicapped teenager be helped

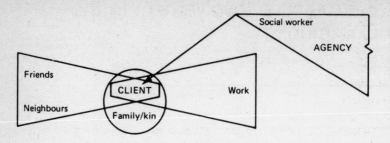

Figure 6.1   The client's social network

into some suitable occupation? Can the social worker join forces with the parents in the use of learning techniques to help a disturbed or deviant child?

There are two distinct, but obviously related, issues. How does the social worker interact with the client's network? And, given that many clients are often rather short of friends, neighbours and relatives, how does the social worker make up for deficiencies in the network? To further complicate the issue, it must always be recalled that social workers are themselves parts of complicated networks which involve their colleagues, other professional groupings, other clients and, not least, their private lives. The remainder of this chapter will outline the various ways in which social workers have sought to make their services available in different community settings.

Detached work

Detached workers try to break into client-networks by 'detaching' themselves from an agency base and setting up shop close to the grassroots or by working without any base at all. The Wincroft Project (Smith et al., 1972) operated from a specially established coffee bar in inner Manchester. Teenagers were attracted to it by the social facilities on offer and social workers mingled easily with them and provided any needed services. Other projects – most of them tending to concentrate on work with adolescents – have been run from council houses, city-centre walk-in refuges or advice shops. In each case, the aim has been to get closer to natural networks of need than is normally possible. Although there is evidence that this can be achieved, it has also been found that the ambiguity inherent in the detached work relationship is very difficult to overcome: the very act of getting closer to the client, dressing like him, identifying with him, becoming a part of his culture, can lead to confusion on both sides. If the detached worker retains loyalty to his agency, what happens when the client challenges the agency or the standards it upholds? If the worker identifies totally with the client, what happens when the agency by whom he is employed makes demands on him which he finds to be incompatible with the client's interests? Even though most detached work has been done under the auspices of voluntary bodies, such dilemmas are commonly recorded, and the task of reconciling conflicting perspectives in social work does not appear to be made easier by the approach. Unless the delicate nature of the worker-client relationship is handled well, there is always the risk that clients who had been led to see detached workers as being much closer to them than other social workers in their experience might feel betrayed if the worker's allegiance to them were ever thought to be in doubt.

Drug users pose particular problems for conventional social work units, and Dorn and South (1984) have described a variety of street agencies sited close to addicts communities and which make themselves available as necessary. The Hungerford Project in London's Piccadilly area is described as a detached unit, but operates mainly through an accessible reception desk. Availability is the keynote, as the project's administrator says in an interview:

> Say, a couple of people could come in who had been living homeless, and we know them quite well, off the street, and maybe one of them is slightly stoned and we would suggest that they come back later and they may or may not want referral to emergency accommodation or whatever.
>
> But we do have quite a large group of young people who are not particularly at the moment wanting to stop using drugs, needing some kind of local support and a bit of advice now and again, maybe getting into trouble with the police and needing a bit of advice about that. Sometimes when we get very busy, we get a very wide range of people who come wandering in. Basically we sort of advertise ourselves as seeing anybody about anything to do with drugs. It could be the person themselves, or a relative or friend or whatever...
>
> (Dorn and South, 1984, p. 11)

The interesting thing about such an approach to detached work is that it tends to be limited to counselling and advocacy – and even that role is sometimes restricted by virtue of the anonymity of the agency base. The Hungerford Project is close to the clients, but lacks the authority or the responsibility of a state agency; this can make it feel safer for vulnerable and frightened addicts, but it almost certainly reduces the scale of aid available.

A particularly remarkable exercise in detached work was launched in Sheffield in 1971, where the probation service opened a unit in Havelock Square, a run-down part of the city. The workers' initial aim was to help drug addicts but later their primary focus switched to work with prostitutes (Morris, 1976). The unit was not expected to operate according to conventional probation criteria; but was 'an utter contrast to the usual office setting in which the typical probation officer works. The probation officers live alongside their clients and offer a 24 hour round-the-clock service', and one of the workers called it 'the ultimate in social work'. The unit had four probation officers, three of whom were living in, and there was a part-time senior in charge. Caseloads were small with an upper limit of ten per worker, and the atmosphere was informal, with clients free to walk in at any time of day or night. The workers said that there were two main planks to the unit's philosophy: first, the honesty between worker and client – 'There are no barriers to hide behind, no secretaries or receptionists; you have to deal with it there and then; you can't say, "I'm knackered, clear off" or get the receptionist to tell the client that you're away'; and second, the residential fact which meant that workers and clients were 'all sharing the same grotty area'.

Morris commented that the unit, though regarded as successful, also threw up the two major problems in detached work: the strain on staff, and the 'whose side am I on?' dilemma. The strain is such that the workers told Morris that a two- to four-year stint was as much as any of them could manage. The unit's originator, Bruce Hugman, left to work on a smallholding in Kent (although he later returned for a time to the probation service); and other workers said that they worry about the effect of their job on their wives and families, or, quite simply, reach the point where they can take no more.

The lack of privacy in detached work is one aspect of the strain, but the absence of the kind of role protection which most social workers enjoy is another:

Freedom entails risks and this is certainly true of the unit... Most of the risks hinge upon that delicate line between legality and the role of the probation officer. 'Where does one stand?' asks one of the workers, 'I have been in pubs with drug users where they have openly injected and have known that they got the drugs illegally. I will say that they're being daft but what more should I do?' It is the ancient dilemma at the heart of social work: either the social worker reports the incident to the police and destroys irrevocably the trust he has established with the client or he turns a blind eye and connives in the commission of criminal acts. (Morris, 1976)

The Sheffield unit survived for nine years, but a decision was made in 1980 to close it down on the grounds that its work did not constitute a high enough priority for probation expenditure. Controversy stayed with it to the end: 'respectable' members of the neighbourhood (which had been refurbished and had moved upmarket during the 1970s) attacked it because they said it attracted prostitutes to the square, and others criticised it because it did not fulfil the reformative expectations that they had of the probation service.

Such criticisms are not specific to detached work. They are equally applicable, and often applied, to more conventional settings. But detached work is necessarily more public, more exposed to view; and, because it lacks a structure and reduces role-clarity, its practitioners are more frequently confronted with the inevitable dilemmas and ambiguities of their task. Although the balance of functions might vary, however, detached workers still find themselves operating the triad of social work behaviours – maintenance, change and the fulfillment of responsibility. The only real difference in their work comes in their attempt to get closer to the target population with a view to fulfilling their agency objectives more efficiently and more successfully.

Community networks

The idea of community, though conceptually controversial in sociology, was given a boost by the English school of community studies that emerged during the 1950s and 1960s and which examined kinship and neighbourhood relations in a wide variety of locations: in inner London and its outer suburbs, in Liverpool, in the mining-belt of Yorkshire, in rural Wales and in Cumbria. Abrams (1980) has argued that the romantic view of neighbourhood relationships prompted by these studies is misguided and misleading, for the sense of community arises, not out of free choice, but as a defensive response to external threats, economic hardship and restricted opportunities for personal and social growth. It follows from Abrams's thesis that any policy which seeks to emulate the community self-help model is inappropriate in a highly mobile society and, because of that, unlikely to succeed.

Notwithstanding such theoretical doubts, there has been a growing interest in the part that the community might play or ought to play in promoting the welfare of its members. A big fillip to this movement was given by Bayley's (1973) study of the plight of the mentally handicapped in Sheffield which led him to conclude that the 'statutory social services are quite unable to cope with the sheer volume of care and support that is needed' (Bayley, 1978). He recognised that the two support networks – one provided by the social services department, the other by the community – could and should co-exist, but that efforts should be made to ensure that their roles complement each other. To characterise this process, he used the term *interweaving*: 'The social services seek to interweave their help so as to use and strengthen the help already given, make good the limitations and meet the needs. It is not a question of the social services plugging the gaps but rather of their working with society to enable society to close the gaps.' It has certainly been established that, so far as the mentally handicapped and the elderly are concerned, relatives play the major role in providing care, and this has led to the cautionary comment that when we refer to 'community care' it is important to recognise that what we are almost always talking about is 'care by the family'. Wilkin (1979), writing six years after Bayley, and having similarly carried out research into the needs of the mentally handicapped, was much more hesitant about the strength of informal networks operating in support of the families of subnormal children. He concluded that, although the extended family did have some part to play, its contribution was not normally relevant to the day-to-day domestic routines, and that friendship and neighbourhood networks provided even less support: 'The cosy idea of neighbourhood mutual support systems conveyed in the concept of community care did not exist for these families.'

The attractions of looking to the neighbourhood for support services have been eagerly grasped by politicians who have – I suspect, wrongly – seen in the idea a cost-free benefit: if what they think of as 'social work' can be put on tap by friends, neighbours and family, then, lo-and-behold, the need to train and employ growing numbers of professional staff would evaporate. The inclination has been given even more encouragement by the widespread publicity given to Keller's neat but dubious assertion (1968) that 'we should expect a negative relationship between public welfare provision and community care arising from primary group and localistic (sic) involvements'.

In 1978, Parker provided a simple guide for the statutory services to adapt to natural helping networks:

1. Workers must begin to identify much more closely with geographical neighbourhoods, or patches.
2. They should build up contacts with other agents and agencies, especially home helps and street wardens who are likely to have 'an encyclopaedic knowledge of the support given by friends, relatives and neighbours of clients'. This involves working with 'perfectly ordinary people who are not hampered either by the labels that society confers on social workers or that social workers confer on clients'.
3. Social workers might aim to mediate within natural networks when problems arise that weaken the caring pattern.
4. It would be helpful if social workers could build up records of the kind of support which clients receive, thus adding greatly to our knowledge of natural caring systems.

This guide heralded a major conceptual development in British social services practice. Patch systems have emerged as a natural evolutionary phenomenon, borne of the recognition that social workers alone cannot always achieve maintenance objectives either as solitary operators or even through the medium of their agencies; some system of partnership with the community is essential.

Patch
There has been no development more significant in British social services during the 1980s than the emergence of the idea of 'Patch' as a model for service delivery. In its most simple form this might mean only that a team of social workers (or even a single social worker) is attached to a clearly defined geographical district, but in its most advanced forms, it means that the office buildings are decentralised, that the social worker coordinates teams of colleagues in the patch, that maximum use is made of volunteers, of informal caring networks and of inter-agency liaison, and that the social workers are therefore both more visible and more accessible to the community.

The idea of a social services department adopting an adventurous community perspective was incorporated into the Seebohm Report, (1968) but it took over a decade for it to become adapted to political and professional reality. It is, moreover, one of the few developments in

British social work which has been prompted from within the profession. It has tended to emerge initially in areas staffed by particularly imaginative, energetic and charismatic officers; others have followed on, recognising an idea that made sense, and now some social services departments are implementing the model from the top.

Normanton in West Yorkshire has become known as the trendsetter; and descriptions of the way 'Patch' works there certainly give the feel of the phenomenon.

A small industrial town of about 19 000, Normanton became the laboratory for the community-oriented ideas of its Area Officer, Mike Cooper. He divided the area into three patches. Each patch team included a social worker (as leader), two patch workers (typically a social work assistant and a care worker), perhaps six part-time community wardens and about 25 home helps. 'Staff were encouraged to make themselves readily accessible to users, to respond flexibly and rapidly to the problems they encountered and to collaborate closely with local people in developing community resources." (Hadley and McGrath, 1983)

It is reported that there is no real division of labour between the qualified team leaders and the social work assistants except that the patch leaders are required to oversee statutory work like child abuse and to be present during days when the team is on duty for the area as a whole. (Sharron, 1982) Even the work of the community wardens has become less routine: they used to visit 30 old people a day from a prepared list. 'Normanton, in keeping with its philosophy of extending the responsibilities of its untrained staff, allowed them to alter their roles and become the front-line in referring any problems of needs to the patch team.' Now the community wardens use their own discretion as to whom they should visit and for how long; they refer requests for home helps and meals-on-wheels to the patch social workers who then assess the needs of the clients; they act as listening posts and bring problems to the attention of the team; they draft in volunteers and double up as community workers.

Sharron describes the work of one Normanton patch warden, Mabel Betts. She has 40 clients, many of them elderly and with medical complaints such as diabetes, angina, or confusion. She lights fires, brings milk or medicine, and cooks meals. With one seriously confused octogenarian, Mabel calls five times a day – the first call at 8 o'clock – and it is that, she thinks, which keeps the client cheerful.

Sharron found that Mabel Betts was very well known in the community; it is through her and the other wardens that the patches have penetrated to the roots of the people, and a major factor in the success of 'Patch' is thought to be the extensive involvement in the team of local people who already know, and are known by, a great many of the prospective clients. Whatever else 'Patch' has or has not achieved, it has undoubtedly overcome the problem of the social workers, who, because of rapid turnover, spiralling career patterns and detachment from the location they are appointed to serve, deal with their clients at arms-length, and never think of them as having complex relationships within the community.

Quite how 'Patch' will develop as we move towards the 1990s is not clear, but a major commitment to community involvement or social care planning (to use Barclay's term) is clearly on the agenda. And the basic patch model has proved more adaptable to different settings than was initially thought possible. Its successful introduction depends on leadership, on departmental support and, increasingly, on trade union cooperation.

Hadley claims that 'Patch' definitely increases accessibility and serves to reduce the emphasis on crisis management, since, through the network, the team gets early warning of impending domestic or other crises before they reach full fruition. 'Patch' increases the public's awareness of social work services, which could obviously have resource implications, but it does enable steps to be taken to preclude institutional admissions wherever possible.

Mike Cooper, the leader of the Normanton initiative, has spelt out two principles that bring 'Patch' firmly within the framework outlined in *The Essential Social Worker*. He sees the chief aim of 'Patch' as being to 'divert people from institutional care while satisfactorily maintaining them within their families and neighbourhoods'. The model aims, above all, to make home-based care the departmental priority for all clients, (Cooper and Denne, 1983), and he and Stacy (1981) outline the argument that 'the place of the qualified social worker in this context is to act as an enabling catalyst who may also have expertise to offer in particular fields of work'. This lends emphasis to the community's reservoir of ability, good will and expertise which can be offered in partnership with the statutory services.

There is a suspicion that the exponents of 'Patch' sometimes get carried away in their contrast of its virtues with the shortcomings of traditional approaches. The idea, for example, that the patch worker is accountable both to the agency and the neighbourhood, is not specific to 'Patch', and Croft and Beresford (1984) have criticised the failure of

'Patch' advocates adequately to gauge client opinion.

Nevertheless, 'Patch' does go further than any of its predecessors in bringing into reality the idea of maintaining the client in ways that both appeal to him and key in with the warp and weft of community life. Politically it is not an especially radical step forward, but it is one that takes the idea of community involvement and makes it into a feasible strategy for a local government department to pursue.

The trained social worker becomes a kind of community manager in the world of 'Patch'; elsewhere, specialists are still needed, and decisions involving responsibility, power and social control will always need to be taken. But these functions are easier to accommodate within the tradition and ethos of social work if departments simultaneously accept their role as community and client supporters, as the doctrine of 'Patch' requires.

Community Care

'Patch' represents an important breakthrough in social services organisation, but as a conceptual element in social work it remains only a part of the full spectrum. It is misleading to imagine that it provides a model upon which the whole of social work can be based. Some critics have, for example, expressed doubts about the extent to which the client population for whom the greater part of the social services budget is allocated is really likely to be helped by a neighbourhood support scheme. A Director of Social Services has put it bluntly:

> Social Services are provided for the most severely frail, vulnerable, and those at the greatest risk of danger or harm to themselves. Although statistically insignificant in the population as a whole, large numbers of people are involved (for example, 880 in Lambeth's old peoples homes, approximately 1550 children in the care of the Council, 1700 meals on wheels delivered weekdays, 2000 meals at weekends). The number over 80 years of age will be substantially more in the future.
>
> The tasks in the form of management and organisation, including staffing, catering, cleaning and transport, require rather more than the enthusiastic efforts of local people and community groups.
> (Osmond, 1980)

Studies in both mental health and the penal system have pointed out that it is usually those with the worst problems who are also the most isolated socially, and in view of the fact that Abrams has suggested that neighbourhood support tends to be given on a reciprocal basis, there is obviously a problem when the giving is all one way – especially if, as is not infrequently the case, the aid offered is not even accepted gratefully by a cantankerous old lady, a disturbed alcoholic or a depressive mental patient.

The role and responsibilities of social work remain distinct from those of the citizen – and even from those of the volunteer or of part-time wardens. That role and those responsibilities require the social worker to put into operation programmes that further the objectives of their department, and it is important that, 'Patch' notwithstanding, a variety of approaches are employed to improve on performance.

A scheme with some similarities to 'Patch' but one targeted specifically on the elderly infirm with the explicit goal of reducing departmental costs by delaying admission to Part III accommodation is the Kent Community Care Scheme.

The Scheme is wholly client-focused (unlike 'Patch'), and those drawn into the spectrum of the scheme must be 'otherwise eligible for admission to residential care' by virtue of their frailty, incapacity or confusion. A budgetary allocation is made which represents two-thirds of the marginal cost of a place in Part III, and within that, specially allocated social workers are free to spend resources as they think fit, normally negotiating a contract for service from an individual or an agency at agreed rates. The aim is to enlist the support of people who will serve the elderly 'more for its intrinsic satisfaction than for material reward', but the fact that there is *some* payment is regarded as critical.

The primary system has involved the employment of locally-based helpers to perform tasks for clients, usually at relatively small cost. Matching client to helper is regarded as important, and sometimes clients have been able to visit the helpers' homes: the social workers have become case-coordinators, and the local helpers' activities have been dovetailed in with already existing services – especially, of course, home helps and meals-on-wheels. Challis and Davies (1980) give an example of the investment of effort required:

Mrs A. is crippled with arthritis, and, since breaking a leg, is virtually immobile. Her home is unsuitable (outside toilet, different floor levels between front room and kitchen), but the package of care has made it possible for her to remain at home against all the odds:

Early morning – Community Care Project (CCP) helper gets her up, dresses her and gives her breakfast; there is a different helper at weekends.
Morning – District nurse helps with washing and dressing her leg.
Lunchtime – Home help provides meal and does other household jobs; a CCP helper does it at weekends.
During day – CCP helper provides tea, social visits and shopping as required; there is also help from friends and neighbours.
Night-time – about 10 p.m. CCP helper assists Mrs A. to bed.
(Adapted)

In their evaluation, the research leaders of the Kent Scheme claim that it is both of proven viability and able to reduce costs in the Department. They quote figures which show that those clients served by the experiment were significantly less likely to be admitted to hospital or residential care during a twelve-month period.

The problem with the Kent Project, as with any front-running experiment, derives from its very innovatory nature. To what extent is it capitalising on (a) the current availability of mainly female labour in a depressed employment market, and (b) the willingness of people to work for less than proper wages because of the 'compassionate' identity of a work task? To the extent that either of these are true, the fear must be that the full national development of such a scheme would involve higher costs, as the normal play of market forces and trade union demands begin to operate – and, when that happens, as Armitage (1979) has argued, the costs of home caring may quickly rise above those of residential care.

The critical role of the trade unions within 'Patch' developments has also been commented on in the literature. In Normanton, a successful campaign for social work assistants to receive significant salary increases to differentiate them from general care workers is said to have worrying implications for the inherent flexibility of role-players within the scheme. Again, however, this only serves to reinforce the importance of departments (and especially social workers) being absolutely clear about objectives in projects of this kind. Soft-centred benevolence and open-ended endeavour is alright to start off with, but the nature of large-scale organisations and the needs of budgetary control demand clarity of perspectives. The only trouble with the idea of pro-active involvement in the community is that it can mean anything from being a parish priest to a youth club-leader or an underground sectional revolutionary. In the context of social work, it is essential that its purpose and identity are distinct, easily understood and in receipt of broad recognition within the profession. The main contribution of both 'Patch' and the Kent Scheme is that they have gone some way towards achieving such clarification.

Probation and the community

In its statement of National Objectives and Priorities for the Probation Service (April 1984), the Home Office invites the service to engage in 'other work in the community' over and above its role in the courts and with offenders. Certainly for a number of years, tentative steps have been made to encourage community initiatives, and some adventurous areas have gone so far as to make specialist appointments. In a survey of community initiatives, Shaw (1983) says that those officers given a full-time brief to act in a detached fashion succeeded in becoming involved in community-based developments, but suffered from being cut off from their institutional base and hence ran the risk of a lost identity. In other words, they might become good community workers, but as a result they lost their probation identity or found it an encumbrance.

In other areas, where teams of officers were encouraged to operate as a 'Patch' team, the problem was usually one of time and resources, and the evidence of achievements gained was very limited. 'In Hartlepool, for example, the only tangible reward for 18 months input by two workers was a week-long play scheme for residents' children during the school summer holidays.' (Barry 1984)

Barry comments that the probation service's attempts at community involvement have suffered from being disparate, isolated and lacking an underlying rationale. There is a feeling that the Home Office's expression of encouragement for action in the area of crime prevention might offer clearer objectives, but even here the boundary between what is appropriate for probation practice and what properly falls within the orbit of the police force is a potential source of confusion.

The significant contrast between the apparently successful introduction of 'Patch' in social services departments and its tentative failure in probation seems to hinge on differences in the availability of resources. Local authority social work starts off with a depth of personnel that the probation service cannot match; moreover social services have considerable scope for diverting erstwhile institutional funding to community work, and this has led to a much more flexible mode of operation.

In fact, the best developments in community initiative to be found in the probation service are quite different, reflecting greater specificity and hingeing on the availability of external funding. Thus, in a number of settings, the service has drawn on Manpower Services Commission funding to enable it to set up schemes to counteract unemployment among its clients; elsewhere a variety of financial sources have been tapped to provide new or better facilities to house homeless ex-prisoners. Given that the availability of just such accommodation is often the deciding factor in whether or not someone is given parole, it can easily be argued that the probation service will be better engaged in such manoeuvres than in vaguer initiatives of a less offender-orientated kind.

Many offenders – especially recidivists in prison – exemplify a major problem for social workers wanting to adopt a stronger community orientation. These clients frequently have no network, and some are actively not wanted by their neighbourhood, so it is arguably better for the probation officer to ease their way back into the mainstream by striving to create work and housing opportunities.

Conclusion

It has been argued in this book that, for the first time in 15 years, a theoretical framework for social work has begun to emerge clearly.

The overall objective of practitioners in post is the achievement of maintenance: maintenance of the state – which presumes a consensus model of politics, though it certainly does not preclude democratic conflict; and maintenance of those citizens who, for one reason or another, are not surviving under their own steam. Social work does not undermine a central emphasis on the preferred dependence on personal responsibility wherever and whenever it can be achieved.

The goal of maintenance, although it involves a commitment on the part of practitioners to provide such elements of support and help as they individually and corporately can, also requires them to fulfil a wide and still growing range of statutory and policy-based responsibilities – often concerned with the movement into and out of residential or institutional care – and to engage in such therapeutic activities as seem to be appropriate bearing in mind the needs, the interests and the views of clients. And now there is a further dimension to the theory: the pro-active involvement of the social worker in the community, which often carries with it resource implications, and can rarely be carried out by the worker in isolation. Agencies have to accept this as a legitimate role for their professionals, and committees and government departments have to be prepared to fund it, for it is centrally relevant to the goal of maintenance.

These various functions are not necessarily all vested in all social workers. Most of the 'Patch' literature recognises the need for specialist operators in fields like adoption and fostering, mental health, and so on (though the difficulty of achieving efficient and speedy access to them is sometimes a cause for complaint). In large departments it is appropriate and natural that there should be a proper division of functions and responsibilities. But, with regard to the community, it seems likely that too many serving social workers have not yet recognised the growing importance of pro-active intervention. This is nicely captured by Black *et al.* in their study of three social services departments: 'Social workers had a willingness to ignore the community and even in many cases dismiss the relevance of volunteers; to adopt a client specialist approach by design or by stealth and to work in a privatised and ad hoc manner in relation to individual cases and other agencies.'

Since Seebohm first mooted, in 1969, the idea of community social work, numerous debates have taken place about the way in which the idea could be activated. Very often these have had a political dimension with the extreme left arguing that social work could and should move into an activist role – fulfilling an explicitly critical role and striving to influence decisions by militant or collective action. Such an idea, though often atractive to students, normally founders because of its apparent impracticality in a hierarchical organisation which is subject to political authority in its own right and employs a wide range of staff not by any means unanimously at one with a marxist or radical perspective.

Thomas (1983) identified *service extension* as an equally legitimate community task, and it is clearly this which has now been taken on board by creative social workers. It enables a degree of campaigning, without requiring staff to oppose democratic authority – after all, as Hadley has said, social workers do have their jobs to consider!

Environmental support has long been recognised as something which the social worker ought to be expected to provide, but for many years this only seemed to be possible through the removal of the client from the community – often with stigmatising and destabilising consequences. Many of the most interesting developments of the last decade attempt to achieve the former without recourse to the latter.

Pro-active intervention in the community demands that the social worker accepts a leadership or management role; that he campaigns for resources either within his own department or elsewhere (through Urban Aid, the Manpower Services Commission or voluntary charities); that he works in full exposure in the local community, making himself accessible and visible; that he attempts to provide facilities on terms that make sense to the client group; that he utilises indigenous support systems and maximises existing networks; and that he accepts a degree of accountability both to the community and to the agency. The role thus offers a glimpse of social work as maintenance in its most developed form.

PART II

Dimensions of Practice

7 First Encounter: The Client Enters an Alien World

Social work and probation offices are heavily stigmatised: they are viewed by all except those who work in them with suspicion, perhaps with awe, and frequently with distaste. It is partly the feeling that a small boy has outside the headmaster's study, the feeling that comes from knowing that therein is vested considerable power from which it is better to keep well away. But it is also the feeling that such places are strongly identified with poverty, misfortune, crime and deviance, and that higher status is normally accorded to those who have no need of them. Thus to go to a social work agency voluntarily is a sign of having 'given up'; to be compelled to go there is a mark, not only of failure, but of shame.

These feelings are frequently reflected in expressions of client opinion, as in these quotations recorded by Mayer and Timms (1970):

'It takes a lot to go to one of those places. You feel very beholden to someone.'
'I said to my daughter that I'm almost in two minds whether to go or not. Well, she said, you try them, mum, and see what happens. But I had butterflies in my tummy all the time I was going there and sitting in the waiting room.'
'I felt belittled by going there.'
'To go for money, to ask them to help you out, seems a right predicament to get into. That was the worst feeling of it.'

Comments such as these lead the authors to conclude that 'clients do not go to social work agencies unless they are sorely troubled'; in another study, 58 per cent of clients admitted that 'it bothered them to be referred' to social work, while one woman said that she had been terrified when she knew that the social worker was coming for the first time: 'I said, "Here is a man coming to see me about the children. What is he going to do?" '(Rees, 1978)

In a society where self-respect is strongly identified with independence and conformity, it is a rare citizen who will walk for the first time into a social services department with his head held high and a jauntiness in his step. That daily recurring fact should be stamped indelibly on the mind of every social worker and every receptionist.

Bombardment

Given a general reluctance, then, to seek out the services of the social worker, what is it that leads an increasing number of people to come into the agency? There are, of course, some – a majority so far as the probation service is concerned – who have no choice in the matter: they are placed on probation, put into the care of the council, or made the subject of supervision orders, and henceforward their relationship with the social worker is enforceable by law.

But in voluntary agencies, and in about half of the instances in local authority departments, the client comes over the doorstep of his own volition – however much he may feel that circumstances or his family have pushed him. Why does he – or, in the majority of cases, she – come?

Table 7.1   *Main problems given at first referral to a Southampton area social services office*

	%
Physical disability/illness/ageing	30
Financial/material	17
Delinquency	15
Child behaviour/family relationships/etc.	14
Housing/accommodation/homelessness	11
Mental/emotional disorder	7
Other	6
	100

N = 2019. Problem not known in 38 cases. Data refer to the year beginning 1 February 1975.
Source: Goldberg *et al.*, 1977b.

Tables 7.1, 7.2 and 7.3 are drawn from different studies but together they provide a useful picture of bombardment and response in local authority settings. As Goldberg *et al.* (1977b) comment, it can be dangerous to draw general conclusions from single studies like these, partly because the criteria employed for classifying cases tend to vary

Table 7.2   Short-term referrals in a social services department

Request for service	N	Proportion of the applicants deemed to be in need of service (%)	Proportion of the applicants who received the service (%)
Social work	514	116	79
Aids	285	108	95
Housing	251	47	12
Information/advice	164	274	243
Investigation/reports	158	138	108
Finance/DHSS	121	67	33
Long-term residential	109	50	16
Occupational therapy	102	151	110
Parking badges for the disabled	92	76	67
Telephone	89	35	15
Handicap Register	68	113	103
Psychiatric admission	64	91	81
Short-term residential	62	81	48
Material aid	57	96	63
Adoption	35	40	31
Childminding	30	107	57
Day care	28	114	75
Adaptations	10	70	30
Counselling	9	711	367
Other	55	265	133
Total	2 303		

Note: The data refer to new referrals closed during a two-month period in a Devon social services department during 1978. They therefore exclude all referrals destined to become long-term cases. Also excluded from the figures are police liaison work over juvenile offenders, and requests for home help and meals-on-wheels.

The first column gives the numbers of clients who asked for the named services. The second column indicates how applicants' requests were re-defined in the light of the social workers' judgements about their 'real needs'. Thus those categories with percentage figures in excess of 100 indicate that many people were deemed to be in need of service who had not originally come asking for it. Conversely other categories, like housing and requests for a telephone, were greatly reduced as a result of the social worker deciding that some applicants were not in 'real need' of the service they had requested. The third column shows which requests were most and least likely to be met: again, where the proportion is higher that 100 per cent, this indicates that more people were given a service than had asked for it.

Source: 'Priorities and workloads, a study of closure decisions', Devon County Council SSD Research Section, September 1979. Reproduced in *Clearing House for Local Authority Social Research*, no. 9 (1979).

alarmingly and partly because patterns of bombardment also differ from place to place: the client groups and the problems presented are unlikely, for example, to be identical in Southwark, Tyneside, Peterborough or rural North Wales. Nevertheless it is possible to make a number of reliable assertions.

1. At referral, the elderly are always the largest single client group.

This stark fact emerges time and again, and is the clearest rebuff that can be given to those right-wing critics who persist in believing that social work is primarily about coping with deviants and scroungers who ought to be out earning their living. Black (1983) studied three area offices in North Wales, East Anglia and Birmingham and found that 53 per cent of all new referrals came from the ranks of the elderly. The pattern held true in all three areas, although in Birmingham the demand from families and children was significantly greater than it was in the rural districts.

2. The service provided to the elderly tends, on average, to be shorter term than that offered to other client groups; in Black's study, families and children made up 37 per cent of long-term cases in the three area teams studied; the elderly came next with 29 per cent; the mentally ill made up 12 per cent; and the remaining 22 per cent were divided equally between the mentally handicapped and the young physically handicapped.

3. Financial and material problems are frequent, with housing and accommodation difficulties also common. Together, in the Southampton study, they account for 28 per cent of all new referrals. But, as the Devon investigation shows, these are often the problem-groups that are among the most awkward to deal with satisfactorily. With regard to housing, for instance, the social workers decided that only 47 per cent of those who came for help with housing had real justification for doing so, and partly as a result of this, but partly too because of the department's inability to satisfy even 'confirmed' needs, only 12 per cent of the applicants for housing help had a service provided. It seems probable that an increasing number of people will come to see the social worker because their living arrangements are unsatisfactory or because they are in financial difficulties – and this despite the fact that down the road there are the specialist agencies, the housing department and the social security, which are manifestly failing to meet people's needs.

4. Those requests most likely to be given a positive response are, not surprisingly, the ones that are the easiest to meet at little or no additional cost. Requests for information, advice and counselling are not only met in full but the facilities are provided for many people who did not ask for them in the first place. Other applicants who were virtually certain to be given what they were asking for were clients wanting aids for the disabled, occupational therapy, or to have their names put on the Handicap Register. At the other

extreme, requests to enter long-term residential care, to adopt a child, to have housing adaptations provided or for a telephone were more than likely to be refused.

5. One important statistic, not contained in these data, demonstrates the short-term nature of most social work in the local authority. In Goldberg's investigation, only 6 per cent of the cases identified during a twelve-month period were 'still receiving continuous social work help' six months after the end of the pick-up period. For the most part, social services departments have become rapid-turnover agencies: of the short-term referrals contained in Table 7.2, the average period before closure of each case was only two-and-a-half weeks. However, there will always be a minority of clients who need to be admitted to residential care, to be given home help, day care or meals-on-wheels, or who will continue to use aids and adaptations provided by the department over a long period of time. Some juveniles will remain under supervision for up to three years or in care until their eighteenth birthday – and it is this minority of long-term clients who have the biggest impact on the department in terms of the resources required and the social work service provided.

Thus social services departments have to be geared up to cope with two quite different types of population: short-term applicants

Table 7.3   The social work response to referrals and long-term cases

	Work with new referrals %	Work with long-term cases %
Investigating/assessing	74	61
Giving information/advice	48	58
Mobilising resources	40	46
Supporting/sustaining	19	54
Advocacy	8	19
Problem-solving	7	34
Supervising/reviewing	6	34
Providing group activity	2	8
Educating/developing skills	1	14
	N = 1 140	N = 754

Source: Social Work in Context, J Black *et al.* (1983)
Note: The figures have been produced by reprocessing published tables in the volume.

with specific needs and long-term clients with both general and specific needs.

6. However, although the crudeness of quantitative data of this kind can sometimes conceal more than it reveals, the kind of social work practised both with new referrals and in long-term casework is shown to have some remarkable similarities in Black's study (Table 7.3). In particular, there emerges in sharp profile confirmation of the theory of maintenance outlined in Part I of this book. Social workers' single most frequent task is concerned with their responsibility to investigate and to assess – to make decisions for the benefit of the client or according to statutory regulations. Secondly, in respect of both new and long-standing clients, they use their contacts and their expertise to give advice and information; and they move into full maintenance gear with a commitment to mobilise resources and, especially in the longer term, to provide personal support and sustenance for those in need. The actively interventionist roles of advocacy, problem-solving and educating or skill-training come into operation only with longer-term clients, and only a minority are likely to find themselves referred into a group setting.

This is the shape of what awaits clients once they have put themselves into the social services departmental orbit.

Reception

Hall (1974), reviewing practice in four social work departments, found that 'the importance of client reception was almost universally undervalued'; and this despite Bessell's (1971) assertion that 'the job of the receptionist is a key one in any agency'. Hall certainly confirmed the significance of the receptionist's role, though not always in the sense that might have been anticipated. He says that he found evidence to show that receptionists were often in a position to operate in three different ways:

1. They could act as guides and advocates on behalf of selected clients in order to get them a speedy and effective social work service. For example, 'when a client was not seen quickly, the receptionist would frequently make further telephone calls [to the social worker] to ensure that the client was eventually seen as quickly as possible.... A client's stated problem might be significantly

exaggerated and urgency stressed when it was relayed to the social worker on duty.'
2. Conversely clients who were thought to be less deserving, less attractive to the receptionist or less in need of help, 'could be suppressed in a variety of ways'. This might mean that they didn't see the social worker at all on that day, or if they did, only after considerable delay.
3. Receptionists were often placed in the position of themselves providing advice and guidance – perhaps because no social worker was available.

The publication of Hall's work undoubtedly had a major impact on office organisation, especially in the large social services departments, but there is ample evidence that much still remains to be done:

There are too many waiting rooms which seem to institutionalise personal failure in the grudging way in which they are decorated or organised or serviced. (McGrail, 1983)

Hall's argument that efficient reception requires the easy availability of both a duty social worker and an appropriate intake system if the power of the receptionist were to be curtailed has been largely accepted.

But even where immediate access to a social worker has been achieved – and there are still many places where this is not so – six basic principles of reception remain important:

1. The receptionist is in the front line and has to counteract the client's feelings of doubt, anger, shame and pain, without becoming involved in a preliminary interview.
2. The receptionist must make the client feel welcome.
3. The receptionist should be expected to ask for the least possible amount of information to meet the duty social worker's needs and privacy in conversation should be arranged. (Hall refers with approval to one office which had separated the waiting area from the reception desk and, in addition, displayed a notice which indicated that clients could ask to be seen by the receptionist in private if they so wished).
4. Receptionists should not be concealed behind an impersonal grille

or window, and, whenever possible, they should not have other duties such as typing or answering the incoming telephone (though the size of the agency is acknowledged to be a factor in this latter respect).
5. Receptionists should be selected with care, always given some in-service training, and encouraged to identify with the aims and ideals of the agency. Nothing is worse than having a receptionist whose ethos is wholly out of tune with social worker's values. She should be able to respect clients rights, and to cope with hostility or depression.
6. The waiting area should be clean, attractive, warm and comfortable.

These principles (derived from Bessell) have not proved uniformly easy to implement. In Northampton, for example, where an architect-designed reception area was provided in 1981, social workers initially resisted the openness and directness of the new system.

> A long and heated debate took place regarding the filter afforded by a receptionist, but management insisted that the client's initial contact should be with a trained social worker. However a compromise was reached over the provision of a counter between worker and client. It was recognised that some reassurance was needed for staff who had experienced the anger, friction and sometimes violence created in a reception area. (Sweet, 1981)

It is crucial that the principles of warmth and openness are not conceded in social work, though it has to be acknowledged that the growing sense of vulnerability and fear felt by receptionists and practitioners in inner city areas is a factor that cannot be ignored and that may ultimately militate against the sense of professional commitment that remains crucial to good practice.

Intake

The function of the intake interview in social work is, first and foremost, *to help the client*, and the overriding thought in the worker's mind must be: 'How can I be of assistance to this person?' A great deal has been made in the literature of filtering and rationing, screening and assessment, decision-making and referral, and, although it is true that all of these somewhat technical processes might be contained within the intake system, if they loom largest in the worker's mind he is likely to have a distant, impersonal and potentially dismissive impact on the client.

Loewenstein (1974) uses a cool, analytical approach to the intake process:

> Whatever form it takes, the initial encounter between client and agency must provide the agency with sufficient information to decide how best to serve this client and to determine if this agency is the best place to provide the needed service. The worker has to ascertain as accurately as possible what the actual problem or enquiry is from the client's point of view, to explore the problem or situation with the client, to evaluate the client's psychological state, to ascertain what coping efforts he might have made, to recommend a course of action, and to facilitate such a course being undertaken by the client. Not only should an intake system filter out clients who are not considered appropriate for the services the agency offers, but it should also act as a filter in passing on cases to other agencies.

All very true, no doubt. But it is much more important for the intake worker to be smilingly efficient, to help the client feel welcome (even if the eventual outcome is a referral to the Housing Department) and to demonstrate that social workers are employed to provide a positive service, than to operate a restrictive policy of rationing and refusal.

For work such as this, knowledge, experience and skill are all needed. So, too, are time and immediate access to a social worker. And it is with a view to meeting these needs that many larger social services departments have now established intake teams. Smaller offices and most probation and voluntary agencies continue to rely on a duty-rota system; both methods have advantages and disadvantages, but both should ensure the ready availability of professional personnel to respond to requests by casual callers or telephone enquiries.

Short-term work

Of those who come through the door of the intake worker's interview room, we now know that, in social services departments, a large majority appear to need only a short-term service. Goldberg *et al.* (1977b) found that the aim of an intake team was 'to deal with explicit requests on a short-term basis unless there are clear indications for more intensive and longer-term involvement': 75 per cent of referrals were closed within two months and 88 per cent were never transferred out of the intake team's caseload.

Goldberg's study found that, in intake work, three kinds of activity predominated: exploration and assessment, the provision of information and advice, and the mobilisation of resources. The third of these included the supply of some kind of practical assistance, in which help with applications, usually for welfare benefits, topped the list. In four-fifths of all cases, intake workers were in contact with outside agencies of various kinds, most often health agencies: GPs, health visitors, hospitals and district nurses.

Something not far short of a revolutionary change in social work skills has been required of the profession in the last decade. 'One-interview work', from being regarded disparagingly, has come to be seen as a crucial, even dominant, part of the social worker's task and, as Goldberg has suggested, it can need very different skills from the traditional model of long-term care. For the trained professional, there is no excuse for not being able to cope with a steady stream of short-term clients and most social work courses now recognise the need to prepare their students to handle immediate crises and issues like welfare rights. But knowledge of one's own working locality – where the boarding houses are, which other service agencies to draw on, what are the potential sources of employment for clients, etc. – can only be accumulated on the job, and the skills required to handle such knowledge are not fundamentally different from the skills required to undertake any other form of social work.

Knight (1978) gives us a nice example of an intake case:

At 10.40 a.m., Nick (a newly-qualified social worker in the Camden intake team) is called downstairs to interview a large, rather bedraggled man who has arrived without an appointment and whose appearance, flies undone and grubby clothes, has alarmed the receptionists. He tells his rather sad story to Nick. Five weeks ago, he was discharged from a psychiatric hospital in Surrey where he had spent the last ten years, with a ticket back to his home in Ireland. But, he tells Nick, his family were not interested in having him back so he returned to London and has been living rough since then. 'His case seems to be a terrible indictment of community care', commented Nick later. 'Ostensibly he came in for some money but before sending him to the DHSS, I wanted to find out more about him and try to offer him something more positive. I couldn't get hold of his old doctor at the hospital to check out the case, and unfortunately our local hostel had no room. But they gave me the address of another one which I shall check out. So I then sent him to the DHSS after I had told them to expect him, and asked him to come back on my next duty day on

Thursday. By then, I should have got hold of his doctor and contacted the other hostel.' He groaned, 'We spend hours and hours of our life on the telephone.'

The idea of rationing

Referrals to social services departments have risen steadily since 1971, although the preferred policy of meeting immediate needs with short-term responses means that a high proportion of 'new' cases are always re-referrals: people who have had help in the past and who come back for more. The question of how many referrals an agency should be designed to deal with is impossible to answer because it depends partly on how you define social and economic policy and partly on felt need in the community. In one sense, there need be *no* limit on the services which the social worker might provide, but, in reality, of course, boundaries do exist. It is this realisation that has led policy-makers in recent years to review the balance of supply and demand, and some departments have tried to set down an order of priorities. Nottinghamshire's is quite explicit:

Priority 1: Life or death situations where immediate investigation and action is required. (For example, allegations of non-accidental injury to children, elderly confused clients and clients displaying active depressive psychosis). And high-risk situations where action is to be taken within 72 hours of the referral being received.

Priority 2: Work with a specific time-span laid down by law or by the Department. (For example, social enquiry reports, compulsory admission to mental hospital, visits to boarded out children).

Priority 3: Preventative work with both families and individuals where there is a prospect of their problems being repeated in the next generation. (For example, work with homeless families and handicapped people where there is a perceived risk to the next generation.)

Priority 4: Work with clients who might need residential care or where there is a prospect of rehabilitation from residential care. (For example, the unsupported and isolated elderly.)

Priority 5: Work with all other clients. (For example, clients in residential care with no rehabilitative prospects, work with solitary drug addicts and alcoholics, etc.)

Within each client group, wherever they appear in an agency's list of priorities, it ought to be possible to outline the precise steps which social workers should take to meet specific circumstances. For example, Wakefield (1976) has suggested five stages in the preferred intake response to the referral of an elderly person said to be 'at risk' – a situation generally acknowledged to take precedence over most other new cases:

1. Clarify exactly what the risk is and what is being asked for. Does the old person know of the referral? Wherever possible, the client's consent should be obtained.
2. Collect basic information about what help is already being given. For example, by the family or the community and in the form of domiciliary care.
3. If the risk appears to be connected with health or hypothermia contact the GP, health visitor or district nurse for a medical assessment.
4. If the request seems to be for general support because of loneliness, etc., and the client himself has called in, consider making a referral to the appropriate voluntary body – Old Peoples' Welfare, clubs, churches, volunteers, etc. In the case of a third party referral, either suggest the client calls at the office, or pass to the intake team for an assessment visit.
5. If the request is for residential accommodation, respond as follows:
   (a) Collect basic information: for example, age, address, reason behind request and consider the need for further investigation by the health visitor or GP.
   (b) Assess the degree of urgency, and the appropriateness of the application. Discuss the alternatives: for example, relatives, friends, neighbours, day care, domiciliary services. Consider providing lists of private and voluntary homes, including the Salvation Army and homes run by the trade unions or occupational welfare groups.
   (c) Establish which domiciliary services are already being provided and consider whether other services might be appropriate and would enable the person to remain in the community. Arrange an assessment visit where necessary and decide how to continue social work contact, for example, where the application for admission to care is accepted but cannot be arranged immediately.
   (d) If the applicant is in hospital, ask for full reports to be sent for consideration.

(e) If immediate admission is arranged attend to the protection of the client's property – and pets – where appropriate.
(Adapted from the *Community Care* Supplement on Intake, with acknowledgement.)

As could be deduced from Tables 7.1 and 7.2, the intake worker has to be prepared to cope with an immense variety of requests, needs and crises, and his responses must be similarly wide-ranging. Most departments now provide operating instructions of one sort or another, and some have developed algorithms to further clarify the process. But although such written guides do seem to be increasingly necessary, especially when there is a rapid turnover of staff, they must be acted on sensitively and in a humane fashion. There will always be a need to aim for and to achieve a nice balance between agency and statutory requirements, the cumulative practice experience of the team and the professional skill and initiative of the individual social worker.

Intake to residential care

If the client feels fearful at the idea of coming to a social work office, how much more apprehensive is he likely to be at the prospect of entering a residential home! It is a giant step to take whether the person involved is a child going into a community home or assessment centre, a psychiatric patient being admitted to hospital, an offender entering a probation hostel, an elderly person being taken to Part III accommodation or a young woman staying in a mother-and-baby home. All of these allocations are, to a greater or lesser extent, subject to the influence of social workers, and inside each institution, too, social workers have an active part to play.

The skilled social worker will always make the process of admission to care less painful, less stressful than it might otherwise have been. Of course, such moves are often crisis events for which adequate preparation is rarely possible, and no matter what the social worker does, however skilful his efforts, the anguish cannot altogether be assuaged. Entering an old people's home, for example, is probably the second most important personal move that many people make in their lives after getting married and setting up an independent household. But even though it is impossible to minimise the pain, or rather, perhaps, especially *because* it is impossible to minimise the pain, the need for a high standard of social work practice is absolute.

The following example reveals a better-than-average model, and one that could be emulated everywhere. It concerns the admission of an old lady to Part III accommodation, which, as Billis (1973) has shown, often involves complex decisions on the part of the social services organisation, but that in the client's eyes, is straightforward though far-reaching in its implications.

> Mrs Marchant is in a hospital bed, having been admitted from her own home with pneumonia. Her mobility is restricted, she has no relatives left, and it is thought that she can no longer cope in the house. The medical social worker reports her position to the area's fortnightly review meeting where fieldwork representatives, heads-of-homes and managers come together. There is a vacancy in *St Cecilia's*, and the matron, having ascertained that Mrs Marchant is not incontinent, says she will visit her. She does so three days later; Mrs Marchant indicates that, despite many regrets at losing her independence, she will be glad not to have to return to her large, cold house, and would like to come to St Cecilia's. Arrangements are made for her to move there from the hospital; she is conveyed by a friendly volunteer, and welcomed, formally by the matron, and informally by the other residents. She will be there for four weeks before the allocation is finalised: this gives Mrs Marchant the chance of expressing her doubts about the move, and the matron of the home the chance of concluding whether or not the arrangement is likely to succeed. The admission is thus made smoothly and with proper concern for the feelings of the new resident, for the interests of the other residents who will have to live with her and for the staff who usually have very clear ideas about the boundaries of suitability for admission to their home.

Conclusion

The successful and sensitive use of intake procedures requires, first, clarity of agency objectives – *why does this social work office exist?* Second, acceptance by the social worker of those objectives – *how can I help my agency to fulfil its obligations?* And, third, a commitment to the use of professional skills of the highest standard attainable. Such skills at intake can be briefly summarised:

1. *Efficiency*, by virtue of the workers' disciplined knowledge of the relevant aspects of practice.
2. Sympathetic *concern* for the client's feelings about his problems and in his relations with the agency.
3. The provision of a positive *service*, and the clear expression of a sense of direction derived from the worker's identification with the aims of his agency and the humanitarian ideals of his profession.

4. *Friendliness* and cheerfulness. The social worker, like the actor or the judge, must never have an off-day. The crisis in each client's life is unique, and the professional role of the worker demands a reliable and a helpful response.
5. *The ability to handle* distress, anger and depression in the client: these are the emotions naturally associated with the kinds of problems brought to the social worker, and they must be accepted as such.
6. *Acceptance of responsibility* for determining what, if anything, should happen next. The client must have the right to refuse further contact, but he should not be left in any doubt about its availability, or about who – the client or the social worker – is expected to make the next move.

The achievement of a high standard of practice requires the constant reiteration of the central importance of these skills in intake. The agency which ensures that they are practised day in, day out, will know that the first encounter of its clients with social work has been made as smooth, as helpful and as responsive as it can be.

8 Who is the Client?
Who Determines the Action?

Despite occasional expressions of unease at the term 'client' in social work ('Clients?! I know what I'd call 'em.' said one Rotary Club stalwart to laughter and applause during the discussion which followed a lunchtime lecture I'd given on social work), it is a word which appears to have successfully made the transition from private, fee-paying counselling to the state welfare sector. The term has stuck and seems likely to be retained.

The idea of 'the client', however, remains fraught with ambiguities, and Pincus and Minahan (1973) have performed an important service by pointing out that a distinction has to be drawn between the *client system* and the *target system*. The client system constitutes the person-in-situation who requests a service from the social worker; the target system consists of the person or the situation on which the worker decides his efforts should be concentrated. Thus in a traditional counselling role, where, for example, a matrimonial couple might come jointly for guidance, ventilation and insight, the client system and the target system are one and the same: the clients ask for help and the counsellor provides it by focusing on the husband and wife as interacting individuals. Or, again, a young married woman, her husband in prison, might come to the probation officer and ask him to help her work out a manageable budget on a limited income. The probation officer might do no more than that, in which case, once more, the client and target systems are identical.

However, in the latter case, the probation officer might decide that his client appears to be receiving less than her due deserts from the social security. At this point, having decided with the client to act on her behalf, he will phone, write to or visit the DHSS office concerned, and attempt to obtain improved allowances: this will mean that, temporarily, he will be engaged in helping his client by tackling a different target system – the state's income maintenance service. (Pincus and Minahan also identify an 'action system', which would be illustrated in this case if the probation officer were to involve the claimants' union in his client's cause – but this refinement is of no consequence to the problem of defining 'the client'.)

In contemporary social work, there are a great many instances where the client and target systems do not coincide; for example:

1. Mrs Blythe comes to the family casework agency and says she wants the social worker to 'do something about my George' (her impossible husband) or 'our Willie' (her delinquent teenage son). Should the social worker instantly act on Mrs Blythe's behalf, and take up the cudgels for her against those targets that she says are disturbing her peace and quiet? Or should he regard Mrs Blythe as both client and target, and, by patient enquiry, set about discovering whether there is some way in which he could help her to cope with her erring menfolk rather more successfully? Or should he, by virtue of Mrs Blythe's arrival on the agency doorstep, regard the entire family as the client-and-target system, and draw up a programme – modest or ambitious, depending on circumstances – aimed at improving the climate of relationships?

2. In situations where a child is deemed to be at risk of abuse by its parents, the conflicts of responsibility can be severe. At the time of a court hearing the law is quite clear in requiring the social worker to regard the child's interests as paramount. But at the same time, the social worker is expected to work with the parents (who therefore can also be regarded as 'clients' in the traditional sense) even though he may feel their immediate interests to be in conflict with those of his 'true' client, the child. The 1975 Children Act has recognised the reality of this conflict by legislating for the appointment of separate solicitors to represent the child and his parents respectively. In the event of the child being taken into care, the agency's responsibilities require the social worker to concentrate on the parents with the aim of improving their circumstances, their attitudes and their behaviour sufficiently to allow the child to be returned to them: they thus become the target-system, while the state – acting on behalf of the child – is in effect the client-system.

In a sense, the distinction between 'target' and 'client' systems might be thought to be primarily one of semantics, and the fact that George or Willie Blythe and the parents of a child-at-risk are defined as 'target-systems' does not in any way reduce the obligation on the worker to relate to them and engage with them in styles traditionally identified with a social work ideology: in particular, this would include an attempt to negotiate a 'voluntary' relationship or contract incorporating a commitment to cooperation and endeavour on the part of the target-system which would effectively convert it into a client-system. Pincus and Minahan's major contribution has been to highlight the importance of *clarifying obectives in practice* – of noting the fact that the worker may have different aims depending on *who* made the first approach and *how* the case relates to statutorily defined requirements. Their distinction between clients and targets has been most commonly taken to push the analysis in a radical direction: to show that the welfare of clients might most effectively be served by seeing community change as an appropriate goal and therefore community agencies and facilities (or their absence) as a target system. Less apparent from their own writing, but crystal clear to any reader familiar with a contemporary public welfare system, is an entirely different interpretation of the distinction and one especially pertinent to statutory social work. This represents *society* or *the state* or *the government* or, if your political analysis requires it, *the ruling class* as sometimes the client-system, and some statutorily-defined consumers of the social services as *targets*: youth custody inmates on compulsory after-care, parolees, persons discharged from special psychiatric hospitals (like Broadmoor) and subject to supervision, juvenile offenders given supervision orders. These are not people who have sought social work help voluntarily, but people who, by virtue of their past behaviour or present condition, are required by law to enter into a social work relationship. They are referred to as 'clients' and will, no doubt, continue to be so called (indeed, it is strangely difficult to devise a suitable alternative designation); but insofar as the common use of the term *client* seems to imply a degree of freedom to withdraw from the relationship and to exercise unlimited control over it, it is manifestly inappropriate. In such cases, the state is both the employer *and* the client of the social worker, and the legally defined 'clientele' is really a target group.

Merely to make this point is always to run the risk of being branded as a fascist, of arguing that the social worker is a purblind agent of an omnipotent state authority. The reality is much subtler than that, and I shall return to it later in the book. For the moment, it is sufficient to assert three things: that the traditional textbook notion of the social worker's relationship with a homogeneous collection of clients is wide of the contemporary mark, and greatly underestimates the complexity of the social worker's pivotal position between the individual and the state; that the power of the state cannot be ignored nor can it be claimed that the social worker is in some sense above its authority; but that, nevertheless, the social worker is delegated to identify and look after the interests of marginal persons who might otherwise be overlooked or penalised unjustly by the state, and this must mean that the social worker is sanctioned to do battle on behalf of designated clients against authority in given circumstances, and to do it in such a way that achieves a measure of satisfaction to all parties.

The question of 'who is the client?' has traditionally been posed implicitly in debates about the notion of client self-determination. Both Plant (1970) and Whittington (1971) effectively killed off the concept as a prerequisite of social work more than a decade ago, but the idea has remained a powerful fiction in the minds of practitioners. Whittington lists the following ways in which the social worker exercises direction or control over the client:

1. His agency function – in probation, child care or mental health, for instance – requires him to use coercion, persuasion or pressure or to have recourse to legal sanctions.
2. His official position gives him power over the client's life – for example, whether or not to use his influence to persuade the gas or electricity board not to cut off the supply of fuel.
3. The agency setting – in a school or hospital, for example – means that the social worker has to conform to institutional norms and employ social work practices in order to achieve approved goals. If he fails to conform, or if he pursues goals not sanctioned by the agency, he can be regarded as out of step with the team and so become alienated – to the possible detriment of future clients.
4. Within the casework relationship itself, Whittington suggests, the worker exerts influence by virtue of his status and the client's perceptions of him. 'The caseworker, though he may profess commitment to client self-determination, non-directiveness and the client's freedom to choose, finds his therapeutic aims greatly aided by the client's susceptibility to his influence and subtle directiveness.'

Whittington concludes, 'To increase the client's capacity to evaluate choices may be a goal of treatment, and participation may be a technique used to this end, but to maintain that treatment is carried out without directiveness because the latter's skilled and subtle nature has made it less easy to observe, requires nothing short of self-deception.'

If this analysis of practice is accepted, then the picture of clients who always initiate action, social workers who only ever respond to the client's request, and target-systems which are attacked (or changed) solely for the benefit of the original client is obviously a misrepresentation of social work as it really is.

Of course, social workers do provide a service, but it is a service offered within a fairly precise social context – one in which, in the public sector, they are employed as state functionaries. (Even social workers working for voluntary organisations are subject to the possibility of sanctions being used by their management committees or the withdrawal of cooperation by sister organisations if it is thought that patterns of practice are departing from consensually defined limits. Moreover most voluntary social service organisations in the United Kingdom are now heavily dependent on state funds for their survival and growth.) Social workers can, must and do defend civil liberties, fight for client rights and criticise abuses of statutory power. But, both in terms of political logic and in the light of actual experience, it is clearly not possible for them to defend the absolute freedom of any one individual nor to embark on a singlehanded assault on the power of the establishment – at least, they *can* attempt to do either or both of these, but their future role and viability in social work may be seriously affected as a result.

A good example of the social worker's feeling of helplessness when confronted with the combined forces of law, community and institutional power is provided by the case of the Robinsons.

Mr and Mrs Robinson and their grown-up daughter, Alice, were all educationally subnormal. In addition, Mr Robinson was stone-deaf and unable to get a job. The family was 'known' to the social services department but rarely demanded attention. Their behaviour, however, was a source of constant irritation to the neighbours who found them aggressive and sometimes offensive. There were no rent-arrears, but eventually, because of constant complaints by the neighbours, the district council decided to evict the Robinsons. Social workers who knew the family were aghast because they could see no viable alternative, but their department was powerless to intervene. Attempts were made to mobilise help, but the district council was clearly within its legal rights, and the eviction duly took place. The social worker's role was to arrange transport and storage facilities for the furniture, liaising with the DHSS and the local cat and dog shelter. The day before the eviction, a high-level and somewhat reluctant decision was taken in the social services department to support the family financially (under the National Assistance Act, 1948, section 21) by providing temporary accommodation in a hotel.

As one of the social workers in the department commented, the case undoubtedly highlights some of the limitations inherent in statutory social work. For such a family as the Robinsons, the primary preventative strategy for social work must be the provision of suitable accommodation. When the council, under pressure from the community, takes that away from them, it is understandable that the social worker should feel that his position is a weak one: 'One of the most vivid memories that remain is the feeling of total powerlessness to make the community care'. (Bowman, 1978)

The community in this instance was a rejecting, not a caring, community. It may be that the law was a bad law – it has now been amended in such a way that the district council today would not be able to offload the responsibility for housing the Robinsons once it had made them homeless. But the problem in principle remains valid. The social worker has to work within the framework of legislation, and subject to the expression of attitudes on the part of the community: he has no power of veto either over the legislature or the executive, and he cannot claim inherent superiority in his expressions of opinion over members of the general public. The Robinsons' neighbours, for example, could legitimately turn round and say to the social worker: 'You don't live next door to these people. You go home every evening to your suburban semi ten miles away. Who are you to talk about community care in our council estate? We've worked hard to make the street a pleasant place to live, and we're sick of the Mad Robinsons disturbing the peace.'

The social worker cannot be an arbitrary dispenser of justice unique to the needs of one family irrespective of others. He *can* act as an advocate on behalf of the family, but he cannot claim absolute priority for them merely because they are his clients.

All through this book I have argued that the primary function of social work is one of reconciliation: enabling the state and its citizens to live together in relative harmony. On the one hand, the state is prevailed upon to find a significant place in society for the handicapped, the deviant, the deprived, the aged and the vulnerable: in this sense, the worker undoubtedly operates on behalf of the underprivileged client. But, on the other hand, those same people are persuaded by the social worker to accept the terms currently offered them by the state. Of course, it remains the social worker's responsibility, not only to get the best terms available now but also –

perhaps in unison with client groups – to press for policy developments that will lead to corporate improvements in the future. This circularity in the social worker's role is critical, and has not always been understood in recent years. The social worker owes allegiance to the client, but it is not an absolute allegiance; he is employed by the state, but he is not a mere tool of the state. The unique nature of social work can only be grasped by recognising that the two halves belong together, *are* reconcilable, and *are* dynamic in their long-term effects on social policy and practice.

Assessment

Assessment is the key to all good social work, and is a constant element in the practitioner's daily routine. It is a process of *learning about* the newly presented client and *reaching conclusions* about recommended action. What is the client asking for? Is it within the department's power to help – either directly or indirectly? Should he be referred elsewhere? Are there aspects of risk which require legally-supported decisions? Is he likely to become a long-term case or will this be the only contact?

Curnock and Hardiker (1979) argue that the assessment process follows, or should follow, a set pattern:

1. The social worker will be involved in a *complex process of interpersonal communication*, usually within the context of an interview. In order to handle this, he must prepare himself carefully for both the setting and the purpose of the meeting, and try to anticipate how the client will react to the occasion. It isn't just a question of gathering facts; it is more a matter of trying *to make sense of* a particular person's problems or behaviour in relation to his unique social environment – and that demands real skill in the worker.

2. In relating the circumstances of the client's position to his personal and social strengths and stresses, the social worker must be able to individualise the situation and see it in the perspective of his own department. Can he respond to the client's situation, given the reality of his agency base?

3. The most critical stage involves the drawing up of a balance sheet of relevant variables which can be defined as *risk, need and resources*. Will the *risk* of keeping a client in the community be too great? Does the client have *needs* which the department can satisfy from its

own *resources*? (If this formula is applied to the Robinson case, it will be recognised that the social worker's frustration derived from the fact that, while living in their own house, the family had their needs satisfied and made few demands on state resources. The social worker's assessment of risk was, however, out of step with that made by the neighbours whose judgment carried greater weight with the district council. After the Robinson's eviction, the social services department quickly decided that the family had been put at *risk* by being made homeless, had *needs* which the department was authorised to meet, and that, at least in the short run, there were *resources* available to cover the cost.)

4. Having reached a conclusion, the social worker will normally share his findings with the client, and either communicate the assessment to the people who asked for it – a committee, a court, a team leader, a doctor – or decide whether to act himself.

5. When the report has been completed and presented, the assessment process ends. It may or may not lead on to intervention.

The skills required in assessment are slowly acquired through training and experience: some are generic and relate to the process of interviewing, observation and analysis; others are specific to different client groups. One way of organising an assessment in child care is illustrated in the following example.

The assessment of young children at home
A Central Council for Education and Training in Social Work study group (1978) concluded that it was not possible or appropriate for social workers to be responsible for fully assessing the development of children they visit, but that they should nevertheless learn to observe and assess a number of critical aspects:

1. *The overall appearance of the child:* Height, weight, skin condition. Is he/she appropriately developed for his/her age? Are there any obvious signs of handicap?

2. *Environmental stress indicators:* Home conditions, crowding, bed-sharing, cleanliness, clothing, nutrition, playthings.

3. *Parental and family relationships:* One or two parents? Quality of interaction between adults. Interaction between parent(s) and child. Handling. Violence.

4. *Areas of family functioning*: Affection, security, parental models,

coping with stress, parental interaction, life experiences, discipline, communications.

5. *Mental state of parents.*

6. *Mental state of the child at risk:* For example, is he sad, dejected, apathetic? Is he unnaturally still or watchful? Is he alert and involved? Is he outgoing? Is he overactive? Is behaviour appropriate for age and sex?

The report emphasises that, in some situations such as court reports and investigations of abuse, certain points need to be considered with special care; for example:

(a) the social worker should talk to each of the children and the parents *separately* and on their own;

(b) he should be especially on the look-out for inconsistencies of detail in how events are related to him;

(c) he should particularly attune himself to signs of stress or illness in the parents;

(d) he should note who sleeps with whom and whether adults and children of opposite sex are regularly sharing beds.

Objectives

Traditionally social workers have operated with relatively vague, even grandiose, objectives: 'to improve social functioning in the client's family', 'to show him that crime doesn't pay', 'to improve her self-image'. Following criticisms of such imprecise good intentions from both inside and outside the profession, the current tendency is to move towards greater specificity of goals. For example, Sheldon (1977) argues that it is not sufficient simply to run a group because of a vague interest in doing so: you have to have some idea of what the group is intended to achieve for its members, and how best to set about achieving it with maximum efficiency. Of course, it is easier to make such an assertion than to pursue it, and much depends on whether and how social work's objectives in general are clarified. They may, for example, quite legitimately include a broad commitment to provide a form of oversight or continuing care which might, under agreed circumstances, not merely justify but require the provision of relatively unstructured visits or interviews.

A recent research overview (Reid and Hanrahan, 1982) confirms the position. The most successful social work interventions occur when the practice structure is clearly defined, when there is a specific problem-focus, when personal behaviour patterns or social skills are identified as targets for attention, and above all when behavioural contracting is used at the heart of the relationship. The best results are likely to be achieved when precise goals are set. For example, a behavioural contracting approach proved highly effective with the families of children who had been removed into foster care: the children came home sooner, and family interaction problems were alleviated.

Contracts

The notion of *assessment,* although it can involve self-assessment, is generally taken to emphasise inequality in the social work relationship: the social worker has the responsibility of sitting in judgment upon the client, who may not always even know, let alone agree with, the social worker's arguments and conclusions. The identification of objectives, too, has all too often been carried out unilaterally by the social worker, even to the extent of indulging in *goal displacement.* Sheldon (1977) talks of this as 'an occupational hazard of some importance', and illustrates it by referring to the woman client who didn't know she had a marital problem when she came to ask about a telephone for her disabled husband. The social worker, unable to supply any telephone, was nevertheless willing and eager to engage in a therapeutic relationship with the client, and so focused on the next most relevant topic – the difficulties of living with a handicapped partner. 'This is all right providing we are sure that we have a real problem in hand; one more pressing than some of the others on the caseload, more urgent than the task of joining in the effort to provide more resources – such as telephones.'

But its 'all rightness' also depends upon the agreement of the woman that it is a legitimate area for discussion, something which, if only to achieve ventilation, she is happy to talk about. If such agreement is not obtained, we are back in the world of *clashed perspectives,* in which the social worker's endeavours may be not only irrelevant to the client but also seen as an intrusive impertinence.

It is largely with a view to avoiding this error that recent years have seen the emergence of enthusiastic support for contracts in social work: the idea that worker and client shall make an explicit agreement to work towards clearly defined goals. As Corden (1980) points out, the presence of a contractual element in social work practice is not new. 'Hamilton (1951) emphasised the responsibility of the worker to make explicit the conditions and terms upon which help could be made available, and Perlman (1957) wrote that "it is the business of forming a pact that is the basis of an ongoing productive partnership between the client and the agency".' Many probation officers have, for decades, required their new probationers to sign the probation order indicating their understanding of its terms and their willingness to conform to the objectives outlined.

The new dimension derives from the emphasis on reciprocity in the contractual relationship between social worker and client, although as we have already seen and shall see again, such reciprocity is not without its problems and its ambiguities. The best summary of contracts is provided by Reid and Epstein (1972):

> The major function of the contract is to ensure that the practitioner and client have a shared understanding of the purposes and content of treatment. The contract is formed at the beginning of service and, unless both parties agree to changing it, serves to guide the course of service.... Use of contracts helps to avoid certain perennial problems in social work practice: misunderstandings between worker and client as to the nature of the former's intentions and the latter's difficulty; lack of clarity on the part of both as to what they are to do together; drift and scatter in the focus of treatment.... If a client is unsure of what he wants from the social worker, then perhaps the first order of business should be to assist him in achieving some sense of direction in using help. Most important, use of contracts with the unmotivated or uncertain client provides some assurance that he will not be treated 'behind his back' for conditions that have not been made clear to him.

There are three special attractions of a contractual approach in social work: it encourages honesty in the working relationship; it encourages the explicit identification of some focus for action; and it encourages an element of reciprocity in the exchanges between worker and client.

Honesty
Rees, (1974) recounts an appalling case in which the social worker, without the explicit agreement of his client, Mr S. – a single father of a family of three, out at work each day for twelve hours from six o'clock in the morning – placed in his house a young 'housekeeper' with two children of her own. The client disagreed with the proposal, but 'not forcefully'. Mr S.'s mother, who rarely saw her son, told the social worker she thought it was a good idea. There were problems of

overcrowding and money; the children fought, and the housekeeper's husband came round wanting his children back. 'In spite of the social worker's clarity about his goals and the amount of time he put into the case, he seldom saw Mr S. let alone discussed with him the rationale for his actions.' This case, in which the social worker surely used his powers of discretion wholly inappropriately, could not have followed such a course if the client's written agreement had been required, and if the respective contributions from the various participants had been more carefully spelt out.

Focus
Although precision is not essential in contracts – there is nothing to prevent agreements being drawn up in general terms – there is little doubt that the use of a contractual approach is likely to encourage greater specificity in identifying objectives. Indeed, the use of contracts in the context of task-centred work requires as much.

Reciprocity
It is in the area of reciprocity that the emergence of contracts is both most exciting and yet also most problematic. Take, for example, the case quoted by Salmon in Reid and Epstein (1972):

In respect of a single mother, whose children were taken into care, a contractual agreement was drawn up between her and the social worker. The mother agreed to:

1. secure a stable job;
2. secure and maintain a flat suitable for her and the children;
3. visit the children (in foster care) regularly;
4. set aside some money each month to be used for the children's needs on their return home. (This condition replaced one which required the mother to contribute to their keep in the council's care.)
5. keep the agency abreast of any change in her situation.

The worker agreed to:
1. regularly discuss and evaluate progress in achieving tasks;
2. recommend return of custody to the mother if tasks were achieved and maintained for six months;
3. arrange visiting schedules with children in the foster home.

The case ended successfully, and the client said that she especially appreciated the openness and honesty of the system: 'This was the first time she'd known what the agency expected her to do before she got her children back.' But supposing, in the course of the six months, that the mother had set up a marital association in the flat with a man thought to be wholly unsuitable as a stepfather (perhaps with recent convictions for child molesting, for example)? The terms of the contract would not have allowed the social worker to take this into account; she would have had to renege on the agreement and the client would have had no means of enforcing it. Corden (1980) comments that 'the justification for a contractual model must be grounded in values rather than in claims about its therapeutic effects', and those values are based on the notion of self-determination for the client and the humane tradition of the social work profession. But we have already seen that self-determination is something of an illusion. If contracts are to become a daily part of the social work scene, then their wording must never go beyond what the social worker knows he can deliver, and machinery must be set up which would enable clients to seek recompense in the event of the worker failing to fulfil his part of the bargain. If this were not to be done, social work contracts would be rapidly seen as another example of fine intentions with no substance.

The contractual approach must begin from an explicit recognition of the inequality that is inherent in the social work relationship. Corden suggests that many clients would welcome an element of reciprocity, and it seems likely that they would not be unrealistic in their expectations of the social worker. Rather than promising to make certain decisions in what must always be an unknowable future, it would probably be wiser practice for the social worker's share of the contract to restrict itself to a commitment of specified forms of help in the immediate future – with further commitments to be renegotiated as time goes by and the relationship develops. In this way, a contract can take due account of the client's preference for short-term concrete services and the worker can avoid becoming overcommitted to long-term service deliveries that may be rendered unobtainable by unforeseen events in the environment.

Who then determines the action?
Clients are not by any means totally powerless. As Miller and Gwynne (1972) have shown, the residents of a residential home can have important effects on the lives of staff and the atmosphere of an institution. Any client in the community can influence the nature of

the interactions that occur between him and the social worker by the style and intensity of his response. And just occasionally, a client can make a lasting impact on the social worker by his strength of personality, his courage in the face of adversity, or even his friendship. But the trend of evidence is otherwise undeniable: the social work relationship is an unequal relationship, it is necessarily and irreversibly so. The client is the petitioner or the recipient; the social worker is the potential or actual giver or restrainer. The client is the object of the social worker's attentions, the social worker the subject of the client's hopes or fears.

It is because of this inequality in the relationship that the obligations carried by the social worker are an essential part of his professional identity: the social worker *must* involve the client in his own self-development as much as possible; he *must* make his own objectives explicit; he *must* be honest in explaining to the client how he is assessing him and his situation; he *must* be frank about the nature of the responsibilities implicit in the social work role. One of the major attractions in the idea of contract work is that it compels just such honesty; it demonstrates to the client that he is not a non-person, an object to be used, a recipient of aid only according to the worker's whim or the agency's arbitrary powers of discretion.

Problems can undoubtedly arise, however, when the client is both vulnerable and difficult – especially in the case of a child or an adult who is essentially unlikeable and dependent. The story of Graham Gaskin (MacVeigh, 1982) highlights the abuses that can still be inflicted on people like him – brutality in foster care, regimentation and fear in residential care, the facelessness of professionals, homosexual exploitation by a voluntary social worker, and rejection by the social services department at the age of sixteen. True, he was full of violence and hatred from an early age, but the statutory child care system must be designed to cope with such characteristics without presuming the inevitability of failure. If it is not doing so, then constant efforts must be made to improve it. In view of this, the development of Children's Rights groups can only be good for the system, and – albeit perhaps painfully – good for social work. At least they serve to remind us all that, because of our privileged position, we are under a permanent obligation always to strive for the highest possible standards of professional performance.

In conclusion, then, the social worker determines the action, but in doing so strives for a negotiated relationship between all parties, and, above all, aims to reach some kind of balance between the client and the state. In that sense the role of the worker is that of an arbiter and can only be sustained if he retains the confidence of both sides – and other interested parties. Such a role allows for maximum flexibility in regard to many different types of client and many different styles of supervision: in this way the label 'social work' can satisfactorily be applied both to the exercise of restrictive control over a high-risk parolee and to the encouragement of a radical self-help group among single mothers. In each, the goal of maintenance is sustainable.

9 Speech: The Social Worker's Basic Tool

Where does social work take place? The only accurate answer is 'anywhere': in an old peoples' home; beside a hospital bed; in the client's kitchen or bedsitter; in a prison cell; in a child guidance clinic playroom; in an office – sometimes warm and comfortable, often not. In all such settings the social worker has to strive for professionalism and maximum effectiveness. So he does, too, in detached or transitory locations: a children's play area, a park bench or coffee-bar, a pub or youth-club, the streets of a housing estate or the eighteenth floor balcony of a high-rise apartment block, travelling in a car (taking a child to a children's home, for example, or a woman to visit her husband in prison) or working with a group of young people on an adventure trip.

No matter what the setting, no matter what the focus, the greater part of social work hinges on the nature and quality of relationships between workers and clients; and the basic tool in such relationships, particularly in the initial stages, consists of verbal contributions by the worker and verbally expressed reactions by him to the client. Groupwork and community work have ostensibly broadened the range of social work settings beyond the traditional twosome or dyad of the therapeutic interview, but even they make considerable use of verbal exchanges: 'You spend so much time just talking to people,' says one community worker.

Hence the continuing importance of the interview. The interview, rather like religion, has traditionally been subjected to eulogy or obloquy, depending upon the perspective of the critic, but, despite doubts about its effectiveness as a mode of bringing about behavioural change, it seems likely always to remain an integral and essential part of social work practice. Its value only comes into question at times when theorists argue or practitioners act on the assumption that the interview is *an end in itself*. In medicine, interviewing is an aid to diagnosis; in personnel management, an aid to recruitment; in commerce, an aid to selling. The social work interview is not normally different from these, although we have recognised that relief from tension can be achieved through counselling.

The interview can take a great many forms and the social worker is likely to have as many verbal exchanges with non-clients as with clients. (Indeed, as we saw in the last chapter, the question of *who* the client is, is not as straightforward as is usually assumed.) Telephone calls and visits to landladies, to Supplementary Benefits offices, to employers or potential employers, to debt-collecting agencies and hire-purchase firms, to the police and to doctors or psychiatrists: all are usually made in an attempt to persuade the interviewee to adopt a sympathetic attitude towards the social worker's client, to moderate a punitive response, to consider giving help, to provide necessary information, or to delay threatening action. Such occasions are, thus, in a very real sense, 'conversations with a purpose' which is the traditional definition of an interview. They have a beginning, a middle and an end, and the social worker must approach them with professional seriousness. All interviews can be subjected to review as Banaka (1971) has suggested:

1. What was the *input*? What questions were raised? What answers were given?
2. How should the input be *analysed*? What inferences could one make about the input – including non-verbal behaviour – during the interview?
3. What is the *output*? What is the end-product? What are the conclusions to be drawn at the end of the interview?

It is a worthwhile principle to adopt in social work that no meeting should take place, no interview be held, unless an output is intended. The hoped-for end-product may not always be achieved, of course; but, if it is not, some thought should always be given to the reasons for the failure (Redford and Goodenough, 1979).

Social work interviews are by no means always plain sailing, and although the apprehensions of those new to the job are sometimes exaggerated, the practitioner certainly has to know how to react to and cope with verbal aggression, threats of violence, tears, total silence or more bizarre behaviour. The necessary skills for dealing with difficult clients and situations can only be properly learnt by simulation or role-play, by observation of the interviewing process through video or a one-way screen, and ultimately through personal experience. But fundamentally the rules are:

(a) to combine flexibility in relations with the client with a clear understanding of the agency's goal,
(b) to be honest about the boundaries of reality: if, for example, a child has been taken into care against the parents' wishes and on your recommendation, the only realistic strategy is to be frank but sympathetic, and to attempt to persuade the family to look forward to and plan for a happier future; and
(c) to recognise that, in difficult situations, the agency expects you to retain control of the interview and the professional identity demands that you do so with real sensitivity to the client's feelings. Angry people will not always stay angry; utter desolation can lead to suicide, but it can also be reversed; psychotic extremes are deeply disturbing, but treatment is often possible and relief can usually be given; tears can be distressing but they may be the key to an honest discussion about underlying problems.

Difficult interviews, then, cannot be avoided in social work; they demand adaptability, gentle strength and resilience in the worker, and these are the characteristics of professional expertise.

The skills of the interviewer
The art of interviewing, like the art of acting, of public speaking or of tactical politics, is dependent on the development of a personal style. No Hamlet, St Joan or Willy Loman is ever quite the same as any other; and the stalwart clients on any agency caseload are similarly aware that every social worker is different – sometimes very different – from all the others. Age, sex, social background and personality: all are inevitably a part of the interviewer's style. But there are nevertheless a number of established principles which should only be varied as experience brings with it the confidence to employ more idiosyncratic, more risky methods – and even then this should never be done without good reason.

Jamieson (1978) has listed ten principles of interviewing which provide the new social worker with useful guidelines for practice. They are not absolute assertions of what is right or wrong, but they have evolved over the years, and have been passed on by word of mouth and the written page from experienced interviewers to newcomers. The following is an abbreviated and amended version of Jamieson's Principles:

1. Try to tell the interviewee how much time is available for the interview. 'No specific time is optimum, though five minutes is probably too short and over an hour too long.'
2. Start where the client is. Explain to him why he is being seen, or, if he asked to see you, ask him why.
3. Try to have sympathy for the client, however unsympathetic a person he may be. The aim must be to make the client relaxed and unafraid.
4. Try to have empathy with the client – to see things through his eyes.
5. Do not be judgmental or condemnatory. Try to show acceptance and tolerance.
6. Smile on first acquaintance. This may help the client to communicate more freely.
7. Do not ask questions that can be answered simply 'yes' or 'no'.
8. Do not put answers into the client's mouth. 'I don't suppose you've ever hurt your child, have you?' is a forcing prompt that clearly reflects the interviewer's perspective and that would make it almost impossible for the interviewee to talk about his feelings, let alone his actions. Ask neutral open-ended questions.
9. On the other hand, it is inappropriate to probe too deeply too quickly in an interviewing relationship, and it is wrong to probe deeply at all unless there is a clear purpose in doing so. Even then, the interviewer should only do so if he has the requisite skill to cope with the responses, and if there is sufficient time to return the client to a normal level of conversational reality afterwards.
10. Don't be afraid of silences when the client is thinking his way forward. But don't prolong silences when to do so would be felt as an uncomfortable and even aggressive act on the part of the interviewer.

Interviews are free-flowing, open events: their direction is never wholly predictable, and the interviewer's contribution can never be accurately programmed. An American psychiatrist, Richard Bealka, has demonstrated how many variations there can be in the counsellor's response to even the most common statement of fact or feeling. He uses a hypothetical situation in which a young client says, 'I don't get along with my parents', and suggests that there are numerous responses that can be made by the worker, all equally suitable and all fulfilling the two important requirements of a successful interview: they allow the client to express his feelings, and they help the counsellor to direct the interview. Bealka's suggested responses are these:

- You don't get along with your parents.
- Your parents?
- What do you mean when you say ...
- I don't understand what you mean when you say ...
- Help me understand what you mean ...
- Give me an example of how you ...
- Tell me more about it.
- Uh-Huh. – and? – For instance? – Go on.
- Oh? – but ... – I see.
- When did you first notice that ...
- How do you feel about it? (Perhaps the most important question one could ask.)
- What are some of the things you and your parents disagree about?
- What are some problems kids like you have – not just you but all kids in general?
- What are you parents like? What is your dad like? What is your mum like? (General questions)
- You seem to be very upset about this.
- You look worried. You look unhappy.
- You say you have trouble getting along with your parents. What are some of your troubles?
- Perhaps you could share some of your ideas about what has caused these problems. (It probably never helps to ask the question 'why'. If they knew why they were having trouble with their parents, they wouldn't be seeing you.)
- Maybe it would help to talk about it.
- Compared with you, what type of people are your parents?
- If your parents were here, what would they say about the problem?

Reproduced, by permission, with minor amendments from material developed by Dr Richard J. Bealka, psychiatrist, Mental Health Institute, Independence, Iowa, USA; and published in Beulah R. Compton and Burt Galaway, *Social Work Processes*, Dorsey, Ill., 1975.

Contexts for interviewing
There are three prime contexts for interviewing clients in social work which can be characterised as a meeting of strangers, structured approaches and long-term relationships.

The meeting of strangers
The single interview as an event in itself, or a single interview followed by a strictly limited number of additional meetings but not leading to a developing relationship between client and worker, is what concerns us here.

As we saw in chapter 7, all social services departments are now accustomed to handling a large number of callers every day: many have never been before, and many will never come again. Some have suggested that social workers are not as geared up as they need to be to deal with this persistent bombardment of enquirers and advice-seekers, but most agencies have gradually come to terms with the demand. It is certainly important that they *should* do so, because of the continuing need for a walk-in service where clients are guaranteed a friendly response to the myriad problems they come up against in their dealings with statutory authorities, welfare organisations and the wider community. Whether such a facility is ideally located in a local authority department, which is itself one of the parties most frequently complained about by clients, is a moot point. But that was certainly the intention of the Seebohm Report, it is the way it has worked out, and whether the staff are paid or voluntary, social workers or ancillaries, Jamieson's principles of interviewing apply with full force. In addition, three single-interview principles can be added:

1. Have a full range of relevant information to hand – a knowledge of welfare rights, of local resources, and of the law directly relevant to social work. Be efficient.
2. Know and be known by your referral routes. If the client would *definitely* be better off somewhere else – in the Housing Department, at the DHSS, at a solicitor's or the probation office – tell him so, make an introductory phone call, and perhaps send a letter of accompaniment.
3. Whenever possible, *do* something. A friendly deed, an earnest of your concern, a recognition of the client's vulnerability: these are worth far more than *just* a smile – and a referral on.

The structured approach

Coincidentally with the creation and growth of large-scale social services departments in the United Kingdom, a major development in social work theory has taken place: the recognition that social work needs structure if it is to be realistically implemented. The origins of this realisation can be plotted historically in the casework literature and are well summarised by Smalley (1970): in social work practice 'too little form or absence of form can waste effort and lead to purposelessness, disorganisation, confusion, amorphousness, or outright chaos'. This view represents a reaction against the time-consuming and often meandering work of psychoanalytically inclined caseworkers of an earlier generation, and it emerged initially in two ways.

First, it was argued that structure should be determined by the nature of the agency within which social work was practised, and that indeed social work could not be divorced from the requirements and expectations of that agency. Second, Perlman developed the idea of social work as *problem-solving*, in which an important first step was to *partialise* the goals and the areas for emphasis.

> The idea of partialisation is simply cutting a dilemma down to its size... Particularly in work with those who today are central to social work's concern – the economically and educationally deprived, the hard-to-reach, the nonintrospective, long-and-chronically deprived persons, the crisis-prone and crisis-ridden – a nearby, reachable, easily imagined goal is the only one that has reality. And though the goal may be as material as getting and using money aid, or as practical as gaining re-entry into school for the drop-out, the rudimentary steps of problem-solving may be involved and taken by client and caseworker. (Perlman, 1970)

From these beginnings, three forms of structured intervention have emerged – each demanding of the interviewer a technically correct approach to the client and his situation.

1. Crisis intervention   Crisis intervention techniques grew up independently of casework theory in the field of psychiatry, but they were eagerly taken up by social workers who saw their applicability to the client in a distressed state. The goals of crisis intervention are to counteract the effects of a crisis, to relieve the symptoms of emotional pain, and to restore the client to a state of being able to function normally. One of the many areas in which crisis intervention has been employed is in counselling the bereaved, and Lindemann has argued persuasively that the crisis of bereavement can best be overcome if the worker helps the client to do his 'grief work': 'to emancipate himself from the bondage of the deceased, to make a readjustment to the environment in which the deceased is missing, and to form new relationships and patterns of interaction that bring rewards and satisfactions.' (Rapaport, 1970). Such a problem-focused approach is said to be likely to achieve a healthy resolution of the crisis.

2. Task-centred casework   Due primarily to the influence of William J. Reid, task-centred approaches have found a ready audience since they emerged out of an experiment which showed that a structured form of short-term service in a voluntary agency secured superior results when compared with conventional open-ended casework (Reid and Shyne, 1969). The attractions of these unusually positive research findings and an apparently more economical approach to social work were, not surprisingly, too much for many agencies to resist.

> Task-centred casework is a structured approach to the process of working with clients. The essential elements of the structuring are the use of a short time limit, the selection of a target problem from the problems presented, the use of tasks to work towards the alleviation of the target problem, and the negotiation between client and social worker on the time limit, target problem and tasks. (Butler *et al.*, 1978)

The definition of *problems* can be, and often is, as broad as 'the marital relationship', but *tasks* have to be selected which are highly specific. For example, to improve communications between husband and wife:

(a) to spend ten minutes alone each evening talking about the children;
(b) using hands to communicate feelings;
(c) using more physical contact, with no expectation of sexual intercourse;
(d) Mr H. to try and take Mrs H. out;
(e) Mrs H. to moderate her aggressive tone.
(Butler *et al.*, 1978)

The task-centred approach has, to some extent, suffered from social work's tendency to become too ambitious in its objectives. Task-centred studies have shown that the technique brings focus to the worker's approach, and, if properly contracted, is appreciated by the client: it makes sense, it is practical, and it demonstrates a degree of professional expertise that is valued by the recipient of the service. Goldberg and Connelly (1981) put it this way: 'We have proceeded from vague and global objectives, such as more adequate social functioning or greater ego strength, to more specific, operationally definable behaviours or feelings. So far, so good.' But, bearing in mind the failure of task-centred experiments in the United Kingdom to achieve major behavioural changes, they acknowledge that 'when the aim is the achievement of more complex behavioural changes, such as non-repetition of self-poisoning or decrease in delinquent behaviour, then the results remain disappointing'.

3. Behaviour modification Again with their origins outside social work – this time in psychology – behaviourist methods have been employed by a small number of practising social workers, more especially in the fields of mental health and residential child care where behaviourism's particular contribution has been to emphasise the importance of consistency and reliability in rewarding good behaviour and punishing bad. Hudson (1978) and Holbrook (1978) have described experiments in which the parents of child-patients in the community have been involved in behaviourally-determined programmes of rehabilitation. The results, though mixed, are sufficiently encouraging to make the model worth pursuing. One problem is that the approach can be quite expensive in the use of staff time in the community, but the frequently-quoted advantage is that it is totally subject to evaluation. The objective is spelt out clearly; the method pre-defined, and the end-product always measurable.

The principles have been specially utilised in Portage schemes in which the parents of mentally handicapped children are trained by social workers and health visitors to employ structured methods in order to further their child's development. 'The programme is based on an analysis of the steps in child development and uses a behaviour modification model. . . . [The social worker] regularly visits the family, provides activity charts in those areas where the child is more retarded and helps the parents to plot their child's progress . . . The centre of attention is on the achievement of carefully defined and clearly understood goals.' Hanvey (1981, p. 40) concludes that the approach 'provides a model of social work which seeks to work *with* rather than *for* those for whom help is sought'.

The present and future of structured approaches 'In the midst of
vagueness, there is precision; in a turbulent world, there is form.' That
is the creed which makes the use of structure potentially so attractive
to some social workers. However, in her study of contemporary
practice Browne (1978) records that very few use any of these
approaches on a day-to-day basis. Even when they do so, the
terminology is often not understood, the theories not employed, and
the structure imprecise. ' "Crisis work" was often used to describe a
crisis for the worker or the agency,' she says – not at all what Caplan,
Lindemann or Rapaport had in mind!

Structured models, or others derived from them, not only require
the worker to understand the methods and to be explicit in his aims.
They depend for their success on a stable work-setting in which the
practitioner is sufficiently trusted by his superiors to operate both
according to agency guidelines and in the client's best interests; they
require the ready availability of adequate resources of space and time,
energy and initiative, and they also depend on the suitability of the
clients presenting for help. One conclusion of Butler's is reminiscent of
an earlier research finding: 'The social worker is best able to make a
good relationship with those who appear to need least help.' (Davies,
(1969) Butler (Butler *et al.*, 1978) says:

> At times the [task-centred casework] structure was not adhered to
> through lack of practice of the practitioner, at other times this was
> because of the nature of the client's situation. The method seems
> easier to apply in situations where the presenting problems are
> fewer in number and where the client is in a secure situation from
> the point of view of relationships and accommodation, and where
> the client is a relatively stable person.

Those who have sought to summarise research findings in social
work have, however, reinforced the significance of structure as a key
to success.

> Time-limited, problem-specific approaches emerge as desirable in
> many areas ... It may become increasingly difficult to justify
> practice approaches of a long-term nature, given the attitude of
> many organisations towards cost-effectiveness. Each social work
> practitioner must resist the temptation to be 'all things to all men'
> ... If the objective of social work intervention is to produce the
> greatest change for the client, then it appears that workers who
> develop time-limited approaches that are planned and
> systematically applied to specific problems have an advantage.
> (Thomlinson 1984)

In the United Kingdom, social workers remain somewhat sceptical of these encouraging noises. On the one hand, it is by no means clear whether structured approaches can ever constitute more than a small part of the total 'maintenance model' of statutory practice; on the other, the theoretical vacuum of recent years has meant that little has been done to prepare practitioners for structured methods. In any end-of-term report, their use in statutory settings still deserves to be regarded as 'promising' rather then 'convincing', and their eventual successful employment depends on greater clarity about their place in the scheme of things and on the development of more sophisticated practitioner skills. Whether they will ever completely replace long-term work with all clients seems much more doubtful than is claimed by those American writers used to concentrating on therapy rather than maintenance – although Thorpe's (1982) damaging claims about the potential for harm in compensatory facilities like intermediate treatment have reinforced the argument for structure, specificity and a focus on limited problem-solving.

The long-term relationship

Traditionally the principles of interviewing and the use of structured techniques are primarily employed with short-term clients. But all social workers – or at least all social work agencies – have responsibility for clients who are in contact with them for periods of time extending from three months up to a virtually unlimited number of years. The Family Service Unit works with families over generations. Probation officers frequently supervise offenders for two or three years and work with recidivists through probation orders, detention centre and youth custody after-care licences, and thence into prison and beyond – such a client may know far more about penal system social work than many a newly trained recruit to the service; local authorities, as well as sometimes taking on FSU-type families, also carry extended obligations to the handicapped, the elderly-at-risk, children in care and others. In the residential sector, Miller and Gwynne point out how, in a hostel for the chronically sick and disabled, the residents – or some of them – stay on 'for ever' while the staff come and go on a semi-temporary basis.

In such situations, the relevance of any one interview can be muted (although Sainsbury remarks on how FSU clients always seem to remember their *first* ever contact). What is of far greater force in long term cases is the overall relationship between client and worker, or between client and agency. And each such relationship is undeniably unique. Consider two examples.

1. Arthur and Jenny and the mounting debts   Arthur Silsden was 19 and on probation. Two years before his court appearance he had married Jenny, hugely pregnant and very nervous. Arthur found the responsibilities of being a husband and father all too much. He had made one suicide attempt in the face of increasing debts, and, when things got on top of him, he took to drink or his bed or both. Jenny, at the time of Arthur's court appearance was also on probation and was living twenty miles away in a mother-and-baby home, called Sun-View, with a view to learning housecraft and domestic skills.

Mr Rowland, the probation officer, hoped that he might get Arthur to recognise and accept his marital responsibilities, and he spent a lot of time talking with him about this. He also tried to help him budget his finances, and combatted an attempt by the Housing Department to gain possession of the council house for non-payment of rent.

After three months, Mrs Forbes-Willoughby, the matron of Sun-View, telephoned Mr Rowland and complained that Arthur, instead of sending money to pay for Jenny's keep, was spending it in the betting-shop; she said that she'd asked Arthur to stay away from Sun-View for a while because she thought he was a bad influence on his wife. Three days later Arthur phoned Jenny to say that he thought it would be better if they separated, and at this Jenny became very upset. Later that day, Arthur turned up at Sun-View drunk and 'looking rather shaken'. He'd had an accident in a 'borrowed' car, for which he hadn't been licensed or insured; the police intended to prosecute.

Six weeks later Arthur was back in court for non-payment of fines, and Mr Rowland told the bench that he was trying to get Arthur into a job so that he could pay his debts which were now considerable. He hoped that things might get better as Jenny was home again having completed her condition of residence at Sun-View. However, whatever else she'd learnt there, she had not mastered the art of resisting doorstep hire-purchase temptations, a persistent weakness of hers. The Silsdens plunged deeper and deeper into money trouble. Arthur, though, seemed happier, and Mr Rowland felt optimistic. He had had almost daily contact with one or other member of the family for over six months, and he felt he was winning.

The next week, however, the Housing Department rang Mr Rowland up and told him that the Silsdens were only paying their weekly rent once a fortnight, and that, as a result, arrears were mounting steadily. Mr Rowland went round to the house, and found the rent man there threatening to evict Arthur and Jenny. A day or two later, Mr Rowland, looking down the morning's court-list, saw that Arthur was 'up' again for breaking into the electric meter. When he saw him, he 'asked him why he hadn't come to discuss the matter with me or even told me that he had broken into the meter, but Arthur just shrugged his shoulders'. (Adapted from Davies, 1974)

2. Marge and Jill and the friendly relationship   Margery Hollick describes herself as a suicidal destructive person. At the time of her first contact with the social worker, Jill Ford, she and her husband Reg had three children aged 19, 17 and 14. The youngest had been referred to the child guidance clinic because of problems at school. Mrs Hollick had made attempts at suicide and had been in and out of the local psychiatric hospitals many times, usually discharging herself. She had known numerous psychiatrists, social workers, casualty nurses and other helping persons, and was critical of many of them.

But for the next three years Marge and Jill forged a relationship that became a classical amalgam of friendship and professionalism:

> Without a genuine liking and respect we would never have got off the ground. Unless these had deepened to love and trust we would never have seen it through. On the other hand, we could never have achieved what we did if we had not both been quite clear that I was her social worker and she was my client .... She knew she had the right to burden me, to make demands on me, because she could trust me to be clear about where the bounds lay.

> Marge brought her tensions to the social worker. She came and talked, and they met approximately once a week for three years.

> There were long periods when she came to see me by appointment and we looked at her past and her present and how they connected and what it could mean for her future – both her very immediate future (how she would get through another day) and for the long term. There were other periods when I visited her, also by appointment, for the same purpose.

Jill got to know Margery's family, especially Reg. Sometimes things seemed to be getting worse rather than better, and then both worker and client sensed the value of 'the uniquely personal and the necessity for unwavering professionalism'. Margery came to know that she could take her wrist-slashing fears directly to the worker; she could share her desperation and terror; and the worker could respond to 'the lost child crying within'.

Ford was concerned how she could manage such a commitment of time, and she describes one critical occasion when she had come into the office early one Monday morning in order to clear her desk before a first appointment at 11.30. Her plans were upset when Marge's neighbour phoned saying that they needed the worker's help. 'I did not feel like going . . . But I had to go.' The worker carefully considered her feelings, the fact that she had made an open commitment to the client, and the fact that she had to be honest – with both Marge and herself. 'Having sorted it out and made my decision I felt light at heart and optimistic as I drove round to her house... But the quality of the decision was vital. Unless I could wholly "will", that part of me which did not "will" would be sure to make itself felt'.

An important aspect of the case lay in the worker's implicit faith in the client: 'I always felt we would make headway, that Marge had within her the capacity to move forward, to grow. I also felt she had the will to do so in spite of the despair which overwhelmed, at times, her sense of having the will.'

The case extended the worker's feeling and thinking capacities to the limit. The first helped her to be aware of Margery's depression and despair; the second to make sense of her thoughts and feelings about the past and the present. These capacities enabled Jill, on one occasion when all seemed lost, to find the reserves of spirit and energy to convince the client that a part of her, an important part, did not want to commit suicide. Why otherwise had the client telephoned at the crucial moment?

The relationship continued until the worker left the district, and even then Marge and Jill remained in touch by letter and occasional meetings. 'There were good times', writes Marges, 'not all was bad, was it? I'm standing on my own feet now, so say a little prayer for me, as I've forgotten how, but that will come in time. All my love, Marge.' (Ford and Hollick, 1979)

These two cases, each unique, but neither untypical of the contrasting patterns to be found in long-term social work, amply demonstrate the way in which the primacy of the individual interview is submerged in the totality of the relationship. In the case of Arthur and Jenny, the wider systems in which client and worker operated assumed major significance. All the interviews were dominated and gradually swamped by the chaotic turbulence of the clients' life-style and the formal and informal responses which it provoked in those around them. In the case of Marge, the ups and downs were no less marked, and Ford identifies critical events and meetings in the three year period, but the crucial aspects of the case are to be found in the recurring evidence of trust, empathy, honesty and courage that characterised the working relationship.

Long-term social work covers the spectrum of client-types from multi-problem families living in a turbulent field into which the social worker is almost inexorably drawn, to men and women who survive on their own but who, in a civilised society, have a right to expect a degree of continuous support from the community. In this category are the lonely elderly, the parents of handicapped children and physically disabled housewives whose plight is known to be especially bitter. Interview style is an important social work quality with this group, as with any other, but, on its own, it is not enough; the skills needed by the social worker are more to do with securing community resources, and coordinating helping networks, as we saw in Chapter 6.

Curriculum development
Social workers are always interested in new ideas for practice, although many may be sceptical of their efficacy – often rightly so. The achievement of innovation is not hindered by any lack of worker-motivation, but depends on the development of practice models which represent improvements on present routines, are appropriate and ethically acceptable, and are capable of being absorbed by existing settings. A shortage of adequate resources is often a handicap to the introduction of new practices, and it is significant that innovations like intermediate treatment, community service orders and day centres have all been made as a result of administrative and political decisions which ensured the availability of sufficient funds to meet capital and running costs.

Ideas such as sculpting and role play (both of which require the social worker to persuade clients to play-act personal experiences or fantasies – for example, marital conflict, child abuse, or going for a job interview) and social skills training (which uses behavioural techniques to help clients improve their ordinary social functioning – such as talking to the foreman, overcoming chronic shyness, or controlling a bad temper) are emerging as having considerable promise for social work. But significantly, it has always seemed to be easier to employ them in a residential or institutional setting than in the community.

One area for development in community practice that has barely been touched is in the writing of *scripts*. Most experienced social workers develop relatively standardised responses to meet recurring needs and informally these are often passed on to younger colleagues: what answers to give to anxious adoptive parents at different stages of the adoption cycle; what approach to use with a man who has just been sentenced to a long term of imprisonment, and how to tell his wife; what to say to a child to reassure him about his forthcoming foster-placement. Obviously every situation *is* unique and every good social worker will develop his own repertoire of intuitive repartee, but there *are* good, bad and dreadful ways of putting things, and it is surprising that social work, which relies so heavily on the spoken word both for its impact and its justification, should not have recognised the value of explicitly making considered judgments on the best ways of coping with frequently repeated themes and queries.

The idea of curriculum development is barely recognised as legitimate in social work, and yet with the investment of increasing resources, not only in team social work, but in group work, day centres and community intervention, it is becoming economically essential for the accumulated experience and wisdom of the profession to be recorded and passed on to each new generation, so that its growth can be cumulative, and each new social worker not have to start entirely from scratch.

10 The Social Worker's Use of Self

Social workers have almost certainly done their profession a disservice in the eyes of the public by their apparent inability to reach agreement among themselves on the kind and complexity of the skills required to do their job well. The problem has, of course, been exacerbated by the continuing willingness of employers to fill social work posts with untrained personnel, a practice which naturally undermines the case that two years' training is needed to produce a good practitioner. It is the argument of this book that, although some facets of social work are in need of de-mystification, it nevertheless remains an extremely demanding professional occupation requiring a wide range of roles and functions. I have defined the central task facing social workers in the statutory sector as one of maintenance, but it is also clear that the key to the profession's identity lies in the recognition that what makes something social work is not *what* is done but *how* it is done. *The way in which* individuals are maintained, *the way in which* their interests are represented in society, *the way in which* society's sanctions, restrictions and powers are conveyed to, and imposed upon, individuals are different if carried out according to social work principles. The good social worker must be carefully prepared for every aspect of his normal duties; he must persistently update the knowledge and skill required for their execution; he must employ real sensitivity in all social relationships, and retain an absolute respect for human life in all its forms; he must espouse a fundamentally optimistic view of human nature; and he must always be ready to use the self to reconcile the often conflicting interests of marginal individuals and the state.

American textbooks down the years – Hamilton (1940), Towle (1945), Perlman (1957), Hollis (1964), Meyer (1976) – have all recognised either implicitly or explicitly that the social worker is potentially his own greatest asset (or liability). Perlman, for instance, says that the style of the helper has increasingly come to be recognised as a potent factor in the therapeutic relationship.

> Ideally this 'style' – this spontaneous, honest expression of the self in the role of the professional helper – flows out from the caseworker's real concern and respect for the client, out of his being

unafraid, either of the person or his problem, and out of his deep
wish to be of maximal help... Style – the helper's ways of relating, of
drawing out feelings, of responding empathically, of stimulating
and guiding thought, of accrediting and affirming, of presenting
reality – is utilised not in a free-form, any-sort-of-dialogue-goes-as-
long-as-it's-lively way. Rather, it is contained within the structure
provided by both the purpose and the process of problem-solving.
(Perlman, 1970)

Social work is the structure *and* the person, the agency and the worker:
without one or the other, it ceases to exist. The self, then, is crucial, and
ironically that assertion can be illustrated as well in the work of an
untrained family aide as it has traditionally been demonstrated by
highly qualified casework intervention.

Grace Batey describes her work with Leslie Wright, a mentally
handicapped man in his late 50s, with whom she has been working for
three years: 'I was visiting for six hours every week, with the aim of
guiding him into patterns of self-help, as far as possible, and with little
real knowledge of how to approach mental handicap.' Gradually the
family aide became aware of his capabilities and limitations: she
showed an interest in the model-kits which he never finished; she
coped with his moods, and developed a sensitivity to his apparently
irrational reactions to instructions which went beyond his
understanding; she accepted his devotion to ritual, and adapted her
approach accordingly; she took him shopping, and learnt the
importance of his participation in decision-making. He has recurring
and painful attacks of haemorrhoids 'which leave him very low. He
has an abhorrence of using either suppositories or healing cream. In
the beginning he suffered agonies rather than face the embarrassment
of bringing it to my notice, but as trust between us grew, he was able to
explain that the blood-stained underpants were what worried him
most of all. So in order to relieve this anxiety, I took the underwear
and washed it myself. Today he has the confidence to let his home help
attend to his laundry.' Grace Batey initiated his attendance at a day
centre, and got him a bus pass 'which opened up new avenues through
travel'. His neighbours care, she says, 'but keep a discreet distance'.
He watches television, buys and talks about his uncompleted model
kits, and hoards. 'He leans close to the one-to-one relationship, and
places great faith in those entrusted with the responsibility of
nurturing his growth and development. He responds to kindness with
feelings of kindliness... He is far removed from the Leslie to whom I
was introduced three years ago and has struggled hard for his place in

the community. Each experience whets his appetite for the next.'
(Adapted from Batey, 1979)

Batey makes no claims for her professional skill; on the contrary,
she emphasises that she was learning as she went by responding to the
client's situation and to his own reactions as they occurred. To wash
the client's underpants may not be everyone's idea of a social work
tactic, but it was practical, it was tangible, and it relieved anxiety.
More than that, though, it demonstrated the worker's willingness and
ability to understand and empathise with the mundane but stressful
realities of a simple man's existence.

There are two sides to the use of self. On the one hand, there is the
client's need to recognise an identifiable person, to know his
idiosyncrasies, his name, perhaps in psychoanalytic terms to
experience a mild transference through seeing in the worker a family
figure of some significance, or, as in residential care, to relate to *one
key worker* who will remain in evidence despite uprootings from
placement to placement and during movement through the system.
On the other hand, there is the worker's own acknowledgement of his
strengths and weaknesses – his height, his age, his sex, his ethnic
origins, his temper, his energy, his prejudices – these are the qualities
he has to work with, for better or worse.

Is it possible to specify and agree on those qualities that make for a
good practitioner? Compton and Galaway (1975) make a brave
attempt, although they sensibly preface their effort by acknowledging
that 'it is difficult to discuss "the helping person" because there are
almost as many kinds of helpers as there are people who need help. . .
There is probably no one person who is an ideal helping person, so that
each of us will probably lack some of the qualities a helping person
should have.' Nevertheless Compton and Galaway list six qualities
which they see as central to effective social work functioning:

1. The enjoyment of being alive: *maturing*, living, growing,
   developing. The acceptance of change: seeing all people, including
   oneself, as being involved in problem-solving.
2. Being a nonconformist, *creative*, intellectually open, receptive.
   Recognising that most solutions to the problems of life are
   tentative.
3. *Self-awareness*, genuineness: self-knowledge, self-respect, self-
   confidence.
4. A *desire* to increase peoples' freedom of choice and control over
   their own lives.

5. The *courage* to confront clients with the reality of their problems, the courage to risk failure in pursuing social work objectives, the courage to cope with unpredictable situations, the courage to face criticism and blame for one's actions.
6. *Sensitivity* to the client's feelings, doubts, fears and movement.

Conversely, they quote Alan Keith-Lucas's claim (1972) that there are four kinds of people who do *not* make good helpers:

1. those who are interested in knowing about people rather than in serving them (coldly objective students of humanity);
2. those who are impelled by strong personal needs to control, to feel superior, to be liked;
3. those who have solved problems similar to those experienced by the people in need of help but who have forgotten what it cost them to do so;
4. those who are primarily interested in retributive justice and moralising.

How is one to react to what are in effect moral imperatives, or at least subjective assertions about the boundaries of personality-type suitable for social work? Certainly to anyone who has himself practised, who knows other practitioners, who sifts through applications for social work training and then teaches and assesses the chosen few, there is no doubt that some people make better social workers than others. I am happier with Keith-Lucas's negatives than with Compton and Galaway's positives. It is not that the qualities sought are inappropriate, but that, taken together, they add up to a sort of catechism of virtue more suitable for a Comtean sect than for an occupational group employed primarily in the public sector. They outline ideals that are normally unattainable, and it is difficult for such a list to avoid the appearance of prissiness, to the extent that it appears to claim that social workers need to be morally superior to other people – a risky, not so say unrealistic, suggestion that can easily be counterproductive. It might be viewed as arrogant, not only by the general public, but more particularly perhaps by closely related occupational groups – the police, nurses, school teachers, the clergy – who, while willing to recognise the special nature of social workers' skills and activities might be understandably reluctant to view Joe Helper in quite the halo-justifying light that Compton and Galaway's six qualities imply. An unfortunate side-effect of social work's good intentions is that its practitioners can sometimes fall into the trap of thinking that they have a monopoly of virtue – an error quite as characteristic of the politically aware younger generation as it was once of an earlier gathering of ladies bountiful. The truth is that if you walk into an average probation office or social services department, you do not instantly get an impression of high moral virtue – nor indeed would most social workers want you to. All the evidence is that the best social workers, whatever they might have in common with others, do not necessarily have much in common with each other. Some are clinically correct, in the best textbook tradition; some are highly deviant, ploughing a lone furrow but respected for their independence by colleagues and clients alike; some are permissive; some are firm in the use of authority.

In the end, it is impossible to be dogmatic about worker-style in social work. But although those with long experience or special ability can afford to employ creative virtuosity in their practice, for all trainees and for the majority of serving social workers, there are basic essentials that have to be aspired to and achieved:

1. First, it must be said again, come Truax and Carkhuff's recommended qualities for counsellors: genuineness, empathy and warmth – plus persuasiveness. These are both personality traits and strategies which the would-be social worker can develop under tuition and perfect. In other words, they almost certainly come more easily to some than to others, but they are skills that anyone can improve with practice. They are not, of course, unique to social work, but they do appear to be broadly essential to *good* social work.

2. A growing amount of evidence suggests that an interest in and a willingness to undertake practical activities are of advantage in social work, and may even be essential in the cementing of a useful relationship. The emotionally and intellectually aloof person is not likely to be welcomed either by his agency or his clients.

3. I have argued that social work is primarily concerned with the goal of maintenance, and it follows that the first-class practitioner must be efficient and knowledgeable in those elements that contribute to its achievement: the exercise of responsibility, the pursuit of change strategies and pro-active intervention in the community. In particular, the good social worker must fulfil the client's expectation of him as an expert both in terms of the *facts* that he knows and of the *tactics* that he pursues in the face of the facts.

4. The qualities of awareness and sensitivity are prerequisites for good
   practice, and that must mean that young adults from a sheltered
   suburban home background, on the one hand, or the sort of people
   covered by Keith-Lucas's negatives on the other, are probably
   unsuitable for social work. The first group need to see something of
   the seamier side of life before beginning social work training –
   perhaps at least to have a glimpse of what it means to raise a family
   on supplementary benefit, or to be out of work for a year, or to live
   in a dingy urban environment; the second group need to be
   excluded altogether unless they can prove the assessment of their
   personality erroneous.

In summary, then, the qualitites required in a social worker can be
reduced to a mnemonic: WE SPEAK PG.

W   warmth
E   efficiency

S   sensitivity
P   persuasiveness
E   empathy
A   awareness
K   knowledge

P   practicality
G   genuineness

Beyond these qualities, the injunction to 'be yourself' is now
recognised as sound advice. Self-revelation, so long as it does not
intrude on the client's problems or dominate the working relationship,
can often be helpful. Each social worker is a unique being, and, since
the use of self is one crucial part of his function it follows that the
development of self-confidence is an appropriate ambition in its own
right. Social work *is* a creative job and the artistry of the practitioner is
a vital component once the other qualities have been mastered.

11 Beyond the Use of Self

In his critique of organised social work, Hugman (1977) argues that 'the business of being a good helper is essentially bound up with being a good person, that is to say, thoughtful, generous, sensitive, relatively unselfish, relatively accepting of self, liberated in spirit, tolerant, reliable, acquainted with weakness and inconsistency, caring, committed, purposeful, capable of joy and sadness, and faithful to a belief in the creative humanity of all people.' His injunction is to '*Act natural*' and to avoid the pretensions of professionalism. There is of course a romantic attraction – in the Rousseauian sense – in such an approach, and it is valuable in its attempt to counteract the conservative and bureaucratic forces that are inherent in large scale organisations, and that will, if left unrecognised, undermine the creative individuality essential to first-class practice. But bearing in mind the central thesis of this book – that social work is of necessity a socially sanctioned activity – it follows that the creative role of the social worker *must* be reconcilable and reconciled with formal and often large-scale structures. I do not disagree with Hugman that the self is of crucial importance – as it is indeed in many service occupations – but I do not think that social work is solely and always about the influence of one person on another, nor do I think that the resources of social work are or ought to be limited to the use of self. The social worker is the front-line agent through which the agency exercises control, fulfils its responsibilities, offers resources for change and development, maintains the individual in society and enables the client's interests to be represented in relation to the state and its citizens. I have argued that the personality of that agent is not irrelevant, that the personal nature of the relationship between helper and helped is a significant part of the process, and I would further conclude that some occupational stability is therefore of value in achieving agency objectives. Similarly it is in the agency's interests to capitalise on the variations of individual ability among its employees and to provide a professional framework which maximises initiative and originality.

However one major area in which initiatives and originality are likely to vary lies in the extent to which social workers are able to go beyond the use of self in their work with clients. Browne (1978) found that casework with individuals and families still dominates the pattern of practice in local authority departments, and comments that 'relatively few from our sample of social workers said that they were using special or different techniques in family intervention'; nor were groupwork or community work regarded by any as a substantial part of their method of working. It is clear from several studies that although one-to-one interviews in the office are not necessarily always the norm, much more could be done to encourage social workers to use their initiative in going beyond the use of self and to enable agencies to provide more broadly-based resources. For example, the development of intermediate treatment has been uneven. In 1983–84, the range of expenditure on IT between areas was enormous, as Table 11.1 shows.

Table 11.1   Expenditure on intermediate treatment, 1983–84

Local authority	Amount spent	Sum per head of population
	£	£
Wandsworth	472 000	1.82
Lambeth	318 000	1.29
Warwickshire	436 000	0.91
Dorset	25 000	0.04
South Tyne	3 000	0.02
Rotherham	1 000	0.004

Source: Chartered Institute of Public Finance and Accountancy

Clearly such variations in expenditure have a direct effect on the treatment strategies that can be adopted by social workers faced with broadly similar problems.

Again, there are wide variations in the extent to which local authorities try to reduce the feeling of isolation among the housebound elderly or disabled. One of the things that social workers may be able to do is to recommend that their departments provide financial assistance for the installation or maintenance of a telephone, but Table 11.2 shows how the provision of this facility differs from one part of the country to another: residents in Islington, for example,

Table 11.2   Help with phone installations and rentals, 1983–84

Local authority	Number of phones installed	Rate per 1000 population	Help with rentals	Rate per 1000 population
Islington	400	2.46	3621	22.26
Wandsworth	595	2.30	3260	12.62
Warwickshire	459	0.96	2014	4.22
Berkshire	83	0.12	670	0.95
Cambridgeshire	67	0.11	49	0.08
East Sussex	30	0.04	23	0.03

Source: *Chartered Institute of Public Finance and Accountancy*

were 60 times more likely to be helped to get a phone installed, and 700 times more likely to be given help with the rental than residents in East Sussex.

Additionally, social workers themselves vary in the degree to which they make use of available facilities; for example, even with a statutory provision like community service orders, McWilliams (1975) has shown that some probation officers will frequently recommend it in social enquiry reports, while others will never do so – and the courts are likely to follow the recommendations made. The same applies to the use of day centres as conditions of the probation order under the Criminal Justice Act 1982; those probation officers who are reluctant to make such recommendations may sometimes not do so because of qualms about the propriety of 'sentencing the offender to social work'; the snag is that such squeamishness can have the unfortunate side-effect of leading to a sentence of imprisonment instead (Wright, 1984).

Because of the varying levels of provision and because of the seeming reluctance of some social workers to make adequate use of even those facilities that are provided, there would seem to be a need for innovation and evaluation in the whole sphere of practice beyond the use of self. There needs to be a much more organised approach to the recording and analysis of imaginative developments in community or group care. Despite a few tentative efforts, the idea of a partnership between practice and research with a view to encouraging the emergence of new and more useful strategies for action has not yet found much favour although the pioneering work carried out in Kent is beginning to be emulated elsewhere. What is needed is for research, practice and management to combine in such a way that innovations can be monitored, feedback provided, and further development stimulated. Too much research has been unimaginative, and too many practice developments have taken place in isolation for growth to occur in any dynamic sense.

In this chapter, I shall note some of the more important recent innovations in practice. It is still difficult, however, to judge their relevance or long-term value – partly because of the rarity of research and partly because of continuing confusion over objectives.

Teamwork

Teamwork, as Harman (1978) says, 'seems almost to have achieved the status of being fashionable'. And, in view of the slightly disarming tendency of some social workers to fall recklessly in love with passing fads and fancies, it is necessary to regard it with some caution. The idea of teamwork can, indeed, mean anything or nothing. At one extreme the mere fact of calling a working group of social workers a 'team' – as happens fairly generally anyway – can lead to the assumption that whatever they do is *ipso facto* 'teamwork'. What seems usually to be meant in the literature, however, is the abandonment of rigid boundaries between each worker's functions, an increase in staff communication (including, perhaps, the more democratic participation of clerical staff and ancillaries), shared assessment and allocation, some shared cases, and a guarantee of adequate coverage during the absence of any staff member. Some teamwork schemes have involved attempts at breaking down the hierarchy of responsibility in an office, with all decision-making being devolved to the group, but such an interpretation does not appear to be inherent in teamwork as such, although there may be other perfectly good reasons for adopting it.

In one sense the idea of teamwork might mean little more than 'good colleagueship': a working environment in which co-workers share each other's burdens, stand in for each other when necessary, discuss problems together and cooperate closely in the course of a working day. Such a model in social work would mean that senior colleagues would come to the aid of a raw beginner if he was faced with a particularly difficult case, or any worker could look to his partners for advice on factual matters – where to find accommodation for a needy client, for example. Another model of teamwork is primarily applicable where the working group have uniform objectives – to galvanise a community into self-help, perhaps, or, more commonly, in the context of an intake team where the daily pressures of an urban environment are better shared. More ambitious is the idea of allocating specialist functions to each member of staff, so capitalising on their respective strengths – rather in the style of a football team in which each player has a slightly different role to play although flexbility is expected as circumstances change. In social work this leads to a form of specialisation, but it also means that many clients are expected to relate to the agency as a whole, and so lose the chance of identifying with one key worker.

Explorations in teamwork have been prompted by an awareness of some of the shortcomings of traditional social work methods and supported by the unitary methods literature which has emphasised the advantages of a more eclectic approach to the client's need (e.g. Goldstein, 1973; Pincus and Minahan, 1973). There is no empirical evidence to suggest that teamwork serves the client better but there do appear to be advantages in internal organisation and efficiency: 'We now seem to be more open and honest about our own and our colleagues' capabilities, and a climate exists where learning from each other is more possible' (Harman, 1978). The Shelton probation studies reveal, however, that initial enthusiasm for radical forms of teamwork can be followed by disillusion, and its use in front-line fieldwork still has to be justified (Millard 1975 and 1976).

An investigation of three social services area teams in Birmingham, Norfolk and North Wales prompts considerable scepticism about the viability of teamwork in the field of routine service delivery. Social workers express fears of reduced job satisfaction (because they prize their personalised caseload most highly), and they express doubts concerning the extent to which the resource-controllers in the higher echelons of the department would be willing to delegate sufficient powers to render teamwork effective (Black *et al.*, 1984). What seems to have happened is that the notion of 'teamwork' has become mixed up with linked questions of community work, the use of informal caring networks through interweaving and the place of specialists in social work. In other words, the very problem of fashionableness has trapped many of the contributing arguments, and the objectives of teamwork *per se* (and even its shape, structure and place within the organisation) are left distressingly imprecise. The Barclay Report (1982) has done nothing to help.

In residential work and day care, of course, teamwork is essential – but that is quite a different story.

Groupwork

There is a large and still growing literature on groupwork and general agreement that it could and should make a significant contribution to social work practice. But as Brown (1979) points out there is almost certainly a discrepancy between the emphasis placed on groups in social work teaching and the reality of fieldwork outside. Part of the difficulty arises from the structure of practice.

In institutional settings, there is a ready-made framework for groups: natural groups exist anyway, and the captive nature of the population makes it relatively easy for selected artificial groups to be brought together by staff. In fieldwork, there has to be a definite initiative, the social worker has to have the time, the space, the energy and sufficient confidence that the effort involved will be worthwhile to maintain both his own and the clients' motivation. All too often, one or more of these essential ingredients is missing, but although it appears that specialist groupwork personnel are uncommon, enough social workers run at least one group in their working lives to ensure that the momentum is maintained. Significantly, the greatest impetus to groups was given by the provision in the 1969 Children and Young Persons Act for intermediate treatment for juveniles who had either offended against the law or were thought to be at some risk of doing so. Such statutory backing persuaded most local authorities to allocate resources to the task, with the result that specialist staff were appointed, funds made available, and premises provided. With such material support, groupwork for teenagers became viable.

It was always a fallacy to see groupwork as a cheap option – a way of seeing eight reporting probationers at once, for example; and although it is doubtful whether anyone ever really believed such a myth, it has taken a long time for there to be official recognition that groupwork is not usually feasible without careful planning and without due consideration to the resource implications. Even now the sophistication of the approach to IT in many areas falls far short of standards normally regarded as minimally acceptable in special education – a field which has much in common with the practice of groupwork with adolescents but which has a far longer and richer tradition of curriculum development.

Other examples of groupwork can be found in:

1. activity work with adult offenders – motor-cycle maintenance, craft workshops, literacy classes, physical training;
2. discussion groups in day care settings – for psychiatric patients or

the elderly, for example;

3. parent-groups in child and family guidance clinics – involving the sharing of mutually experienced problems, role play, or the simple relief of anxiety and tension;
4. groups for would-be foster parents – partly for training purposes, partly to cope with apprehensions and doubts, and, occasionally, perhaps, to complete the vetting process;
5. groups for similar clients: prisoners' wives, alcoholics, the parents of children in care, women who have been the victims of violent assaults by their husbands, ex-mental patients.

Sometimes groups struggle for survival, sometimes they thrive, and occasionally they exercise their own initiative and grow into self-help groups with an existence and a will all their own.

Techniques in groupwork are limitless, and can be either verbal or action-based, or a mixture of the two. Ambitious leaders with the necessary facilities can make imaginative use of video, audio-tapes, role play or sculpting; or the group can be community-directed, towards some mutually agreed goal of bringing about a desired local development – creating a children's playground, for example. At this point groupwork merges imperceptibly into community work.

There has to be a good reason for starting a group, but it doesn't have to be highfalutin. The simple exchange of views and feelings by people suffering from stress is a perfectly valid justification, as is the provision of a place in which the isolated can find company. Reasons don't have to have a curative, therapeutic or transcendental base to justify the social worker's effort. Indeed the need for groups will often emerge naturally, and requires only a sensitive, alert and committed social worker to pick up the cue, and a facilitating agency to provide the means.

The real beauty of groupwork lies in the scope it offers for the social worker to operate in a creative fashion, while at the same time responding to client interests and needs in a way that wholly characterises the social work ideal. Two examples illustrate the point.

1. Working with Agoraphobics
Two final year students aimed to set up a programme to meet an apparent need to help agoraphobics in Bristol. Their first idea was to take the clients out into panic-inducing situations, but this was vetoed by the would-be participants who also overruled the social

workers' view that membership of the group should be tightly limited. Meetings were held, and those who came did so because they wanted to make contact with fellow-sufferers. Attendance over eight meetings varied from 6 to 17, with a considerable turnover. The workers had a clear therapeutic goal, despite scepticism on the part of some of the attenders.

Since everyone would have had a personal struggle even to arrive at the meeting, a welcoming atmosphere was deliberately created. The schedule, although planned, was not rigidly adhered to, the first two meetings being taken up with members talking about their agoraphobic condition. In the next three weeks, paper exercises, discussions and encouragement by the workers to venture out led to discussions about risk, dependency and the members' feelings of resentment about their condition. Session 6 focused on achievements with the lighthearted use of 'gold stars' for anything that deserved a special accolade. This positive emphasis was valuable because of the group's frequent tendency to dwell on setbacks. At this stage, the idea of continuing the enterprise through self-help groups was mooted by the workers, and the last two sessions were used partly to plan these and partly to share feedback about the group experience.

The members valued the opportunity of sharing experiences, and liked the relaxed atmosphere and the encouragement to meet phobic situations. Improvements in behaviour were reported, and two self-help groups were established as a result of the initiative. The role of group members in reinforcing for each other the importance of personal effort seemed to justify the approach (Hutchen, 1984).

2. A Telephone Group

Gibbons has developed an imaginative technique for using the telephone as a primary treatment resource, and has formed Telelink Groups, using British Telecom's ability to provide conference facilities through telephone link-ups.

She selects a group of six or seven people, who are usually blind to a significant degree, and arranges for telephone links to be established at a specific time each week. The groups normally run for between 45 and 60 minutes. The technique involves members imagining a clockface, choosing a number with which to identify him or herself and then, initially, allowing the worker to coordinate conversations. The groups normally run for eight weeks, and develop from the first week when the leader goes round the group clockwise engaging in conversation until, later, the members develop group skills and are able to respond spontaneously and freely as if they were face-to-face. In one case, the group has developed to a stage where the members actively seek problem-solving work and education; they have had guest speakers and have listened to articles on specific subjects as a basis for discussion.

Members do not normally meet each other, but some have afterwards enjoyed one-to-one telephone contact. The technique is particularly suitable for visually impaired clients, because it minimises the difference between them and the sighted leader.

Group membership is warmly regarded by the members, and they can and do move into further groups after the eight weeks are over. Some groups now meet without the leader (Gibbons, 1984).

The use of volunteers

> Volunteering is as essential to humane social services as highly-trained professionalism, and the professional who disregards this ... is liable to make the most cruel mistakes. (Crossman, 1976).

That may be so, but it is also true that the use of volunteers requires not only skill but some imagination, for the addition of a volunteer can further complicate the already delicate balance between the social worker, his agency and the client. One survey (Hatch, 1978) found that 15 per cent of the general population had done voluntary work of one kind or another 'in the past year', and the social worker is in a key position to make sure that those who give their time freely are used to maximum effectiveness.

What might volunteers do? One answer is 'almost anything', and certainly the range of their activities is likely to grow. One study in the probation service identified the following as some of the main tasks which volunteers undertook:

> Prison visiting; groupwork with prisoners during their sentence; looking after children during their mother's visit to prison; providing transport to prisons; running canteens at prisons for visiting families; teaching art, craft and literacy to offenders; helping offenders find work; support and advice to offenders and their families; helping the homeless; running hostels; baby-sitting; helping families to budget; practical work (collecting luggage, repairing and decorating a client's home); writing letters to lonely

prisoners; participating in pressure groups for penal reform; supervising offenders ordered to do community service; providing holidays for mothers and children; organising a clothing store at the probation office. (Clark, 1975)

Volunteers in social services departments can be employed in similar ways but considerable attention has been paid in recent years to the possibility of using them as *good neighbours* in the community: to carry out the job of providing an immediate point of contact for those in need, to keep an eye on those at risk, and generally to supplement the resources of the social services departments at grassroots level. Some authorities have started paying 'street wardens' token amounts of money because of their belief in the importance of the job and their recognition of the responsibility that it carries.

Finally, the role of volunteers, operating in a variety of capacities, is central to community care and 'Patch' developments, using, as they do, Bayley's notion of interweaving. Gone is the idea of the volunteer as a marginal figure in caring, and in its place have come schemes in which the social worker may conduct, coordinate and mastermind operations, but volunteers act out the central roles. Furthermore, as they become more experienced in the function, the scope for them to take leading initiatives is not denied.

The more traditional arrangement which still holds sway in many probation and social services departments is for one or more volunteers to be 'attached' to social workers – sometimes to specially designated liaison officers but more commonly to ordinary fieldworkers who may or may not have been adequately prepared for the task of supervising them. For example, a volunteer might be allocated to an old peoples' home and come under the wing of the warden. I have seen this work successfully, with an imaginative volunteer visiting the home regularly during afternoons, working with some of the residents to produce a weekly news-sheet, using a tape-recorder to engage residents in an oral history project about their childhood in an industrial town, playing board-games, or just chatting and listening.

Alternatively, volunteers can operate in a more detached manner, cut off from professional departments and working within relatively autonomous community groups or care schemes. The Volunteer Centre has advocated the use of Bridge Groups for volunteers which avoid the risks of isolation but give volunteers a greater degree of autonomy than is sometimes possible in professional agencies.

One of the best existing projects known to us using the Bridge Group model is the Chest, Heart and Stroke Association volunteer scheme. The aim is to help those who have had a stroke to recover speech, concentration, memory and so on. Each of the patients (who are living at home) has a small team of about three to six volunteers working with him on a rota basis. The aim is that he will receive a visitor on most days of the week, to provide concentrated intensive work. This method of organisation is very successful in meeting that crucial need of volunteers – to limit their commitment. A volunteer knows that if he cannot for any reason do his turn there are a number of colleagues willing to fill in for him. This means that many people who have not hitherto agreed to be a volunteer in any capacity, for fear of the conflicting demands of family or work, have been prepared to come forward... If any volunteer wishes to do so, he can join more than one Bridge Group, alongside a different group of colleagues. (Bruce and Darvill, 1976)

Recruitment can stretch from insertions in parish newsletters to negotiating access to nationwide or regional television for a phone-in programme. In between come the use of informal networks, posters in schools, offices, libraries, advertising in the newspaper and the issuing of press-releases. Community Service Volunteers (CSV) might be approached if there is need for full-time help, and the New Careers movement encourages agencies to employ present or former clients in voluntary associate posts. If the work has a strong community focus, it is essential to recruit indigenous neighbourhood workers.

There is some disagreement over the extent to which volunteers should be trained for their task, and much will depend on the nature of their work. If they are expected to give precise advice about welfare rights, for example, they are going to need a detailed briefing; but in most cases the art of successful volunteering requires more modest qualities. One apparently successful project was praised by its volunteers because:

1. it had clear objectives, which they could understand and aim to achieve:
2. they had some discretion to make their own decisions;
3. there was reasonably rapid feedback from clients;
4. there was good teamwork between the volunteers and the professionals;
5. they enjoyed good leadership, with a volunteer as the coordinator;
6. they had professional support and recognition;
7. the work was varied; and

8. there was a limit to the commitment demanded of the volunteers, because of a pairing and rota system.
   (Hare, 1977)

Projects, of course, are not designed primarily to satisfy the needs of the volunteers but, at the same time, there is now a lot of evidence to show that volunteer-satisfaction is a pre-requisite of service for the client. And volunteer-satisfaction will often depend on the skill and commitment of the professional social worker (Davies, 1977).

Community work
Some social services departments employ community workers but Stevenson and Parsloe (1978) found that their activities tended to be carried out independently of the mainstream social workers, and although there is disagreement over the extent to which the community work role is legitimately one for the local authority and even whether community work is a form of social work at all, there is no doubt that the activities of most social workers often make them aware of the need for community action and community development, and sometimes prompt them to become involved themselves. The worker, for example, might see the deprivations suffered by young children and poor families in an urban environment and, despairing of any foreseeable improvement in their conditions, encourage them, or even lead them, into becoming more vociferous in their demands for fair treatment. Such a role is understandable and defensible but there is evidence that many social workers find it difficult to reconcile it with their more normal duties. As Black *et al.* (1983) say of their area team social workers, 'they wanted to be involved in the community but did not see it as their job to do community work'.

The Barclay Report's insistence on talking about *community social work* as a preferred model has, in some ways, only fudged the issue. It is clear from the emphasis of *The Essential Social Worker* that contemporary practice requires the professional to operate within, and in direct contact with, the community, but I remain quite satisfied that community work as such benefits from being conceptually distinct from most of the tasks which contemporary social workers are expected to fulfil. In the sense that both have a role to play, it is unnecessary to debate whether social work is a more worthy or more necessary activity than community work, or vice versa.

Problems undoubtedly arise, however, because of discrepancies in funding, with community work being very much the poor relation. Until some way is found of pumping public money into programmes which encourage community development, it is always likely that the relatively well-off statutory sector in social work will find itself envied and attacked by those who see community work as a preferable strategy of social concern.

Although community work takes many forms, the most common approach is to work with community groups – either those that already and naturally exist, or these that are prompted into being by the injection of funds or the allocation of staff. The worker's aims can be many and varied, though they are usually concentrated on developing local facilities, campaigning for additional resources, or making explicit the views of ordinary citizens and pressure groups on significant issues concerned with human welfare.

Briscoe (1977) argues that the community approach can co-exist with service delivery: the essential difference being that service delivery is externally determined, with new developments depending on the sensitivity of workers, management and politicians to local needs, while the community approach maximises the involvement of the recipients of aid, both in the way in which it is distributed and in the development of an overall service strategy.

Hence, the community work perspective brings us back to the client's voice, but strengthens it by force of numbers, and sometimes by bypassing the social worker and exercising direct influence on politicians and managerial decision-makers. Herein lies the as yet unresolved dilemma for those who would like to see community work as an integral part of statutory social work – and there are good reasons for thinking it incapable of resolution: if community work leads inexorably in the direction of political confrontation, as it certainly appears to, the community worker employed by the political authority is inevitably in an ambiguous position – and the ambiguity is double-edged. There may well be limits in the extent to which he can take on his employers on behalf of the community he serves; and he will always be vulnerable to the suspicion that his employers are clandestinely exerting influence on him to moderate the views of his community group. In this sense of being on the boundaries of society, there are similarities between his role and that of the social worker. But whereas the social worker's role is primarily one of reconciliation, the community worker's model is almost inherently conflict-orientated, and that means that the critical question, 'Whose side are you on?' is always being posed. And for the worker to be on the side of a community *against* the political authority demands a degree of independence that is not normally found in a statutory social worker. Hence, despite the pressures in that direction, the conclusion has to be drawn that social workers can never ultimately make good community workers unless contracts are drawn up by their employers which guarantee them a degree of freedom that they would not normally expect – and the experience of the Community Development Projects, which went some way in that direction, suggests that such a step might be unlikely to be sanctioned on a large scale.

New careers and community service

Just as the 1970s saw a spate of research studies reflecting client perspectives, so too did they produce the idea that clients themselves might give as well as receive help. The principle was established in two different settings.

From America came the New Careers movement with an impact on the US Poverty Programme, penal policy and mental health. It sought to provide opportunities for clients – probationers, for example, or ex-psychiatric patients – to secure posts in social work. Paradoxically the movement had its origins in Britain at the Henderson Hospital in Surrey where Maxwell Jones developed the idea of the therapeutic community in which patients were helped and cured as much by their contact with other patients in groups and in ordinary living situations as by the clinical and nursing staff.

In the colder economic climate of the 1980s, New Careers has not developed as its pioneers hoped it would. There is limited evidence that social services and probation agencies have become more sympathetic to the employment of ex-clients in some capacity, but they have not been widely recruited into the ranks of social work itself. Indeed, they have tended to find more opportunity within pressure group organisations, voluntary bodies and the wider field of community work, and this has, if anything, served to reinforce the clear distinction between client and worker.

The New Careers ideal was one of the factors which led to the establishment of the Community Service Scheme for Offenders in 1972. The combination of extracting reparation by requiring an offender to repay something to the community and providing a positive experience which might have a rehabilitative effect has proved to be a uniquely successful penal innovation. Administered by the probation service, community service orders have become so popular among magistrates and judges that they are now challenging probation as the most commonly made order in the United Kingdom's repertoire of community corrections for adult offenders. The task of organising community service schemes, recruiting specialist personnel and developing supervisory styles quite different from those traditionally used in the probation service has had a major impact on the practitioner, and has placed the probation officer in the role of coordinator and catalyst rather than caseworker. Community service has now been made available as a sentence for juveniles, and this step confirms it as the most radical development in the practice of social work with offenders since the overriding influence of Sigmund Freud waned in the 1950s.

Coping with unemployment

Unemployment has become almost endemic in the United Kingdom (see Table 11.3), and, inevitably, the competition for jobs has led to a situation in which the clients of the probation and social services are often among the hardest hit. There are offices in parts of the North West and on Tyneside where unemployment in the client group varies between 80 and 100 per cent. The requirement on probationers that they should 'lead an industrious life' which has traditionally been

Table 11.3   The rise of unemployment in the United Kingdom

	Number of unemployed claimants (thousands)	Unemployment rate %
1961	292	1.3
1971	751	3.3
1976	1 302	5.5
1979	1 296	5.3
1980	1 665	6.8
1981	2 520	10.4
1982	2 917	12.1
1983	3 105	12.9
1984	3 160	13.1

Note: In 1982, regional rates varied from 8.7 per cent in the South East to 16.5 per cent in the North and 19.4 per cent in Northern Ireland

Source: Department of Employment statistics.

interpreted to mean that they should obtain and hold down a job is no longer enforceable; parole release which initially depended to a very large extent on the ex-prisoner being sure of having somewhere to live and somewhere to work is now regularly granted irrespective of the man's employment chances. How, indeed, could it be otherwise? If skilled, able-bodied, law-abiding men cannot get work, what chance has the recidivist, the psychiatric convalesent or the untrained adolescent drop-out?

The social worker sees the pain and the disillusionment of unemployment close at hand, but traditionally there has been only a limited amount of active help that he was willing or able to give. To some extent this reluctance reflected the psychopathological view that unemployment was merely a symptom of other personal problems that the worker had to deal with (Campling, 1980). Now, however, it is based on what the workers would see as a 'realistic' perspective on economic circumstances: 'There are so few jobs around that to become involved in clients' employment problems would be a losing battle,' said one.

Since Campling explored the attitudes of social workers towards unemployment as a focus for intervention, the structural situation has continued to deteriorate, and social workers risk losing their credibility if they seek to deny the uncomfortable fact that most of their clients have no hope at all of getting a permanent job. The dole queue, the pool tables, the street corner, and the loss of any sense of meaning in adult life – these are the psychological forces impingeing on the client, and the worker has to start by recognising this fact.

Gradually, attempts have been made to get beyond the now outmoded strategy of ringing the Job Centre or contacting a friendly employer, and these nearly all require major commitment on the part of the agency and a willingness to negotiate working links with voluntary organisations or government-sponsored job creation schemes. For some time, the probation service has administered special workshops almost on a kind of prison industries model: undertaking wood and metal crafts, seeking contracts in light industry assembly work and packing. The centres tend to be staging-posts for long-term unemployed probationers or for others coming out of prison with nothing else to look forward to.

The same type of approach has been developed for the mentally handicapped, but there is some disagreement about whether it is best to provide sheltered workshops or to arrange outside work experience. There are examples of both types:

1. At Oakfield in Bromley, the aim is to prepare the clients for work by providing opportunities in carpentry, packing, printing and clerical work, light engineering or domestic and kitchen work.
2. At Birkbeck in Waltham Forest, by contrast, the aim is to leave behind the old image of intensive contract labour. The supervisor has 'found no limits to clients' ability to work, given the right opportunity. He has been getting people out one, two or three days a week into jobs in restaurants, hairdressers, cleaning cars, gardening, basic car maintenance, industrial work, painting and decorating, furniture removals and leaflet distribution'. (Crine, 1983a)

The Manpower Services Commission (MSC), with its vast commitment to provide temporary work experience and job training has proved willing to cooperate with social work initiatives in different parts of the country. In Norfolk, largely as the result of one probation officer's extra-mural commitment, a Community Programme enabled 14 offenders and others to spend up to a year in environmental work and in building new premises for a community centre. In a research analysis of the experience, Gosling (1984) has emphasised the feasibility of the approach, but also draws attention to its disadvantages: social work agencies are not normally geared up to cope with the problems of personnel management, budgeting and development that are associated with industrial operations; the officer's commitment can be seen, at best, as a spare-time bonus for the service's benefit, and, at worst, as an intrusion on his normal duties, with consequential costs for his colleagues; the short-term nature of contract jobs puts maximum emphasis on the search for work and funds, and allows little scope for the project getting into a cruising gear.

What seems to have happened is that, faced with the enormity of the problem of unemployment, a small number of creative social workers and agencies have taken the initiative and sought to develop a limited number of work opportunities within the organisation; made possible by the availability of pump-priming funds, there is as yet no sense that the development is more than a marginal element in professional practice. The business of getting a job remains the responsibility of the individual, and the business of creating an economic framework within which jobs are available remains the responsibility of the government. The social worker, responsible for the welfare of designated clients, can only go so far in his role of mediation, but for the client who benefits, any distance is better than none.

The provision of intensive care

It is only relatively recently that it has been recognised that contact between social worker and client is, in quantitative terms, quite severely restricted. Probation research has shown that routine supervision after the first three months of a court order is likely to involve no more than twenty minutes a fortnight; and even the IMPACT experiment (Folkard, 1976), which was intended to provide a more intensive facility, failed to increase worker-client contact beyond an hour a week. One of the reasons for this might be an economic one: the marginal costs of using a social worker are now around £5.00 per hour and real costs probably at least £10.00 per hour. But a more cogent reason is because intensive use of professional staff time conflicts with the normal role of a social worker and the client's expectations of it. Routine duties are many and various but they determine the shape of the social worker's day, and often there are difficulties in reconciling these with the client's most pressing needs. Of course, social workers *can* exercise some control over the use of their time, but the outer limits are surprisingly constricted: the worker may decide to spend two or three hours working one day intensively with a family; the commitment may extend to a whole day or to a repeat performance the next day or the following week; he may even embark on a short programme of planned contacts using behavioural methods or casework over a period of seven or eight weeks. But such options, on the face of it rather attractive, are rarely taken up and, at best, demand a restricted focus on one or two selected clients. Moderately intensive work may thus depend on the worker being allowed to carry a specialist caseload or being relieved of routine duties, and even then there is a risk of other clients getting short shrift in order to enable the worker to carve out space for strategic involvement with the privileged minority.

It is however increasingly recognised that the provision of intensive care must normally mean going beyond the use of the field social worker. Although it is sometimes suggested that the range of available resources can be seen as lying along a continuum, and that they should be employed in direct proportion to client need, the reality is rather less neat and tidy – not least because there is confusion bordering on chaos regarding the status and consequent financial value of different agents employed to provide intensive care. Indeed one of the least logical aspects of the social services field today is that many of those used most intensively have traditionally been lower paid than those operating in the fieldwork front line or in administration: there is a full range of domiciliary care staff – home helps, social work aides, providers of meals-on-wheels; there are day centres for the elderly, for psychiatric outpatients and for offenders on probation; there are child minders and playgroups; and, above all, there is residential provision for every client group imaginable. Most recently there has emerged a tendency to employ 'volunteers' to provide a degree of regular daily contact with a client which would be quite impossible for the social worker to contemplate: for example, a Trackers Scheme uses young Community Service Volunteers to attach themselves almost full-time to young people thought likely to get into some sort of trouble if left to their own resources.

Clients for whom such intensive facilities are made available must inevitably begin to see their original social worker as much more marginal to their needs and circumstances; and the future relationship between the fieldworker, whose function is largely one of processing, decision-making and facilitating, and the panoply of additional provisions is, to say the least, problematic. Should the social worker have high status, low status or equal status vis-à-vis those who are engaged in a full-time caring role with the client? Such a question, of obvious importance for all staff, their trade unions and their clients, arises because of the piecemeal way in which social service provisions have grown, and since Seebohm, because of the way they have been brought into ever more complex relationships with each other. The conundrum is aggravated by the fact that client need for intensive involvement by the state also tends to bring in services outside the range of the social work system – especially the health service and the penal system. At what point, for example, does a disabled old person need hospitalisation rather than residential provision? And at what point does the potential responsibility of the probation service end and the role of the prison service begin? Such 'boundary disputes' are both critical to agency efficiency and inevitable in a complex organisational structure.

A whole range of developments – 'Patch', community care schemes, intermediate treatment, day care, probation control units – have emerged because of the need for an approach that increases the intensity of impact without requiring either the cost or the potentially stigmatising effect of residential care. In each case, the social worker is involved in an essentially managerial capacity with a team of other workers to fulfil specialist functions or to assume a particular attachment to one client.

Day care

Almost all social work clients might now find themselves having access to (or even being required to attend) facilities which go far beyond the traditional office interview but which fall short of residential admission. There are day centres for probationers and ex-prisoners (and, since the Criminal Justice Act, 1982, attendance at them can be required as a condition of a probation order); there are family centres for children in care or subject to supervision orders where entire families or any one or more members of them can be given daytime shelter, stimulus and care; there are day centres for the physically handicapped which have been described as having four main functions – occupation and leisure, work preparation, training or treatment, and education; and there are, in almost all health areas, psychiatric day centres which represent a major part of the government's plan to switch from hospital care to community care for the mentally ill.

Although day centres vary in their emphases, their common aim is to provide somewhere to go for people who, for whatever reason, cannot or ought not to be left at home all day and cannot or will not go to school or work. Day centres for the elderly range from luncheon clubs in church halls to purpose-built establishments with a wide range of activities available. Some research studies have suggested that day centres for the elderly all too often to not provide enough for the attenders to do, and, those located in old peoples' homes seem to be particularly lacking in activities. (Edwards and Sinclair, 1980).

At the other extreme, Crine (1983b) has described the highly organised timetable of the Vale Centre, a Leeds project for psychiatric day care. The centre runs on therapeutic lines with splendid facilities for relaxation, craftwork, cooking, art therapy, and groupwork. The groups include therapeutic role-playing, creative writing, drama and educational groups. The centre operates in close liaison with local group homes and hostels, and it claims a good record in helping its clients into MSC employment schemes. The style of the centre has evolved, and is very much in the style of its leader.

Although client studies reveal some ambiguity in the feelings of those who attend, the fact remains that people do use day centres, and almost always voluntarily. A critical note is sounded, however, by Michael Bender (1983), who faults many day centres for the poor quality of their performance and for being insufficiently responsive to the clients' own preferences. He says that they lack clear objectives, run the risk of institutionalising those who attend them, and are ineffective with regard to their apparent aims. He thinks that where there is a training or therapeutic function to be done, this should be based on a specific short-term contract and specified goals and, where – as in most cases – the aim is simply to occupy the clients, then this should be done in a way that takes into account the consumers' interests: bingo, films, craft and hobby equipment, a bar and coffee room. Such facilities could well be provided, not by the social services department, but by the local authority without the consequent risk of stigmatisation.

Bender's critique raises vigorously the question of where social work ends. Certainly, there is a case for arguing that its inclination to extend too far into the mainstream will both dissipate its value and risk unnecessary stigmatisation. Maybe the role of social workers is to advocate the growth of day care and community-based facilities, but then to normalise them as far as possible, by involving the mainstream departments of health or education in their administration.

Liaison with other agencies
The social work department's work with the client, even though it does have a certain uniqueness, does not exist in a vacuum, and one prerequisite of service is the development of good working links with other agencies – with school teachers and doctors, in particular. The emergence of case conferences has formalised some of these associations, though not always to everyone's mutual satisfaction. Indeed the nature of the occasions and the formality of the procedures can be frustrating: in a well-known *Lancet* editorial (1975) one paediatrician describes how he had to cancel a spina bifida clinic in order to be at a case conference which, 'like the others, was attended by eight highly trained, highly paid professionals, who sat solemnly round a table discussing a robust healthy child with a bruise on his bottom'.

Inter-agency links would be better for spontaneity and flexibility. Intermediate treatment has led to much closer cooperation between schools and social workers, and the development of juvenile liaison panels has meant that probation officers, social workers and police officers meet regularly to monitor their mutual interest in children thought to be at risk.

One sphere where, from tentative beginnings, we now see frequent advances is in respect of social worker attachment to medical practices. Following experiments in South London, there has been a steady increase in the extent to which social workers hold sessions in surgeries or, more adventurously, take a full-time office base there. Close working relationships between the doctor, the health visitor, district nurse and social worker usually follow, although attachment schemes have not been a universal success story. Marshall and Hargreaves (1979) have spelt out some of the pitfalls of attachment schemes: professional isolation, problems of accountability, inadequate interviewing facilities and a failure of the GP to understand the social worker's role or capabilities.

Rushton and Davies (1984) acknowledge that the doctor's attitude is crucial, but say that other factors which lead to successful attachment schemes are careful planning, the existence of a group practice in the surgery, and the self-reliance and adaptability of the social worker. The main advantages of attachment are thought to be the ease of referral of patients who might not otherwise find their way to the social worker, the fact that a significant proportion of GP patients are suffering from forms of depression and might benefit from counselling, and an apparent increase in job satisfaction for the social worker. Rushton and Davies conclude:

> The informality of work carried out in a health setting has great advantages for social work. It is possible that the out-posting of social workers to work with other disciplines may become more common rather than less so in the future. The same thinking applies to collaborative as to patch thinking, taking social workers out of offices to where people are. (Rushton and Davies 1984)

There are barely any spheres where closer collaboration is inappropriate: workers who know each other are more likely to trust each other and so work together for the client's benefit – hence the functional importance of superficially marginal occasions like local luncheon clubs where workers can talk informally about matters (and cases) of mutual concern.

One especially important area for liaison occurs within the social worker's own department: the quality of cooperation between fieldworkers and residential care staff is often criticised – either because fieldworkers are said to lose interest in their clients once they are admitted or because residential staff resent their intrusion and fail to pay sufficient attention to the importance of their residents maintaining their associations with home and the outside world. Money is a major factor here, as travel costs in large county areas can be prohibitive, although letter-writing is better than nothing. But the separate identity of residential and field work staff can also hinder good relations. Suggestions are often made that each person in care should be allocated to a *key worker* who then retains contact with and responsibility for him throughout his moves in and out of the residential care system, but, although it is manifestly a good idea, the feasibility and advantages of such a method have never been properly tested.

In the probation service there have been improvements in communication between officers and the staff of probation hostels since wardens were designated as senior staff and were slotted into the organisational hierarchy. Greater problems, however, continue to be experienced in the probation service's working relationships with prisons where a sense of alienation between custodial goals and the social work approach has generally prevented the development of liaison and integration. In 1982, a new sentence of 'youth custody' was introduced with the intention of involving probation offices much more actively during the time of sentence. Again, though, resistance on the part of the prison service and reluctance on the part of many probation officers appears to have made progress difficult. In Essex, Foad (1984) found that attempts to encourage supervising officers to visit clients sentenced to youth custody were unsuccessful in nearly 50 per cent of the cases; she discovered that the most successful approach to inter-agency work involved the designation of specialist staff not only to liaise with youth custody centres but to become responsible for specialist supervision.

Conclusion

We have reviewed, too briefly, a range of caring agents beyond the social worker's self. The impression gained is of a system still in a relatively early stage of evolution but developing rapidly, albeit in no clearly identifiable direction. The common thread is that of the environment – the setting in which the client lives and the community upon which the social worker draws for support and supplementation.

Social work 'beyond the use of self' is necessarily *an agency* phenomenon rather than a matter of personal initiative on the part of the worker: it tends to involve the allocation of resources, often on a major scale, and to follow the making of policy decisions either in management teams or in committees of councillors or civil servants. Moreover innovations like 'Patch', IT, family centres, day care and the payment of volunteers raise issues that go far beyond the matter of professional skill or worker accountability: they require the design of organisational structures; job definitions and wage differentials mean active union interest; and the allocation of significant budget funds leads to demands for tight monitoring of effectiveness and efficiency. The one-to-one social work relationship was undoubtedly much simpler, but these developments come about in recognition of client interests, and the trend is likely to continue. They throw into even stronger relief the question of whether the term 'social work' as a blanket description of work done is likely to remain appropriate, since it covers such a multitude of organisations, sins and virtues.

In many cases, now, the social worker's use of self is no more than a beginning, a mere passing element in a relationship that takes in the provision of accommodation, group support and community involvement on a large scale. As the welfare services evolve, as the need for provisions 'beyond the use of self' becomes more insistent, both administrators and practitioners will have much to do to improve their methods and to allocate their resources to maximum effect. The professional worker is likely to assume increasingly a grass-roots managerial role in this situation, and to move far beyond the traditional counselling and home visiting functions where it all began.

PART III

In Conclusion

12 Essential Knowledge

'The main task in social work education', says the report of a Training Council Working Group, is 'to equip students with the knowledge and skills essential to effective social work practice' (CCETSW, 1975). But what knowledge *is* essential to social work practice? How do you identify the necessary skills?

It is traditionally assumed, both by aspiring social workers and by course planners, that there is a necessary and close – even an integrated – relationship between social work practice and the social sciences. Because of this, would-be social work students often begin their academic careers by doing a sociology or, less frequently, a psychology degree; some social work courses are explicitly labelled Applied Social Studies (thus carrying the quite false implication that anyone who sets out to apply social science theory to any field of practice must be a social worker). Even the august body of the Privy Council lays down that all social work students must have a sound knowledge of not only human growth and development but of the social sciences as a whole. The formally-taught parts of most social work courses are heavily biased towards sociology and/or psychology, and most rely on at least some social science lecturers whose experience of social work is only slight and whose commitment to it is often suspect. Indeed it is by no means uncommon for social work students to be taught by sociology lecturers whose view of their intended career is frankly jaundiced.

Sociology as a discipline, of course, is just as likely to be concerned with the study of factories, schools, the stock exchange or royalty as with the function of social work. Indeed, if you were to bring together a random selection of a hundred sociologists you would probably find only as much interest in social work as you would find in any like gathering of intelligent, publicly-concerned people. Why then has the myth developed that a knowledge of sociology or of psychology will provide an appropriate basis for practice? There are at least three reasons.

The first, and possibly the chief, reason is to be found in the coincidence of academic history. Social work teaching first took place alongside the early development of sociology; the two subjects shared, to a limited extent, some of the same people – right-wingers in the Charity Organisation Society, socialists among the Fabians. And although sociology quickly broadened its base and vigorously sought to thrust aside the contaminating taint of do-gooding, the taught courses in universities and polytechnics continued to take place under the same roofs, to share some of the same teachers, and, in the 1960s and 1970s – after a lapse of half-a-century – tentatively to compare their respective perspectives once more.

The second reason is linked, but different, and derives from what Howe (1980) has termed the homophonics of their respective designations. If nothing else, social science (or sociology) and social work *sound* as though they are or ought to be related. Indeed, a great many intelligent outsiders (even within the ranks of higher education) tend to think that they are one and the same. This assumed association has been encouraged in the last two decades by the interest of some sociologists in the plight of the poor and the deviant (both client groups of the social work services), and by the simultaneous growth of research activities in social work. Most social work researchers, myself included, have been or are sociologists, or at least use sociological methods of enquiry – albeit often very crudely. But merely because social work is subject to sociological investigation, it does not follow that sociology provides necessarily the best or most appropriate theoretical framework for practice. Sociologists, after all, can carry out enquiries into football management, amateur dramatics, drug peddling, occupational therapy or trade union organisation: such studies in themselves do not turn these spheres of activity into applied social sciences nor do they usually lead the practitioners to the conclusion that sociology has proved itself capable of improving the quality of their performance. Social work, however, perhaps because of its similar sounding label, has been uniquely vulnerable to colonisation by sociologists. The problem is epitomised within social work research itself, most of which is not research directed at improving practice but is carried out by social scientists putting social work under the microscope and generally finding fault with it. There is nothing wrong with such studies, just as there is nothing wrong with the same sociologists studying assembly-line production workers or school teachers. The end-products might well further the ends of sociological theory, but it has to be said that few, if any of them, have yet made any contribution to social work practice.

The third reason is that social work, which, as we have seen throughout this book, covers a wide range of statutory and semi-official functions in society, has been faced on the one hand with the fact that its tasks are both demanding, stressful, often controversial and all too frequently impossible to fulfil to everyone's complete satisfaction, and on the other with a chronically impoverished knowledge base. Understandably, therefore, the temptation to hope for explicit direction from high status disciplines in the social sciences was irresistible. At various times, sociology, psychoanalysis and learning theory have had – and still have – considerable attraction. And of course, they do have some part to play in any social worker's armoury of understanding. But they are by no means the whole of social work and it is increasingly doubtful whether, even together, they constitute more than a very small part of it.

To what extent, then, does the social worker need to be given a sophisticated knowledge of theory in the social sciences in order to be a good practitioner? Is a graduate in sociology likely to be better at predicting the risk of non-accidental injury than a graduate in English literature? Even if an awareness of social processes will be helpful to the practitioner – as it undoubtedly will – does every social worker need to understand the associated subtleties of critique and controversy?

It would be wrong to be over-dogmatic on this issue, but equally it would be wrong to reiterate uncritically what has become the conventional wisdom that the social sciences are a top-of-the-list essential ingredient in the preparation of all social workers for practice.

Let us briefly examine three major contributions from the social sciences and consider their implications for social work:

1. Maternal deprivation. The influence of the psychoanalyst John Bowlby over British child care practice since World War II has been considerable. The 1948 Children Act was passed in the wake of wartime evacuation when children, removed from their homes 'for their own safety', were often found to have suffered serious emotional disturbance as a result. Bowlby's work also had its origins in wartime Britain, and the publication in 1951 of his miniature classic, *Child Care and the Growth of Love*, provided the new children's departments with a theoretical *raison d'être*. Thenceforward his teaching formed the backbone of those courses in human growth and development which were deemed to be an essential part of social work training. Even now, with Rutter's *Reassessment* (1972) and Bowlby's own adaptations of his thesis in *Attachment and Loss* (1969, 1973, 1980), the importance of the mother-child bond or of providing a secure and consistent alternative attachment in infancy is broadly accepted as a critical doctrine by most practising social workers.

As a result, they find themselves striving to prevent the break-up of a natural family at almost any cost because of their ideological position that for a child to be brought up in a consistent family setting is almost invariably preferable to disrupting that arrangement and removing the child elsewhere. (The concept of the blood tie is really a red herring.) And that remains true, so goes the accepted social work philosophy, even when the family seems by 'ordinary standards' to be grossly unsuitable for child care.

The argument has its origins firmly rooted in developmental psychology. Rutter's corrective to the effect that, *provided a thoroughly suitable alternative is available*, breaking the mother-child bond is not *of itself* intrinsically destructive has also been absorbed by a later generation of social work students. In attempting to act on that, however, we see that social workers are confronted not with theoretical constraints, but with practical reality: for most of them know, from their working experience, that their commitment to the mother-child bond, however much it might seem to the public and the media to be a dubious and dangerous home-spun philosophy, is rendered comprehensible, not only by book-learning, but by their awareness of the variable quality of the available alternatives. If residential child care and fostering provisions were always as good, as consistent and as stable as the best of them are, then the social worker's decisions would be easier, and the removal of a child from home could be effected with rather less anxiety than is often the case today.

Hence the weight of theory has to be considered alongside practical policies and administration – with, more recently, the pressures of public opinion, the press and some representatives of the legal profession (as for example when coroners, judges or magistrates criticise social workers for not removing a child before it is seriously injured or killed) introducing further complicating factors. It isn't argued that the theories are *wrong* or irrelevant, only that they are but one strand in a complex pattern of human interactions, and that the social worker has to reach his decision or recommendation in the light of *all* the evidence available. There is no theoretical text which will accurately predict the balance of risks in any case between child removal and maintaining the status quo. Only the social worker can decide. And in that decision, sensitivity to social and psychological reality, experience, practical ingenuity and political acumen are of more importance at grass-roots level than social science theory – once the principles of it are established, understood and accepted.

2. Stigma   The concept of stigma is the most practical manifestation of the interactionist perspective in sociology and social psychology. People are judged by their fellows according to socially defined criteria in a wide variety of ways: they are seen as clever, poor, overbearing, smelly; they are thought of as bullies, inadequates, troublemakers, lunatics – or, in contemporary schoolboy parlance, spastics. People become aware of their labels, irrespective of whether they are reality-based or not, and they learn to handle social relationships in the light of them. They may try to cast them off and sometimes they may succeed; but if they have had a leg amputated, have criminal convictions against them, are of exceedingly low intelligence, are black or white in skin colour, are permanently blind, or have been adopted, these are facts which, to a greater or lesser extent, are a part of their identity, and where they are known and knowable are always likely to be taken into account by others. For example, I was recently concerned with a very competent social work student who seemed to be having some difficulty getting on with his fieldwork teacher on placement. These things happen from time to time, and the fieldwork teacher concerned, though able and well-intentioned, was not universally popular with her colleagues. I took the view that the student simply had to accept the reality of the situation – which was in no danger of getting out of hand – and recognise that, in our working lives, we all occasionally have to accept people with whom we feel degrees of incompatibility. A colleague of mine, however, when the matter was mentioned in the course of a staff meeting, pointed out that the student concerned was an adopted child, and suggested that this circumstance was the cause of his difficulites with the fieldwork teacher. I thought the interpretation dubious, impossible to prove or disprove, and of no practical relevance, and said so. But it illustrates in a simple way how quickly even sympathetic people tend to pin labels on others. On that occasion, the student concerned was not aware of this discussion but undoubtedly he, like all adopted people, had had to learn to cope not only with his own feelings about his childhood origins, but with the realisation that other people too were conscious of his adoptive status, and used it as a reference point.

As Goffman (1963) points out, most other people have some stigmatising characteristics, though the severity of them differs enormously. To be young or to be old, to be a Catholic, a Jew or an atheist, to be a native or an alien, to wear spectacles or a hearing aid, to be a student, a coalminer or a stockbroker, to be an adulterer or a tax-fiddler: all can be grounds for stigma and most can be grounds for acclaim – depending on the company in which one is moving at the time.

Many of the social worker's clients, however, are heavily and unambiguously stigmatised by a lot of people: the hard-core drug addict, the family regarded by their neighbours as a scourge on the community, the downward-drifting young adult sentenced to prison, the homeless recidivist, the severely subnormal child, the confused and incontinent old lady. Empirical sociology has contributed to our understanding of the feelings of such people and of those close to them (the parents of the handicapped child, for example, may feel more heavily stigmatised than the child himself), but it has provided little or no help on whether anything can be done to counteract or overcome them. On the contrary, the social scientist's contribution has been to show that would-be helpers – including the social worker – are themselves not only caught up in the stigmatising process, but are capable of aggravating it quite severely. Most recently this argument has been applied to intermediate treatment, a programme intended to increase leisure-time and adventure opportunities for children and teenagers found guilty of committing crimes or thought likely to get into trouble in the future. But, say the sociologists, merely by involving the kids in IT – whether it means taking them to the funfair, climbing in the Lake District or running a therapeutic group – social workers are subjecting them to a labelling process which will confirm society's view of them as mischief-makers. They are being *selected out* for special treatment, and, no matter how good the intentions (as in remedial teaching), it can and does lead to their peers and elders viewing them in such a way that their delinquent tendencies may thereby receive reinforcement rather than reduction.

3. *Inequality*   The debate about the iniquity of unequally distributed wealth has dominated Western politics, implicitly or explicitly, for a hundred years. The foundation of socialist states and the difficulties they have experienced in fulfilling their egalitarian hopes; the continuing debate among educated opinion in capitalist societies

between the virtues of liberalism, self-interest and socialism; and the apparent ability of most privileged classes always to withstand attacks on their status, and to re-position themselves so that they adapt their advantaged base to changing circumstances, all these are critical aspects both of contemporary social life and of political and social theory. Although, some of the grosser excesses of inequality may have been moderated in the United Kingdom during the twentieth century, much relative poverty survives, opportunities for advancement are unevenly distributed and variably acted upon, and even compensatory policies tend to benefit middle ranking groups rather than the poor (Townsend, 1979). The renaissance of right-wing economics during the 1980s has, moreover, lent official sanction to cut-throat policies of competitiveness that necessarily lead to the weak and the old suffering most severely. Moreover, as worldwide news coverage has become more thorough and, through television, more pervasive, our awareness of international inequality grows: some people in some countries are far richer than most Britons, but a much greater number of people in the world are unimaginably poorer. Some countries have greater extremes of privilege and deprivation; others claim to be achieving a better and fairer distribution of goods and services. And over it all hangs the critical question: What are the respective roles of central planning and of personal motivation and initiative? Politicians are obliged to 'know the answer', but the critical academic may be forgiven for having doubts. Where does the social worker stand in the face of it all?

Courses in politics or in social administration have tended to be taught either implicitly or explicitly in such a way that presupposes the social worker's commitment to a completely egalitarian philosophy. They have rarely recognised – unless it be to criticise him for it – that the social worker is an inherent part of the machinery of state, and must in practice operate within contemporary policies, whatever his ideological complexion. Of course, the social worker's own political perspective impinges on his working life. Radical socialists will look for structural changes, perhaps of a revolutionary kind, and will claim the right to use their position as social workers and trade unionists to further their ends; social democrats will seek to influence policy by campaigning for changes aimed at ameliorating existing conditions without destroying social stability; conservatives will broadly defend the unequal status quo in society. But, although no firm evidence is available, it is clear from reading books and articles by social work authors at different points on the political continuum that their actual performance in practice is not likely to vary in direct relation to their ideological beliefs.

The social administration view of inequality, then, although of obvious general interest to the social worker, is, like the concepts of maternal deprivation and stigma, swamped as a key to practice by the multifarious elements that impinge on everyday social work from all directions. Empirical studies of real-world social work show that the practitioner's objectives are not the achievement of equality – that must be a matter for politics – but are concerned with encouraging client independence, counselling and advising, stage managing compensatory practices for the disadvantaged, and carrying out the legislative requirements of society in respect of large numbers of vulnerable and deprived clients. It cannot be denied that social work, though still essential, would be rendered considerably more feasible and more defensible in a more equal society than ours, but neither can it sensibly be argued that it is the business of social work *per se* to bring that about.

Social administrators, like some sociologists, have fallen into the temptation of seeing social work as a legitimate vehicle for the pursuit of their own intellectual ideas. It is only now that social work, having in turn been seduced by the attractions of such respectable academic associations, is beginning to realise that they do not offer the best or most appropriate means of developing the skills necessary for good performance.

Social science and social work

The contribution of the social sciences to social work has been primarily a negative one. In almost all its empirical work, sociology has countenanced caution against unduly optimistic expectations in practice, has shown that various *change* or *control* strategies are normally of only limited value and may be counter-productive or have unanticipated adverse consequences, and has demonstrated that social workers themselves, though often liked and respected as individuals, ought not to ignore the social and political significance of their occupational base. With the exception of some recent highly specific contributions from learning theory, it is difficult to pinpoint any positive contribution that social scientists have made to the practice of social work, any contribution, for example, that has meant that social workers now operate in a significantly different manner from the way they performed 20 or 25 years ago.

There is a good deal of agreement that insufficient attention has been paid to the respective virtues of education and training in social work, and a frequent comment made by team leaders in the field is that some newly-qualified social workers are often rather better at critically analysing society's response to social problems than at practical action. The blame for this is generally laid at the door of the training courses but the explanation for it and any attempt at rectifying it are almost certainly more complicated than that. Universities and polytechnics produce perfectly competent engineers, vets, dentists, computer technicians and accountants. All training courses produce some able practitioners and most courses produce a lot. The feeling emerges that – apart from the small number of frankly incompetent social workers who squeeze through the training system (Brandon and Davies, 1979) – the production of practitioners who are in some senses alienated from and hostile to the system in which they are likely to be employed is a function of the personal attitudes of some students and the impact on them of the critical literature emanating from the social and political sciences.

It would be quite out of step with my own established perspective to argue that the critical literature should be in any sense proscribed. On the contrary, it is clearly essential for social work education to be able to cope with external attack in an honest and vigorous manner. But I have come to the view that social work, though an imperfect response to often chronic conditions of unending complexity, is a legitimate strategy to cope with the need to maintain society in a stable state and to respond humanely to personal needs and social conditions among marginal groups. It seems to me not inappropriate to expect every new entrant to the profession to share that modest view. If as a result of sociological, political or economic critiques, serious doubts remain about social work's legitimacy or viability, then one must wonder whether such a person is capable of fulfilling the basic responsibilities of a social worker.

Social work education is now strengthening its syllabus in the teaching of practice skills, and there are already signs that, in order to make room in the timetable for due weight to be laid on these, the emphasis on some aspects of the social sciences will have to be reduced. My guess is that the problem has been a short-term one in the wake of the radical upheaval in social work during the 1970s, and that we are now moving to a phase when education will be better able to design and teach curricula directly suited to the needs of practice.

Paradoxically, as this happens, it may well have the coincidental effect of encouraging a new generation of research endeavour in social work, directed not at exposing the shortcomings of the subject (something of which we are only too well aware) but at creating and developing new styles of practice and new tactical interventions in order to contribute constructively to the growth of professional skill.

What then is essential knowledge?

It is neither easy nor satisfying for me to come to the conclusion that the social sciences have so far been disappointing in their contribution to social work theory or practice. I am myself a sociologist; I enjoy reading sociology; and I practise a variety of sociological research methods in my academic work. I acknowledge that it is possible that sociology may yet succeed in proving that social work is irrelevant and misguided in its assumed social role. If that were to happen, and if the major political parties were to be persuaded by such analysis, then it would be better if social work ceased to exist. I have explained and, I hope, demonstrated in the pages of this book why I think that that is a false analysis, and why, if social work as we know it did not exist, its various functions would have to be taken on by other occupational groups who might well not acknowledge the same humanitarian commitment that characterises professional social work now.

But though it is theoretically possible that sociology might undermine or destroy social work, and although sociological research might contribute to the future development of the subject – its record to date is rather modest – the crux of the matter emerges when we return to the critical question posed earlier in this chapter: Is a social worker who has a sociology or a psychology degree *necessarily* a better social worker than one with neither? Does an absence of theoretical sophistication in the social sciences lead to second-rate practice? In both cases, the answer has to be a resounding *no*. Of course, the social worker should have some knowledge of modern society: culture, class, conflict and social change. Of course, there should be an awareness of relevant psychology: the human life cycle, role, abnormal states. But, to be frank, such knowledge can be learned relatively quickly and painlessly, using Open University style training modules, and it should comprise only a relatively small part of the social work syllabus. The temptation, especially when such material is taught at postgraduate level by specialists in the subject, is to embark on a critical consideration of the issues in a way that is intellectually stimulating but that can have the effect of inducing paralysis in practice. Social scientists engaged in teaching social work students find it hard to come to terms with the fact that practice has to go on in an imperfect world, a world that must make do with imperfect knowledge and often unproven theories. For teachers continually to emphasise the shortcomings of social work, to suggest that it can damage the interests of the poor, and will always fail to overcome the overbearing influence of social inequality, makes no contribution to the improvement of social work practice. Assuming the kind of knowledge of social affairs and the psychology of man that any alert reader of, say, the *Guardian* or *New Society* might be expected to have, another critical question suggests itself: Are the theoretical social sciences more essential to the social worker than any other subject? And again the answer has to be *no*. There are four spheres of knowledge that are of more relevance and that *are* essential in the statutory sector: skills in social work practice, a knowledge of relevant law, a sound and up-to-date knowledge of welfare rights, and a sensitivity to, knowledge of and (preferably) experience in the local conditions within which the agency operates. If these spheres are covered, and if they are combined with good sense, strength of personality, intelligence, flexibility and experience of human relations in general, then good social work will be guaranteed whether or not the practitioner is able to lay claim to being a social scientist as well. Sophistication in the social sciences might give added kudos, might speed promotion, might lead to an academic career, might enable him to write clever articles in the social work press or journals, but there is absolutely no evidence that it will make him a better social worker – and that, after all, should be the aim of the training system. There *is* a role for social science in social work but it is not at the heart of basic training. Now let me consider, all too briefly, the four spheres of knowledge that I have dubbed basic to good practice.

Practice know-how
Three of the four spheres of knowledge indicate what I think the social worker should *know about*. But the first, and the most basic of all, is *know-how*. To write about practice skills would require a book in itself, but such skills cannot be learnt merely by reading. Like playing a piano, they have to be done, not just thought about or discussed. Almost the whole of this book is concerned with practice skills. If the reader accepts my thesis on the nature of social work, he will have a good idea of the kind of skills the worker needs to develop: adeptness

in assessment and decision-making, confidence in human relationships, the demonstration of sensitivity to the client, ability to influence people in positions of power, fluency in report-writing, flexible and practical responsiveness to volatile social circumstances, ability to give appropriate help in a wide variety of situations, and awareness of treatment strategies that meet the client's needs. Performance in all these can be improved by training, but although all social work courses attempt to tackle such skill-teaching, the quality of instruction is extremely variable, and many rely, hopefully rather than realistically, on placement supervisors to carry the main burden. There is no doubt that the greatest need in syllabus development in social work education is for the teaching of practice skills to be codified and for national guidelines on teaching methods to be devised, but that can only be done when and if there is general agreement on the nature of social work skills. This book has made an attempt to move towards some kind of consensus on objectives and skills in the belief that training for the profession will be incapable of improving its performance unless we can reach some agreement on the present state of the discipline and the nature of its role in society. Social work will never stand still, but unless we can find an acceptable perspective on contemporary practice skills any thoughts of our moving forward rather then merely shifting our ground with every passing fashion will be seen for the fanciful optimism that it assuredly is.

Knowing about ...

A commonly stated criticism in client-perspective studies is of the youthfulness and inexperience of many social workers called on to tackle the horrific entanglements that characterise the lives of some clients. It *is* a problem: I shall always blush with shame at the memory of the stumbling attempts I made as a rather naive young man of 23 or 24 to respond to the complex needs of large mums with large families or to counsel would-be divorcees whose harrowing experience of interpersonal relations far outstretched mine. Although many clients do prefer older social workers, I suspect that it is not primarily because of their greater experience of life, but because they are presumed to know more about the things that matter to them. But such knowledge in a professional should not be expected to come *only* from experience. After all, there are young nurses, young policemen, young doctors, young school teachers, and although all of them may get better as they grow older, it is reasonable for their clienteles to expect that they have learnt the basic facts necessary to their chosen career. The same must also be true of social work.

Social workers, however, and many social work courses, too, have tended in recent years to be rather smug and superior about such learning: the very idea of rote learning, in particular, will be enough to make the young sociology graduate studying social work spit out the insult, 'Positivist'! For two decades, the fashionable emphasis in social work education has been on critical analysis – at first on the unconscious mind processes of the client, later on the social, political and economic deprivations of the weak. The academicisation of social work training has inevitably aggravated the trend, with postgraduate courses in particular finding some difficuty in holding the balance between the scholarly expectations of higher degrees committees and the practical demands of a vocational qualification. Basic knowledge – of law, welfare rights and the routines of good practice – has risked being downgraded to second-class status, or even being excluded from the process of assessment altogether. This is not to say that there is an irreconcilable dichotomy between analytical skills and practice skills. On the contrary, there is some evidence to suggest a fairly close correlation between the two (Hack, 1973). But it does mean that social work education cannot entirely refute the allegation that its objectives and syllabuses have sometimes been out of step with the needs of the field – and of the client. Intellectual ability is clearly important in an occupation as demanding as that of social work, but it must at all times be combined, not merely with the fundamental personality characteristics of empathy, genuineness and warmth, but also with a sound knowledge of those facts centrally relevant to the social worker's ordinary activities. The client has a right to expect that a qualified social worker should not be ignorant of basic information, and courses accordingly have the responsibility to ensure that, as far as possible, their products meet the clients' expectations.

... the law

Social workers – even if they happen to have a law degree – are not employed as lawyers. They have a social work identity and are required to function accordingly. It follows that, although we have argued that the advice-giving role of social work agencies could be strengthened to the community's benefit, the giving of strictly legal advice is not something within the province of social work. Nevertheless every social worker will be a better social worker if he knows something about the legal principles which underpin social policy and practice, and if he knows, to perfection, the minutiae of legislation as it affects him and his clients – including significant case law as it emerges. The legal frameworks that govern practice are by no means all precisely defined (intermediate treatment, for example, though authorised by statute, and subject to specified time limits, otherwise provides its operators with a virtual *carte blanche*), but precisely because they are so variable it is essential for the social worker to know which laws facilitate action, which laws restrict it, and how. The student's task has been made a good deal easier than it used to be because of the publication of a steady stream of texts and articles summarising and commenting on relevant legislation. It is not the purpose of this chapter to provide a comprehensive account of all the law that a social worker should know, nor in the space available would it be appropriate for me to try to do so. Instead I can illustrate the range by noting ten key subject-areas and posing, in respect of each of them, one critical question. (The answers to the questions, together with recommended references, are contained in the appendix on page 245).

1. *The making of care and supervision orders in criminal cases:* What are the legal grounds for taking a child who has committed an offence into the care of the local authority?
2. *Protecting a child from its parents:* What are the legal obligations on a social worker when confronted with a risk-situation in non-accidental injury?
3. *Adoption:* What is the guiding principle in adoption proceedings?
4. *Mental subnormality:* What difference does a mentally subnormal person's age make to his legal rights?
5. *Mental illness:* What are the duties and powers of the approved social worker?
6. *The elderly in care:* Under what circumstances may an elderly person be taken into the care of the local authority against his/her will?
7. *The chronically sick and disabled:* What are the statutory duties of local authorities with regard to the chronically sick and disabled?
8. *The homeless:* What constitutes 'priority need' among the homeless or potentially homeless?
9. *Adult offenders:* What are the obligations on an offender made the subject of a probation order?
10. *Acting on behalf of the client in court:* Under what circumstances

may the social worker act in court on behalf of a client?

Of course, there is a risk that some naive persons might imagine that simply by learning the answers to these and other similar questions they will be entitled to call themselves social workers. It must be apparent from the complex range of professional functions that have been outlined in this book that nothing could be further from the truth. But it is almost as wrong to assume that one can be a good social worker whilst being in ignorance of the statutory context within which the practitioner has to operate. Relevant law *is* essential knowledge for practice, and its omission must lead to sloppiness, inefficiency, and a betrayal of the client's own best interests.

... welfare rights

While the role of social work as a statutorily defined activity has been steadily growing, there has emerged the almost contradictory need for a welfare rights service to make people aware of their position vis-à-vis the law, to ensure that they receive what is duly their's and, when necessary, actively to defend their interests against the encroachment of the all-powerful state. Can social workers assume that role – either generically or by the employment of welfare rights specialists in their agencies?

The question is still a controversial one. To postulate an adversary relationship between state and individual (Inglis, 1977, for example, has said that the relationship between the citizen and the bureaucracy is the 'central and lethal tension in all advanced societies') would suggest that welfare rights ought to be defended by a separate profession; but to argue, as I do, that the task of social work is fundamentally to achieve a reconciliation *between* state and individual leads in the direction of requiring the social worker to straddle both sides of the relationship, to engage in two-way negotiations, and therefore to assume as much responsibility for the rights of individuals as for the functions of the state. It is not, perhaps, an ideal arrangement (or perhaps it is *too* idealistic, presuming on the ultimate sense of absolute fairness in the practitioner), and special arrangements need to be devised to cope with situations in which the social worker finds himself in conflict with his own department; but, in terms of practical politics, it is improbable that a fully-fledged welfare rights role will ever be taken on by any group of people other than social workers. They thus emerge as the best welfare rights officers we are likely to get.

Social workers, however, do not fulfil that role at present, and there is some evidence of widespread resistance to it at all levels. Burgess (1979) has argued that social services managers are reluctant to encourage welfare rights activities because of the complex political repercussions that might ensue, and many social work students, including some of those with a radical view of their future occupation, are deterred by the intricate detail that needs to be learned in order to become a welfare rights expert. Certainly few social workers have made the effort to grasp the nettle: 'a recent study ... found that for many the problem was finding and maintaining a reliable source of information, given that they themselves lacked the time, the energy and sometimes the motivation to ferret out the details.' (Parker, 1979, on Melotte). I am not convinced that time and energy are the chief deterrent. If, as I now believe they should, social workers were to take on the role of welfare rights officers as an integral part of their maintenance function, the teaching of the intricate detail would need to be provided during basic training and then regularly updated as required. Nothing would bring greater strength to the social worker's position than for him to assume a major responsibility for representing the legitimate rights of the client in all his dealings with the welfare state – including his contacts with the social services department. Specialists might have a part to play but the main burden should fall on the shoulders of ordinary social workers. This could only happen were the welfare rights function to be sanctioned both by political committees and the administrative hierarchy. But above all it would demand a changed attitude on the part of practitioners, students and social work teachers: knowledge about welfare rights is crucial to the social work task; ignorance about welfare rights must lead to the social worker being only half as useful as he might be. It is sad but significant that the recent improvement in the quality of books on law for social workers has not been paralleled by a similar development in respect of welfare rights.

Information technology is, however, a field which is likely to have something to contribute to the provision of an efficient welfare rights service. The fact that assessment of personal circumstances and detailed access to complex knowledge about rights and resources are both within the capability of electronic data processing is a clear indicator that computerised facilities should be developed. Furthermore, clients have expressed the view that they would prefer to employ a video display unit to check their benefits and rights than have to rely on human contact. Certainly, developed properly, modern technology could cut down waiting time, improve reliability and make a real contribution to social services performance.

In the meantime, there are at least eight basic fields in which welfare rights knowledge is crucial:

1. Rent rebates and rent allowances;
2. Rate rebates;
3. Education welfare benefits: free school meals, clothing awards, education maintenance awards;
4. Family Income Supplement (FIS) – especially for low-paid workers with children;
5. Free milk and vitamins; help with dental and optical charges;
6. The rights of tenants in the public and private housing sectors;
7. The exercise of advocacy in clients' relations with the fuel boards;
8. Supporting or representing clients in tribunals – for example, with regard to national insurance, supplementary benefits and housing or medical appeals.

The acquisition of knowledge, competence and confidence in these and similar areas would enable the social worker to make a direct contribution towards improving the client's lot – not only because there could be material gains, but because the demonstration of practical aid would lead to better relations between worker and client, thus facilitating the delivery of a full social work service. The two hurdles to overcome are staff motivation and the inaccessibility of much of the relevant information. But, although the task will not be easy, the explicit recognition that social work should incorporate a high quality welfare rights element would enable it to be tackled. In particular there would have to be significant changes in the required curriculum of social work education (with welfare rights knowledge being rigorously assessed), determined leadership in this new direction by departmental heads, and the efficient production of detailed and regularly updated rights guides for social work personnel.

... local resources

No matter how well a social work student has been trained, there is one sphere of knowledge that can only be acquired when he takes up his post, but which is nevertheless undoubtedly an essential element in professional competence: knowledge of his local scene, the problems it presents and the resources on offer. Every time a social worker changes his job, even if it is within the same city, he must begin afresh the task of getting to know his neighbourhood, its social and demographic structure and the availability of helping agencies. His pocket reference book must be radically revised, and he must go out of his way to become known by those who are most likely to be influential in his working life and the lives of his clients. The social worker and the probation officer are at the hub of a network of services, and until knowledge of the network is mastered they can only provide a second-rate service.

Twelve keys to the local community

1. First of all, know your way round your own agency. Who are the specialists to whom you can turn for guidance – not just designated consultants or advisers, but long-serving social workers who will have a wealth of detail to convey as a result of their previous experience? If you need to call on your agency to exert influence on a client's behalf, whom should you turn to? What are the hierarchial lines of responsibility for sanctioning services and funds? How can you get answers and approval for action speedily and helpfully? (The answers to the last two questions might not always be compatible.)

2. Get to know and be known by the local social security office. Although your work may bring you into professional conflict with the staff there on occasions, this will be easier to handle if there is mutual familiarity and understanding. You will be a better advocate if your credibility is established. You will be more help to a client if you can communicate easily with the staff there. And you may be of help to the social security office if they know they can refer potential clients to social workers whom they have met.

3. Identify the voluntary social work agencies. Some will be traditional/conservative; others will have a radical perspective; sometimes the identities will overlap or change with time. Voluntary and statutory agencies are acting on the same stage, and, although their roles may differ, they need to understand each other's functions.

4. What self-help groups are there? Many are invaluable, especially for the provision of long-term support in highly specific circumstances. Clients' groups and feminist groups are an

important new resource on the social work scene.

5. Are there any local charities that can give occasional help with money or material aid?
6. You should become quickly familiar with the psychiatric services in the district, Studies have shown, for example, that social workers who are able to forge close and sympathetic working relations with psychiatrists are far more likely to get a speedy and helpful service for their clients. Moreover knowledge of which psychiatrists specialise in which conditions can also be utilised for the client's benefit.
7. It is rather a tall order to expect social workers to develop a rapid working knowledge of the entire health sector in their locality. But social workers have to work with general practitioners, district nurses, health visitors, geriatricians and paediatricians, and there is little doubt that the social worker who is known to and trusted by medical personnel is in a stronger position than one who is seen by them as an unfamiliar layman.
8. Know the local labour market, liaise with the Department of Employment staff, build up a list of potentially sympathetic employers.
9. Know the penal system and court services locally; establish a working relationship with relevant personnel in the police force.
10. To know local schools in detail and in depth will take time, but contact with special schools should be a priority, as should the establishment of links with specially designated teacher/counsellors in other schools.
11. Draw up and maintain a list of suitable lodgings and landladies.
12. Get to know the general availability of residential provision both inside your own department, in other departments and throughout the voluntary sector.

A major problem in social work recently has been the rapid turnover of basic-grade staff; the problems that have arisen from this are twofold: first, many able social workers have never fulfilled their potential in post because their short stay in any one office has been insufficient to make maximum use of the local network of facilities; and secondly, the frequent changes of staff not only make it difficult for other agencies to know who the local social workers are, but antagonise them to such an extent that they may be less-than-otherwise willing to greet the numerous agency newcomers and spend time establishing working relationships. If successful social work is at least partially dependent on an effective network of community resources, its development is clearly not helped if the person primarily responsible is constantly changing. Rapid turnover is a particular problem if it occurs within a 'Patch' system, and that fact is a major argument for maximising the use of indigenous personnel, permanent residents and locally respected community leaders.

It is partly to try and counteract the problems of ignorance caused by rapid staff turnover that a case has been made out for depersonalising the information system in any social work agency. Streathfield and Wilson (1979), for example, have argued that there is an agency responsibility in this respect. They suggest that the 'who knows what?' problem can be resolved by having a card (or computerised) index subdivided into organisations, individuals, problems, etc. Each card should have addresses, phone numbers and names of contact persons – including the most knowledgeable social worker in the base agency. Such a system, like any information index, would need to be continually updated, but it would undoubtedly share the burden and overcome the obvious inefficiency of every social worker striving quite independently, and often very selfishly, to develop only a personal network. Private networks – rather like a policeman's information network – must remain a part of the social worker's daily routine, but they should go hand-in-hand with an agency approach to the total problem.

In conclusion

In their book on practice theories in social work, Curnock and Hardiker (1979) argue persuasively that the way social workers operate reveals the kind of learning they have absorbed; the authors suggest that social workers employ 'an assemblage of sign-posts' – for example, an emphasis on individualised ideologies, and an inclination to draw up a balance sheet of risks, needs and resources. Although Curnock and Hardiker detect some elements of social science knowledge in all of this, they do not know and cannot say *how* this knowledge was obtained – whether, for instance, it was dependent on extensive original reading, or whether it was derived from a distillation of literature handed down as a part of the profession's conventional wisdom. Thus, although they go some way towards defending the importance of the social sciences as a foundation-stone of practice, it is not possible to extract from their work those aspects of sociology or psychology which are of the greatest proven value in social work.

Despite the importance of Curnock and Hardiker's work, the argument of this chapter remains valid. For the practice of social work a knowledge of the social sciences is less crucial than training in basic skills and a knowledge of law, welfare rights and the local scene. These skills and this knowledge have to be maintained; the learning process must be dynamic. Practice develops, the law changes, rights and benefits are affected by legislation and government decisions, the local scene evolves.

Social work went through a sticky patch in the 1970s, and one of the reasons was its failure to establish itself as a profession in command of essential knowledge; too many social workers did not believe in the validity of, or the justification for, their own job. Such an error might be forgiven in retrospect, occurring as it did in the wake of the ill-planned Seebohm reforms, the too rapid recruitment of badly-prepared staff and an unfortunate theoretical vacuum in social work education.

Even in 1984, newly qualified social workers were saying that, in many cases, their courses had not prepared them adequately for practice and had got the balance of critique and technical training wrong (Davies 1984). The errors of the 1970s must not be allowed to continue into the 1990s; the training curriculum must adapt itself to the demands of practice, because, if it does not do so, the clients will suffer, and society will be confirmed in its traditional disillusionment with social work.

13 The Essential Social Worker

For social workers to be considered essential to society, they do not have to prove themselves *more* essential than anyone else. Theirs may not be the most critical of all occupations: they are not primary producers, nor are they directly concerned with public or private health. But neither is social work the most easily dispensable job in a civilised community. Social workers bring a humanising force, a caring component into the increasingly large-scale welfare setting – a setting which, though created for the best of reasons, can so easily slide into heartlessness and become alienated from the compassionate intentions that fired its originators. The social work tradition that has evolved over ninety years decrees that welfare functions in respect of the elderly, the handicapped, the deviant and the deprived shall be fulfilled in a manner that respects the individuality of those involved, that always recognises potential for survival and growth and that reflects an absolute commitment to care. Society could survive without social work, but it would be a society with a very different attitude towards its marginal citizens: one which shut its eyes to suffering, disposed of its offenders (as by transportation), bricked away the mentally ill, created vast impersonal orphanages and workhouses and ultimately resorted to the convenience and economy of the gas-ovens.

We need to continually remind ourselves of how often in the past communities *have* built walls around the unwanted – the riff-raff, the scroungers, the throw-outs, the has-beens, the spastics, the undeserving – all those people to whom fate and the neighbours have not been kind. Social work is politically sanctioned to devise, administer and run systems which seek to make more humane provision for those unable to cope alone, and, to that extent, social work is best understood as having a function in society just like any other job. On a number of occasions in these pages I have sought to demonstrate this by making use of analogies with other occupations – school teaching, nursing, and so on. A less obvious but still appropriate comparison can be made between social work and the police: not that the social worker's aims are always the same as those of the policeman – on the contrary, the two jobs, though sometimes complementary, are often in tension with each other. But both the policeman and the social worker are public servants; both are given a relatively open-ended brief and have considerable powers of discretion; both are faced with tasks that are regarded as being simultaneously important and yet ultimately impossible to achieve to everyone's satisfaction. In one respect, however, the police force has more successfully managed the limitations of its social role. Neither society nor policemen themselves expect perfection; people only dream of, they do not anticipate or look for, a crime-free community, and when offences are committed, on the whole the public does not blame the policeman.

There *has* been, however, a tendency to assume that social work can rid society of child abuse, hypothermia and even – ironically – juvenile delinquency. There may be more than one reason for such fallacious thinking, but an undoubted component has been the profession's own inclination to justify its existence on the grounds that it could cure or prevent all manner of human ills and shortcomings, and to appear willing to accept responsibility for clients' behaviour when it clearly was in no position even to monitor let alone control it. But if social workers have not always resisted the mantle of omnipotence, the responsibility for proffering it is surely that of parliament and policy-makers whose optimistic vision of a planned society has led them to ignore the fallibility of man and his ultimate right to choose the untidy, the undesirable or even the criminal option.

Social work is a by-product of an unequal and imperfect society. To that extent, its radical critics are right; social work can be said to tend towards the perpetuation of an unfair social order because it exists to ameliorate its worst effects. But the radicals are also wrong, as evangelicals have always been wrong, in their belief that they and they alone hold the key to the achievement of perfection – a state of material and sociological grace in which there will be no place for social work or its practitioners. Such a view reflects not so much a misconception of social work as a misconception of man and of social and political reality. All the evidence of psychology, sociology and history points to the high probability of imperfection in human behaviour, society and the social process: any style of practice which ignores that evidence is doomed to disillusionment and can be persisted in only by restricting basic human rights in a way that is itself incompatible with social work values. Of course, political theorists and social and economic policy-makers must work towards improvements in the way society is organised; but their task is rather like that of an artist-in-oils trying to paint while riding on a fairground waltzer – the contrary forces are always paramount. The pattern and process of social, economic and psychological reality is too complex to be explained by one analysis, too complex to bring under total control. Social workers have to operate not only from where the client is at but also from where society is at. And neither the client nor society ever stand still.

Social workers are essential because of the frailties of human genetics and the ageing body, because of aberrations of human behaviour, because plans go wrong and people die, because all political and economic systems produce victims and label deviants, because human nature and human life are occasionally vicious, and because people – especially people in families – sometimes fight with and hurt each other. Social work has emerged as one of the twentieth century's attempts to cope with such problems as best it can.

Social work copes with them, I have argued in this book, not by giving absolute priority to self-determination, but by emphasising the right of the client to a say in his own destiny and his right to enter into dialogue with the state on matters that affect his freedom and his welfare. The essence of social work is maintenance: maintaining a stable, though not a static, society, and maintaining the rights of and providing opportunities for those who in an unplanned, uncontrolled community would go to the wall. The profession of social work is living testimony to a political commitment to safeguard and further the welfare of all citizens. The agencies within which social workers operate employ them in order to comply with society's desire to so manage affairs that scarce resources are distributed fairly and humanely, that critical decisions are arrived at with due regard for the needs and feelings of all parties involved and that provisions for the disadvantaged are made in such a way as to ensure maximum scope for personal and communal development. Such functions need to be carried out in any modern urban society, but the *way* in which they are carried out is of importance to the state of civilisation – and it is the aim and the claim of social work that its principles of humanity and concern can and should raise the standards of welfare practice to the highest levels attainable.

Such standards are neither easily achieved nor automatically sustained. The pressures upon them, especially in institutional settings, and the expressions of hostility towards them (ranging from the exasperation of relatives and the cynicism of the media to the pure strains of fascist doctrine never far below the surface of the public's consciousness) all mean that the social worker's defence of his professional commitment and of the rights of his client frequently involve him in emotional battles and induce in him a feeling of isolation in the community – again perhaps not unlike that experienced by the policeman. At such times, the worker needs the support of his colleagues and the respect of his agency; he needs to be able to feel that, although there are contrary forces in society, nevertheless his role is recognised as legitimate by the community at large.

The social worker also needs to feel that his commitment to the unique qualities and essential rights of all citizens – however weak or vulnerable they may be – is one that is shared and supported by the political authority which, as we have seen throughout this book, is his undoubted employer. If social work has been brought into existence during the twentieth century by social democratic forces concerned to create a compassionate community, then any hint that there has been a radical switch of political philosophy in government, especially if it is one which undervalues the social worker's role, will be found to affect morale and induce confusion.

Since the election of the Thatcher Government in 1979, British social work has been receiving mixed messages. As we saw in chapter 1 (Table 1.1), the growth in financial commitment to the personal social services has not declined significantly. But a Conservative emphasis on self-help and on a yearned-for return to Victorian values, the seemingly uncontrollable rise in unemployment, and the emergence of conflict, competition and confrontation as political virtues have all seemed to signal a climate hostile to social work. To the extent that a polarisation of political perspectives has been a consequence of Thatcherism, to the extent that the richer are more generously rewarded than the poor, and to the extent that the working class – and even more so the lumpenproletariat – seem to be viewed with disdain ... to that extent, social work as a tangible expression of society's commitment to conciliation and consensus becomes difficult to sustain.

It is unfortuante that the emergence of right-wing values in politics has occurred simultaneously with an emphasis on the need for improved management in social work. Certainly social work in its time of rapid growth *did* suffer from weak management, poor quality of recruitment, unclear objectives and inadequate standards of training. But there is no necessary relationship between conservatism on the one hand and disciplined administration on the other; socialism just as surely requires improved performance and proper attention to quality control if it is to maintain credibility in the eyes of the public and the professionals. The next decade is going to see a great deal more attention paid to the raising of performance standards and the use of effective modes of evaluation, no matter whether the government is dominated by the left or the right. What is important from social work's point of view is that this should occur in a political climate which continues to respect the central values of contemporary welfare practice so painstakingly built up: the provision of a humane service to those in need, the achievement of reconciliation between the state and its citizens – without oppression on the one hand or violent deviance on the other – and the efficient use of compensatory resources in such a way as to avoid demeaning the recipient or undermining personal independence.

Such an approach can only be adopted and pursued in a society where consensus is the foundation of all political action – and the responsibility for ensuring such a climate rests, as it always has done, with those in positions of power and privilege. The clients of the social services have little of either.

The practice of social work can be seen as a form of pastoral care in a secular society. Like the mediaeval church, contemporary state welfare agencies have a variety of functions – punitive, protective, compensatory, watchful – and, like priests, social workers are at their best when their attention is focused on the needs of individuals or small communities; it is then that they act to represent the interests of ordinary men and women to the state and vice versa. Social workers exist because of the pastoral commitment of the modern welfare state. But such a commitment is neither simple, nor unified, nor unchanging. The maintenance task carried out by the social worker must inevitably at times lead to debate and even to conflict between the various parties – hence the need for a strong welfare rights role in contemporary practice, and hence the inevitability of social work challenging some traditional perspectives in institutional settings like prisons and hospitals. But social work *per se* is not about revolution. Neither, of course, is it about the uncompromising, relentless and naked imposition of state power. Social work operates within, and represents the interests of, the state by which it is sponsored; it asserts the primacy of the individual and to that extent is a product of the evolution of social democracy in the twentieth century. The social worker is jointly accountable both to his client and to the agency, and, because of this duality, social work must inevitably reflect a degree of tension and ambiguity, and be increasingly ill-at-ease and eventually untenable in any society under absolute rule or in a state of anarchy.

Social work is not and can never be wholly apolitical because its practice depends on the state regime respecting the basic rights of all citizens. Political battles may have to be fought and won in order to defend the climate within which social work can be practised. Social workers will find themselves challenging legislation or administrative conventions which undermine their position vis-à-vis the client. But, in the end, social work is not about winning, just as life (except in the shortest possible term) is not about winning. It is about reconciliation and compromise – reconciling the personal and the political, the individual and the state, different individuals with each other. Each social worker will apply the principles of reconciliation in slightly different ways – hence the importance of the use of self – and some will adopt longer time perspectives than others. Some will tend more towards an identification with the state, others more towards an active sympathy with the individual; all will vary in their attitudes from case to case, on different occasions, and perhaps as they themselves grow older. But all will sense the professional cohesion which unites them and commits them to their reconciliatory task.

Of course, I recognise that some critics will reject such a pluralist interpretation of what social work is or ought to be about. I can only argue that this representation seems to me to best fit the empirical evidence of how and why social workers are employed, of what their agencies and clients expect of them, and of how the vast majority of social workers respond to those expectations. Indeed I would go further and suggest that when a social worker tries to go beyond the maintenance/reconciliatory role to anything other than the most modest degree, client, agency and political forces combine to counteract such 'inappropriate' excursions and to bring the worker back into the professional mainstream or to eject him altogether.

Moreover, although the model I have presented is fundamentally a modest account of social work's identity and role, it does contain an ultimate irony. If it were to be accepted as not only the necessary but the correct framework for social work practice, this would open the door to all manner of ideas for radical growth and development. Social work's relative paralysis of recent years (in some respects, even, its regression) has derived from a lack of faith in its ascribed role in society. That mood has in turn followed on, first, from a bevy of research critiques most of which began from the erroneous assumption that social work was first and foremost to do with the achievement of change; secondly, from a sense of political ambivalence induced by a yearning in some for radical solutions and an impatience with the focus on individuals; thirdly, from a lack of theoretical leadership because those who wrote about social work were too often ignorant of real-world practice as the social workers knew it; and, fourthly, from a sense of post-Seebohm confusion about the nature of the social work task and doubts about the willingness of local authorities to support it.

It is now time for social workers openly to acknowledge both the limitations of their task *and* its crucial importance to the survival and growth of a compassionate democracy. Most social workers came into their job with ideals, and most manange – despite public and academic sniping – to retain them. They need now only to be allowed to apply them in their daily work.

There are two spheres for theoretical development in the future: one is concerned with practice, the other with manpower.

I have earlier referred to the need for social work to make a commitment to the idea of *curriculum development*. It is not that new ideas in practice are absent; indeed, as we have seen in these pages, they exist in abundance– community service, social skills training, self-help groups, 'Patch', and so on. It is rather that they emerge, spread and then often disappear in a haphazard fashion that suggests both a lack of theoretical clarity and more especially an absence of intellectual discipline. What is missing is the potentially fruitful partnership between thinking practitioners, research staff and academic theorists which would provide the ideal environment for core developments. There is a long way to go, and the pattern of curriculum development in education has shown the need to allow sufficient time and space for some false starts: proposals and ideas have to be tried, tested and possibly rejected or amended, and generous resources have to be allocated to thinking about, planning, designing and evaluating alternative schemes. With the development of many different kinds of day care, the continuing growth of IT and community service and the growing numbers of highly dependent people in all age-ranges and client groups, it is perfectly clear that social workers in the local authority and probation services must start taking a more active approach towards the development of imaginatively designed programmes for practice.

Sociology, too, has a part to play in this if its exponents can only see their way to contributing towards innovation and growth instead of being seduced by the academic attractions of sitting in proud and austere judgment on the shortcomings of present practice. Research must learn to contribute within given perspectives and not only to question the appropriateness of those perspectives. If the framework is accepted and if the legitimacy of social work is acknowleged, then it cannot be beyond the wit of practice, theory and research to join together in order to improve standards of performance more determinedly than has happened in recent years.

The second sphere for development concerns the use of manpower. Here, there are conflicting strains in operation: on the one hand, an ideologically egalitarian pressure to assert that everyone is or can be a social worker and that professionalism is an undesirable concept; on the other, the real-life trend towards longer hierarchies, greater salary differentials, and union activity to protect or amend relative positions in the occupational pecking-order. I have argued throughout this book that the phrase 'social work' is exasperatingly neutral in failing to clarify just what its practitioners do. But it is now clear – clearer, indeed, as each year goes by – that those who are employed in positions traditionally labelled as social work are emerging as grass-roots community managers, carrying discretionary powers and welfare responsibilities that extend beyond mere *caring*. Social workers are community entrepreneurs; their job is maintenance, and they approach it by imaginatively balancing a variety of skills and roles, in which the coordination of other operators in the agency and the community plays an increasingly important part.

Lack of clarity about social work's objectives and boundaries has posed problems for administration and practice until recently. As this book has outlined, these problems have now almost been overcome, and, as a result, the skilled deployment of personnel and the creative development of practice strategies are realistic goals for social services and probation departments alike.

It is the job of trainers and educators, of managers and professional associations to work within the framework of a theory of maintenance, to develop skills and tactical wisdom with a view to raising practice standards and encouraging developmental strategies in relation to the three key elements of social work: the exercise of statutory and departmental responsibility, the achievement of change, and pro-active involvement in the community – all used with the aim of supporting and encouraging the clients of the social service system.

Social work is essential in two ways. First, because of the tasks which social workers are called upon to perform – if they did not do them, others would have to be employed to do so. And secondly because of the democratic and humanist values they espouse in the course of carrying out their functions. They and their mode of working are essential because of the state's aspiration to accommodate a caring community and to respect the absolute right of every man, woman and child to independence and growth. Of course the state, and its employees fall far short of the ideal, but that is no reason to abandon it or to deride the efforts made to achieve it. Social work will almost certainly change beyond recognition by the end of the twentieth century, but the foundations laid by its pioneers over ninety years are sound and enduring; this century has seen many improvements in the way basic welfare functions are carried out, and there is every reason to assume that the trend can be maintained.

APPENDIX

Law and the Social Worker

Ten questions and answers

by Caroline Ball, Barrister at law

Appendix: Law and the Social Worker

1 The making of care and supervision orders in criminal cases
What are the legal grounds for taking a child who has committed an offence into the care of the local authority?

Children who commit offences may be brought before the juvenile court either in criminal proceedings or in civil care proceedings under s. 1(2)f of the Children and Young Persons Act 1969. In practice, the option to prosecute rather than bring care proceedings is almost always exercised, since criminal proceedings provide a wider range of possible disposals of which the care order is one. Initially care orders could be made in criminal proceedings providing only that the offence was one for which an adult could be imprisoned, thus avoiding the burden of establishing a need for care or control as well as the commission of the offence.

In response to research evidence and public and professional disquiet that criminal proceedings were providing a 'back door' into care following the commission of often very minor offences, and in circumstances in which local authorities might not have been able to prove the need for care or control, the criteria for the making of care orders in criminal proceedings were considerably tightened by provisions inserted in the 1969 Act by the Criminal Justice Act 1982 s.23-s.24. A care order can now only be made in criminal proceedings if the offence is a serious imprisonable one *and* the care or control test is satisfied. Additionally, a court considering making a care order in criminal proceedings must offer the juvenile the opportunity to be legally represented (Children and Young Persons Act 1969 s.7 (7), s.7 (7A) and s.7A).

Supervision orders made in criminal proceedings may have requirements written in to the order, breach of which may mean the offender being returned to court and either fined or made the subject of an attendance centre order (Criminal Law Act 1977, s.37). Although requirements may be written in to supervision orders made in care proceedings there is no similar sanction for their enforcement. On proof of a need for care or control which cannot otherwise be provided, a supervision order made in either care or criminal

246 The Essential Social Worker

proceedings may be discharged and replaced by a care order (Children and Young Persons Act 1969, s. 15).

The best guide
Ball, Caroline (1984), *Child Care Law File,* 2nd ed., University of East Anglia, Norwich, p. 16.

2 Protecting a child from its parents
What are the legal obligations on a social worker when confronted with a risk-situation in non-accidental injury?

The legal obligations of a local authority social worker, as a representative of the authority, when confronted with a risk situation in non-accidental injury are laid down in the Children and Young Persons Act 1969, s. 2. They are to investigate any information suggesting that there are grounds for bringing care proceedings and if, after such investigation, it appears that there are grounds, that the family is unwilling to accept voluntary supervision or place the child voluntarily in the care of the local authority under the Child Care Act 1980, s. 2, and that no other authorised person is immediately involved and likely to instigate care proceedings under s. 1(2) of the Act, to do so on behalf of the local authority.

If, before such proceedings can be brought to court, emergency action is needed to protect a child at risk, any person, though most usually a social worker, may apply to a court or to a single justice, on the basis that they have reasonable cause to believe that grounds for care proceedings exist, for a place of safety order under s. 28 of the Act. The order authorises the detention of the child in a place of safety which may be a community home, police station, hospital, surgery 'or any other suitable place the occupant of which is willing temporarily to receive the child' (Children and Young Persons Act 1933, s. 107(1)), for a specified period of up to 28 days. Because of instances of abuse of parents' rights through over-use of this power, justices increasingly require evidence to be given on oath when application is made, and often only grant place of safety orders for the minimum period necessary to bring the child before a juvenile court.

The best guide
Hoggett, Brenda (1981) *Parents and Children,* 2nd ed., Sweet & Maxwell, Chapter 5.

3 Adoption
What is the guiding principle in adoption proceedings?

The guiding principle in adoption proceedings is laid down in the Children Act 1975, s. 3 which provides:

> In reaching any decision relating to the adoption of a child, a court or adoption agency shall have regard to all the circumstances, first consideration being given to the need to safeguard and promote the welfare of the child throughout his childhood; and shall so far as is practicable ascertain the wishes and feelings of the child regarding the decision and give due consideration to them, having regard to his age and understanding.

The wording of this section was considered at great length when the bill was being debated and the 'first consideration' form of words represents a compromise between making the child's interests the central issue and recognising that the finality of the severance of the tie justifies more weight being given to the natural parents' interests than is now considered appropriate in other proceedings relating to children. The test of the welfare of the child being the 'first and paramount consideration' laid down in the Guardianship of Minors Act 1971, s. 1 is, for instance, applied in wardship cases, in custody issues in divorce and matrimonial proceedings, and will be applied to custodianship cases when these become available.

A considerable number of judicial decisions in adoption cases involving dispensing with parental consent, made both before and since the implementation of s. 3 have resulted in a body of case law on the fine distinctions involved in interpretation of 'first consideration'. For a detailed review of relevant cases, and an indication of current judicial interpretation of parental 'reasonableness' in refusing consent to adoption, see the judgment of the Court of Appeal in *Re; ReW 1983 4 Family Law 615.*

The best guide
Hoggett, Brenda (1981) *Parents and Children* 2nd ed., Sweet and Maxwell, Chapter 11.

4 Mental subnormality
What difference does a mentally subnormal person's age make to his legal rights?

In the Mental Health Act 1983 the term 'mental subnormality' has been replaced by that of 'mental impairment' which is defined in s. 1 of the Act as being:

> a state of arrested or incomplete development of mind (not amounting to severe mental impairment) which includes significant impairment of intelligence and social functioning and is associated with abnormally aggressive or seriously irresponsible conduct on the part of the person concerned...

The need under the new definition to establish the association of impairment with aggressive or irresponsible conduct replaces the previous requirement that the condition should be susceptible to treatment or training. Under the 1983 Act the person's age no longer, as it did previously, makes any difference to their legal rights.

The best guide
Hoggett, Brenda (1984) *Mental Health Law*, Sweet and Maxwell. Chapter 2.

5 Mental illness
What are the duties and powers of the approved social worker?

The provisions of the Mental Health Act 1983 seek to ensure that approved social workers, who replace mental welfare officers, have a fully independent professional role to play in relation to the mentally ill. To this end, local authorities are obliged to appoint sufficient approved social workers to fulfil their statutory obligations and to provide them with adequate training and assessment in mental health work and law in accordance with the scheme devised by CCETSW in 1983.

The duties and powers of the approved social worker (ASW) fall into three broad categories; that of making arrangements for the compulsory admission of patients into hospital or into guardianship in the community; the entry and inspection of premises in which mentally disordered persons may be living; and the apprehension and return of patients compulsorily detained who abscond from hospital. Each of these categories require consideration in greater detail:

1. Compulsory admission of patients to hospital

The Mental Health Act 1983 s.11(1) provides that applications for compulsory admission to hospital, for assessment or for treatment, may be made either by an ASW or by the patient's nearest relative (as defined in the Act). Although either a nearest relative or an approved social worker may make an application for admission for assessment without consulting the other, mechanisms exist for informing social service departments and nearest relatives if such an admission is made without their knowledge.

When an ASW is proposing to make an application for admission for treatment under s.3 of the Act he must consult the nearest relative and in the face of that person's opposition may not make the application unless he first applies to the court to have the nearest relative replaced on the grounds that the objection is unreasonable. For judicial interpretations of 'unreasonable' in this context see 'W v. L' *Mental Health Patient*, 1973, 3, A11ER 884.

Before an ASW makes any application for admission to hospital he must interview the patient and satisfy himself that detention in hospital is necessary.

2. The inspection of premises and the removal of patients

Where there are premises in which there is reason to believe that a mentally disordered person is either being neglected or ill-treated, or if living alone is unable to care for himself, an ASW has a duty to inspect those premises. If it is necessary in order to gain access, he may apply to a magistrate for a warrant authorising a named constable to enter the premises, if necessary by force. The constable must be accompanied by a doctor and an ASW.

3. The conveyance and return of mentally disordered patients to hospital

ASW's, amongst others, are empowered under the Act to convey patients who are subject to compulsory powers to hospital, and to return such patients if they are absent without leave. They may apply to a magistrate for a warrant authorising a constable to search premises for such patients.

The best guide
Rashid, Stephen Parvez (1984) *Mental Health*, Social Work Law File, University of East Anglia, Norwich, Chapter 7.

6 The elderly in care

Under what circumstances may an elderly person be taken into the care of the local authority against his/her will?

Although there is often considerable pressure from local communities to persuade local authorities to remove elderly people who are seen to be living alone in dirty and often squalid conditions, and who may be a considerable nuisance to their neighbours, to hospital or other suitable accommodation, the National Assistance Acts which give local authorities such powers have to be very strictly interpreted if the civil liberties of the elderly are not to be abused.

The National Assistance Act 1948 provides for the compulsory removal from their homes, for the purpose of securing necessary care and attention of persons who:

s. 47(1)   (a) are suffering from grave chronic disease or, being aged, infirm or physically incapacitated are living in insanitary conditions and
(b) are unable to devote to themselves and are not receiving from other persons, proper care and attention.

In order to secure the removal from their home of a person who falls within the definition in s. 47, the 'proper officer' – now the community health officer for the area – has to certify in writing to the local authority that it is in the interests of the patient, or necessary for preventing injury to the health of, or serious nuisance to, other persons, on the grounds stated in s. 47(1), that the patient should be removed to hospital. The local authority may then, having given seven days notice in writing to the patient, apply for an order to the Magistrates Court for the petty sessional division in which the patient lives. Before granting such an order the court must be satisfied on oral evidence of the truth of the allegations on the certificate, and either have heard evidence from the person in charge of the premises to which the patient is to be sent, or be satisfied that they have had seven days notice of the intended admission. The order authorises the patient's removal to those premises for an initial period not exceeding three months, which may be extended by a further three months on application to the court.

At any time after six weeks from the making of the order the patient, or anyone acting for them may, after giving seven days' notice, apply for revocation and the court 'if it considers it expedient to do so' may revoke the order (s. 47(6)).

An emergency procedure was made available under the National Assistance (Amendment) Act 1951 s. 1 and it is now the procedure most commonly used. The community health officer and another registered medical practitioner, usually the patient's general practitioner, have to certify that in their opinion the grounds in s. 47(1) exist and that 'it is necessary in the interests of that person to remove him without delay'. In these circumstances the local authority, or the community health physician if authorised by his authority to do so, may make application to the Magistrates Court, or to a single justice, for an order under the section. This order may be made *ex parte* and without the justice seeing the patient, unless they elect to do so, provided that the grounds are established on oath and the applicant can show that arrangements have been made for the patient's accommodation.

Orders made under the emergency procedure only last for three weeks in the first instance.

The best guide
Rashid, S. P, and Ball, C. (1984) *Mental Health, Disability, Homelessness and Race Relations.* Social Work Law File, University of East Anglia, Norwich, pp. 64–66.

7 The chronically sick and disabled
What are the statutory duties of local authorities with regard to the chronically sick and disabled?

Legislation to ensure the provision of adequate services and resources for the chronically sick and disabled has largely fallen short of achieving its goal because so much of it is of an enabling rather than a mandatory nature. This was particularly true of the general duty laid upon local authorities by the National Assistance Act 1948:

> s. 29: A local authority may with the approval of the secretary of state, and to such an extent as he may direct in relation to persons ordinarily resident in the area of the local authority shall, make arrangements for promoting the welfare of ... persons who are blind, deaf or dumb, and other persons who are substantially and permanently handicapped by illness, injury or congenital deformity or such other disabilities as may be prescribed.

It is significant that it has been those provisions of the statute originally welcomed as a 'charter for the disabled' – the Chronically Sick and Disabled Persons Act 1970 – which are mandatory which have achieved a measure of improvement in provision, whereas the implementation of enabling clauses falls a long way short of the high hopes of those who introduced the legislation. The 1970 Act required local authorities to compile a register of the disabled in their area in order to identify the extent of the need for the provision of services and resources and has, most importantly, compelled those authorities with responsibility under the 1948 Act to make available as of right under s. 29 the following facilities to persons in need who are ordinarily resident in their area:

(a) practical assistance within the disabled person's home;
(b) the provision of, or assistance in obtaining, wireless, television or similar recreational facilities;
(c) the provision of, or assistance in taking advantage of lectures, outings, games and other recreational activities outside the home;
(d) transport to such services as are provided under s. 29;
(e) assistance in arranging for works to adapt the home or provide additional facilities to secure greater comfort, safety or convenience;
(f) the provision of holidays, whether under schemes arranged by the local authorities or other persons;
(g) the provision of meals for that person whether in his own home or elsewhere;
(h) the provision of a telephone or assistance in obtaining a telephone and any special equipment needed to use it.

In addition the statutes mentioned and others place on local authorities statutory duties with regard to housing, the provision of home helps, the parking of the cars of disabled people, access to public buildings, and the provision and advertisement of suitable public conveniences.

Housing

The National Assistance Act 1948, s. 21 provides for the provision of so called 'Part III' accommodation (s. 21 being the first section in Part III of the Act), that is to say under s. 21(1)(a): 'residential accommodation for persons who by reason of age, infirmity or any other circumstances are in need of care and attention which is not otherwise available to them' and to charge for such accommodation according to the patient's means (s. 22).

In addition the 1970 Act provides that every housing authority when discharging their duty to consider housing conditions in their district, and the provision of additional accommodation 'shall have regard to the needs of chronically sick or disabled persons' (s 3(1)).

Home helps
The Health Services and Public Health Act 1968 s. 13 lays a duty on local authorities to provide or arrange for the provision of home help for households where such help is required 'owing to the presence of a person who is suffering from illness, lying-in, an expectant mother, aged, handicapped as a result of having suffered from illness or by congenital deformity or a child who has not attained the upper limit of compulsory school age' and to make such charges as they consider reasonable having regard to means.

The orange badge scheme
The Chronically Sick and Disabled Persons Act 1970, s. 21(1) provides for 'a badge of a prescribed form' to be issued by local authorities for cars and other vehicles used by, or carrying, disabled persons; special exemptions from parking restrictions are made for cars carrying the orange badges to facilitate shopping and access to public and other buildings.

Access to public buildings and the provision of public conveniences
S. 4(1) of the 1970 Act lays down requirements for the provision of access, parking facilities and sanitary arrangements, suitable for the needs of the members of the public who are disabled, for all new buildings to which the public are to be admitted, though a proviso that the provision of such facilities is 'both practicable and reasonable' provides a loophole for failure to comply. The Act as amended also makes provision for access to universities, colleges and local education authority schools and to places of work.

The best guide
Rashid, S.P. and Ball, C. (1984) *Mental Health Disability, Homeless-*

ness and Race Relations, Social Work Law File, University of East Anglia, Norwich, pp. 55–65.

8 The homeless

What constitutes 'priority need' among the homeless or potentially homeless?

The Housing (Homeless Persons) Act 1977 lays the responsibility for providing accommodation for homeless persons in their area, who qualify under the Act, on local housing authorities. In order to qualify, applicants must be homeless, have not become so intentionally, and must have a priority need. A person has a priority need under s. 2 if:

(a) He/she has dependent children living with him/her or who might reasonably be expected to live with him/her. The wording of the provision is intended to avoid the 'Catch 22' situation of children being in care so there was no priority need and the children not being able to leave care because there was no accommodation; or

(b) He/she became homeless or threatened with homelessness as a result of any emergency such as a flood, fire, or any other disaster; or

(c) He/she, or anyone who either does or might reasonably be expected to live with him/her is vulnerable because of old age, mental illness, physical disability or other special reason; or

(d) She, or if a man, a woman who either does or who might reasonably be expected to live with him is pregnant, no matter how long or short lived the pregnancy.

Those who cannot establish a priority need are still entitled to advice and assistance from housing authorities, for instance about rent and rate rebates, available lodgings, housing centres and related issues.

The best guide
Arden, A. (1983) 'The Housing (Homeless Persons) Act 1977', *Legal Action Group,* Chapter 2

9 Adult offenders

What are the obligations on an offender made the subject of a probation order?

When a court proposes to make a probation order on an offender the meaning of the order and of any requirements within it must be explained to the offender in ordinary language and he must consent to its being made. Once the order is made the offender is under obligation, to be under the supervision of a probation officer for the duration of the order (it may be from a minimum of six months to a maximum of three years) and to comply with any requirements in the order. The law relating to the making of probation orders is laid down in the Powers of the Criminal Courts Act 1973 as amended by the Criminal Justice Act 1982.

The standard requirements, which are to be of good behaviour, to lead an industrious life, to keep in touch with the probation officer and notify him of any change of address and to report to him and receive visits at home from him when required to do so, are commonly included in all probation orders. In addition, if the court considers them to be necessary to secure good conduct or prevent the commission of further offences, other requirements relating to residence, attendance at day centres and medical treatment, may be written in to the order.

A requirement as to residence may be made if, after considering reports on his home surroundings, the court requires him to live in a particular house other than his own home, or an approved probation hostel, or, in special circumstances, in a non-approved institution, for a period specified in the order. If the court is satsified on the medical evidence that such an order is appropriate, it may require the offender to receive medical treatment during the whole or part of the probation period.

Where a court has been notified that a day centre is available to probationers, and has received a report as to the feasibility of the plan and that the person in charge of the centre or any third party involved consents, they may make a requirement that the probationer attend the day centre for up to 60 days.

If a probationer is in breach of any of the requirements in the order he may be brought back to court and, if it is considered appropriate, be admonished and continue under the probation order, or be dealt with differently for the orginal offence, or he can be fined a maximum of £50 or made the subject of a community service order or an attendance centre order (if male and under 21). If the offender is punished differently for the original offence the probation order ceases to have effect but if fined or made the subject of a community service or attendance centre order the probation order can continue.

The best guide
Jarvis, F. V. 1980 *Probation Officers Manual* 3rd ed., Butterworth,
Chapter 3 and Criminal Justice Act 1982, Schedule 11.

10 Acting on behalf of the client in court
*Under what circumstances may the social worker act in court on
behalf of a client?*

Legal aid exists to enable those who cannot afford to pay for it
themselves to have legal representation in court, provided certain
criteria which differ for civil and criminal cases, are satisfied.
However, there are still many cases in which representation is needed
but for one reason or another legal aid is not granted. In such cases
social workers can be of great help to their clients either by actually
representing them, with the permission of the judge, in the county
court, or by sitting with them and offering advice as a so-called
'McKenzie man' in the magistrates court.

Only clients and their legal representatives, if they have one, have a
right of audience in any court, but in the county court anybody may,
with the permission of the court, represent a party to the proceedings
(County Court Act 1959, s. 89), and it is unlikely that a social worker
would be refused permission to do so if an explanation was given as to
why his client needed help and why he was not being legally represented.

There is no provision for lay representation in the magistrates court
but the Court of Appeal's decision in *McKenzie* v. *McKenzie* (1970, 3
WLR p. 472) lays down the principle that a party to legal proceedings
is entitled to have someone in court with him to take notes and give
advice, and this applies as much to defendants refused legal aid in the
criminal courts as to parties in civil proceedings. The so-called
'McKenzie man' cannot address the court, but can speak to the
defendant and in that way remind him of points to make and suggest
questions to be asked, particularly in cross-examination which is the
part of court procedure which most defendants (and some lawyers)
find particularly difficult. The magistrates court is bound by the Court
of Appeal's decision to allow the presence of a 'McKenzie man' and it
has been suggested that where they are reluctant to do so they may
decide to grant legal aid in cases where they previously refused it; this
could be a satisfactory consequence for the client of the social worker's
willingness to assist him in court.

Caveat
It must be added that the possibility that it may be appropriate for a social worker to act in court on behalf of a client makes it essential that social workers should be familiar with both court procedure and basic rules of evidence; they are not expected to act as legal representatives but ignorance or incompetence could result in their intervention jeopardising, rather than helping, their client's cause.

The best guide
Hodge, Henry (1977) 'Aid and Representation in Courts', *Social Work Today,* vol. 8, no. 41, 26 July, p. 13.

References

Abbreviations: *BJSW – British Journal of Social Work*; *CC – Community Care*; *SWT – Social Work Today*.

Abrams, Philip (1978) 'Community care: Some research problems and priorities', in Barnes and Connelly (1978), pp. 78–79.

Abrams, Philip (1980) 'Social change, social networks and neighbourhood care', *Social Work Service*, no. 22, February, pp. 12–23.

Armitage, Mary (1979) 'The cost of caring for the elderly', *SWT*, 10(38), 5 June, pp. 15–16.

Atkins, Norah (1981) 'The best possible start in life', *SWT*, 12(45), 28 July, pp. 14–15.

Bailey, Roy and Lee, Phil (1982) *Theory and Practice in Social Work*, Blackwell.

Balbernie, R. (1966) *Residential Work with Children*, Pergamon.

Banaka, W.H. (1971) *Training in Depth Interviewing*, Harper and Row.

Barclay Report (1982) *Social Workers: their role and tasks*, Bedford Square Press.

Barlow, Gerald (1978) 'Why did we go for behaviour modification?' *Social Work Today*, 10(15), 5 December, p. 22.

Barnes, Jack and Connelly, Naomi (eds) (1978) *Social Care Research*, Bedford Square Press.

Barry, Michael (1984) 'Crime prevention, community work and probation policy', MA dissertation, University of East Anglia.

Batey, Grace (1979) 'The world of Leslie Wright', *CC*, no. 275, 2 August, pp. 24–5.

Bayley, Michael (1973) *Mental Handicap and Community Care*, Routledge and Kegan Paul.

Bayley, Michael (1978) 'Someone to fall back on', *CC*, no. 207, 5 April, pp. 42–3.

Bealka, Richard J., psychiatrist, Mental Health Institute, Independence, Iowa, USA; quoted in Compton and Galaway (1975) p. 203.

Bean, Philip (1980) *Compulsory Admissions to Mental Hospitals*, Wiley.

Beaumont, Bill and Walker, Hilary (1981) '*Probation Work – Critical theory and socialist practice*', Blackwell.

Bender, Michael (1983), 'Day Centres – For what and for whom?', *CC*, no 445, 13 January, pp. 20–21.

Bessell, Robert (1971) *Interviewing and Counselling*, Batsford.

Bettelheim, B. (1950) *Love is not Enough*, Collier-Macmillan.

Billis, David (1973) 'Entry into residential care', *BJSW*, 3(4), Winter, pp. 447–71.

Bird, Nicholas (1984) *The private provision of residential care for the elderly*, Social Work Monographs.

Black, Jim *et al.* (1983) *Social work in context*, Tavistock.

Boswell, Gwyneth (1985) *Care, control and accountability in the probation service*, Social Work Monographs.

Bottoms, A.E. and McWilliams, W. (1979) 'A non-treatment paradigm for probation practice', *BJSW*, 9(2), Summer, pp. 159–202.

Bowlby, John (1951) *Child care and the Growth of Love*, Penguin.

Bowlby, John (1969, 1973, 1980) *Attachment and Loss*, volumes 1, 2 and 3, Hogarth.

Bowman, A. (1978) 'Meanwhile back in Ambridge', *SWT*, 9(23), 7 February, pp. 8–10.

Brandon, Joan and Davies, Martin (1979) 'The limits of competence in social work', *BJSW*, 9(3), Autumn, pp. 295–347.

Brimelow, Mary and Wilson, Judy (1982) 'Ourselves alone', *SWT*, 13(21), 2 February, pp. 12–13.

Briscoe, Catherine (1977) 'Community work and social work in the United Kingdom' in Specht and Vickery (1977), pp. 182–94.

British Association of Social Workers (1978) *The Central Child Abuse Register*, BASW Publications.

Brown, Allen (1979) *Groupwork*, Heinemann Educational.

Brown, Barrie (1978) 'Behavioural approaches to child care', *BJSW*, 8(3), Autumn, pp. 313–26.

Browne, Elizabeth (1978) 'Social work activities', in Stevenson and Parsloe (1978), pp. 77–136.

Bruce, Ian and Darvill, Giles (1976) 'Over the defences: the volunteer in the area team', *SWT*, 7(9), 5 August, pp. 294–6.

Burck, Charlotte (1978) 'A study of families' expectations and experiences of a child guidance clinic', *BJSW*, 8(2), Summer, pp. 145–58.

Burgess, Paul (1979) 'Representation and advocacy in tribunals: a social work role?', in Parker (1979), pp. 189–212.

Burgess, Robin *et al.* (1980) 'Working with sex offenders: a social skills training group', *BJSW*, 10(2), Summer, p. 133–42.

Butler, Janet, Bow, Irene and Gibbons, Jane (1978) 'Task-centred casework with marital problems', *BJSW*, 8(4), Winter, pp. 393–409.

Butler, Neville *et al.* (1979) 'Uncovering a gap in the services, *CC* no. 173, 3 August, pp. 14–16.

Butler Report (1975), Committee on Mentally Abnormal Offenders, Cmnd 6244.

Campbell, T.D. (1978) 'Discretionary "rights"', in Timms and Watson (1978), pp. 50–77.

Campling, Jo (1980) 'Social work for the out of work' *SWT* 12(14), 2 December, pp. 11–12.

Caplan, Gerald (1964), *Principles of Preventive Psychiatry*, Basic Books.

Carter, Jan (1974) *The Maltreated Child*, Priory.

Central Council for Education and Training in Social Work (1975) 'Education and training for social work: a working group discussion paper', CCETSW.

Central Council for Education and Training in Social Work (1978) *Good Enough Parenting. Report of a Study Group*, CCETSW.

Challis, David and Davies, Bleddyn (1980), 'A new approach to community care for the elderly', *BJSW*, 10(1), Spring, pp. 1–18.

Challis, David, Davies, Bleddyn and Holman, Jon (1980) 'Bringing better community care to fragile elderly people', *SWT*, 11(22), 5 February, pp. 14–16.

Chartered Institute of Public Finance and Accountancy (1980) *Personal Social Services Statistics, 1978–79 Actuals*, CIPFA.

Cheetham, Juliet (1980) personal communication.

Cheetham, Juliet and Learner, Eva (1972) 'Social workers and women requesting a termination of pregnancy: Report to the Lane Committee on the working of the Abortion Act', (Privately circulated report. A summary is contained in the Report of the Committee on the Working of the Abortion Act, Volume II, Statistics. Paras 464–73. HMSO, Cmnd 5579–I, 1974.)

Clark, A.T. (1975) 'Volunteers accredited to the probation service: A national survey', Hertfordshire Probation Service.

Colwell inquiry: see DHSS (1974).

Compton, B.R. and Galaway, B. (1975) *Social Work Processes*, Dorsey.

Cooper, Michael and Denne, John (1983) 'A problem of coordination', *CC*, no. 456, 31 March, pp. 16–18.

Cooper, Mike and Stacy, Graham (1981) 'Translating community based care into action' *CC*, no. 347, 12 February, pp. 15–17.

Corby, Brian (1982), 'Theory and practice in long-term social work',

BJSW, 12(6), December, pp. 619–638.

Corden, John (1980) 'Contracts in social work practice', *BJSW*, 10(2), Summer, pp. 143–61.

Corney, Roslyn (1981) 'First time clients', *CC*, no. 355, 9 April, pp. 21–23.

Corrigan, Paul and Leonard, Peter (1978), *Social work practice under capitalism*, Macmillan.

Cosgrove, Julie (1983), 'Shelter in a storm', *SWT*, 14(44), 26 July, pp. 13–15.

Cree, Gordon, Robertson, Margriet and Short, Maggie (1979) 'Behavioural casework in mental health', *SWT*, 10(42), 3 July, pp. 22–4.

Crine, Alistair (1982) 'Opus 82', *CC* no. 249, 16 September, pp. 14–17.

Crine Alistair (1983a) 'Two-way squeeze' *CC*, no. 455, 24 March, pp. 14–16.

Crine, Alistair (1983b) 'Taking risks and making changes', *CC*, no. 470, 21 July, pp. 14–16.

Croft, Suzy and Beresford, Peter (1984) 'Patch and participation – the case for citizen research', *SWT*, 16(3), 17 September, pp. 18–24.

Crompton, Margaret (1979) 'Applying to foster', *CC*, no. 282, 20 September, p. 25.

Crossman, R.H.S. (1976) 'The role of the volunteer in the modern social service', in Halsey (1976).

Crowley, Margaret (1982) *Preparation for foster-care practice*, Social Work Monographs.

Curnock, Kathleen and Hardiker, Pauline (1979) *Towards Practice Theory*, Routledge and Kegan Paul.

Davies, Martin (1969) *Probationers in Their Social Environment*, HMSO.

Davies, Martin (1974) *Social Work in the Environment*, HMSO.

Davies, Martin (1977) *Support Systems in Social Work*, Routledge and Kegan Paul.

Davies, Martin (1984) 'Training – What we think of it now', *SWT*, 15(20), 24 January, pp. 12–17.

Dawson, Hilton (1983), 'Working with Mr A', *CC*, no. 451, 24 February, pp. 17–18.

Day, Beryl (1977) 'Unmasking child abuse', *CC*, no. 153, 16 March, pp. 18–20.

Department of Health and Social Security (DHSS) (1974) *Report of the Committee of Inquiry into the Care and Supervision Provided in Relation to Maria Colwell*, HMSO.

Department of Health and Social Security (DHSS) (1976) *Guide to Fostering Practice*; a *Working Party Report* (Chairperson, Janie Thomas), HMSO.

Devon County Council Social Services Department Research Section (1979) 'Priorities and workloads, a study of closure decisions', reproduced in *Clearing House for Local Authority Social Services Research*, no. 9.

Disraeli, Benjamin (1867) speech in Edinburgh, 29 October.

Dockar-Drysdale, Barbara (1968) *Therapy in Child Care, Papers on Residential Work*, Longmans.

Dorn, Nicholas and South, Nigel (1984), *Drug-related Social Work in Street Agencies*, Social Work Monographs.

Eaton, Barbara (1979) 'Foster care in Camden', *SWT*, 10(35), 8 May, pp. 18–19.

Edwards, Carol and Sinclair, Ian (1980) 'Debate: segregation versus integration', *SWT*, 11(40), 24 June, pp. 19–21.

Fellows, Gill and Marshall, Mary (1979) 'Services for the homeless elderly', *SWT*, 10(35), 8 May, pp. 16–17.

Fletcher, Harry (1978) 'Council house evictions – a new tribunal experience', *SWT*, 9(32), 18 April, p. 19.

Foad, Kathleen (1984) 'Youth custody through-care practice in Essex', Advanced Certificate dissertation, University of East Anglia.

Folkard, Steven (1974 and 1976) *IMPACT*, volumes I and II, HMSO.

Ford, Jill and Hollick, Margery (1979) 'The singer or the song: an autobiographical account of a suicidal destructive person and her social worker', *BJSW*, 9(4), Winter, pp. 471–88.

Foren, Robert and Bailey, Royston (1968) *Authority in Social Casework*, Pergamon.

Gibbons, Jane (1981) 'Task-centred methods of intervention after deliberate self-poisoning', in Goldberg and Connelly (eds, q.v., pp. 23–44.

Gibbons, Jennifer (1984), 'Live wires', *SWT*, 15(24), 20 February, pp. 14–15.

Glassner, Barry and Freedman, Jonathan (1979) *Clinical Sociology*, Longman.

Goffman, Erving (1963) *Stigma*, Prentice-Hall.

Goldberg, E. Matilda *et al.* (1977a) 'Exploring the task-centred casework method', *SWT*, 9(2), 6 September, pp. 9–14.

Goldberg, E. Matilda *et al.* (1977b), 'Towards accountability in social work: one year's intake to an area office', *BJSW*, 7(3), Autumn, pp. 257–83.

Goldberg, E. Matilda *et al.* (1978) 'Towards accountability in social work: long term social work in an area office', *BJSW*, 8(3), Autumn, pp. 253–87.

Goldberg E. M. and Connelly, Naomi (eds) (1981), *Evaluative Research in Social Care*, Heinemann Educational Books.

Goldstein, Howard (1973) *Social Work Practice: A Unitary Approach*, University of South Carolina Press.

Goldstein, Joseph, Freud, Anna and Solnit, Albert J. (1973) *Beyond the Best Interests of the Child*, Free Press.

Gosling, Martin (1984), 'Community programmes in probation practice', Advanced Certificate dissertation, University of East Anglia.

Hack, Kenneth (1973) 'A study of predictors of success on a social work course', *BJSW*, 3(2), Summer, pp. 189–207.

Hadley, Roger (1984) 'The idea of major change by casework alone seems indefensible' *SWT*, 15(50), 27 August, pp. 16–19.

Hadley, Roger and McGrath, Morag (1983) 'The Normanton experience', *CC*, no. 488, 17 November, pp. 23–4.

Haimes, Erica and Timms, Noel (1984) 'Counselling and the Children Act 1975', *Adoption and Fostering*, 8(3), pp. 42–46.

Hall, Tony (1974) *The Point of Entry*, Allen and Unwin.

Hall, Tony (ed.) (1980) *Access to Birth Records*, Association of British Adoption and Fostering Agencies.

Hallett, Christine and Stevenson, Olive (1979) *Child Abuse: Aspects of Interprofessional Cooperation*, Allen and Unwin.

Halsey, A.H. (ed.) (1976) *Traditions of Social Policy*, Blackwell.

Hamilton, Gordon (1940: revised 1951) *Theory and Practice of Social Casework*, Columbia University Press.

Handler, Joel (1973) *The Coercive Social Worker*, Markham.

Hanvey, Christopher (1981) *Social Work with Mentally Handicapped People*, Heinemann Educational Books.

Hare, Edward (1977) personal communication.

Harman, John (1978) 'A teamwork approach at IMPACT', *SWT*, 9(36), 16 May, pp. 15–17.

Harris, John (1981) 'Christine and her shouts', *SWT*, 13(8), 27 October, pp. 10–11.

Harris, Robert (1977) 'The probation officer as social worker', *BJSW*, 7(4), Winter, pp. 433–42.

Hatch, Stephen (1978) *Voluntary Work: A Report of a Survey*, Volunteers Centre.

Hawker, Maurice (1984) 'Welcome to care!!', *CC*, no. 501, 1 March, pp. 23–25.

Hazel, Nancy (1976) 'Child placement policy: some European comparisons', *BJSW*, 6(3), Autumn, pp. 315–26.

Hazel, Nancy (1980) *Fourth Report of the Kent Family Placement Project*, Kent Social Services Department.

Hildebrand, Judith (1977) 'Abortion: with particular reference to the developing role of counselling', *BJSW*, 7(1), Spring, pp, 3–24.

Hill, Michael (1978) 'Resources' in Stevenson and Parsloe (1978), pp. 225–46.

Hoghughi, Masud (1979) 'Myth, method and utility', *SWT*, 10(29), 20 March, pp. 11–17.

Holbrook, Daphne (1978) 'A combined approach to parental coping', *BJSW*, 8(4), Winter, pp. 439–51.

Hollis, Florence (1964) *Casework – A Psychosocial Therapy*, Random House.

Home Office (1984). 'Probation Service in England and Wales – Statement of National Purpose and Objectives'.

Horsley, Gail, (1984), 'The language of social enquiry reports', Social Work Monographs.

Howe, David (1979) 'Agency function and social work principles', *BJSW*, 9(1), Spring, pp. 29–47.

Howe, David (1980), 'Inflated states and empty theories in social work', *BJSW*, 10(3), Autumn.

Hudson, Barbara (1978) 'Behavioural social work with schizophrenic patients in the community', *BJSW*, 8(2), Summer, pp. 159–70.

Hughes, Brian (1976) 'Are case conferences all at sea?', *CC*, no. 141, 15 December, pp. 18–19.

Hugman, Bruce (1977) *Act Natural*, Bedford Square Press.

Hunt, Linda (1979) 'Conflict, pressure and the psychiatric emergency', *SWT*, 10(42), 3 July, pp. 20–1.

Hutchen, Jill (1984), 'Welcome to the world', *CC*, no. 494, 12 January, pp. 24–26.

Huxley, Julian (ed.) (1961) *The Humanist Frame*, Allen and Unwin.

Inglis, F. (1977) 'Them, us and the welfare state', *New Society*, vol. 39, 17 February, pp. 330–1.

Jackson, Michael P. and Valencia, B. Michael (1979) *Financial Aid through Social Work*, Routledge and Kegan Paul.

Jamieson, John (1978) 'What is an interview?' *CC*, no. 199, 8 February, pp. 18–19.

Jones, Carolyn and Jones, Ron (1974) 'Treatment: a social perspective' in Carter (1974).

Jones, Howard (ed.) (1975) *Towards a New Social Work*, Routledge and Kegan Paul.

Jones, Maxwell (1977) *Maturation of the Therapeutic Community*, Human Sciences Press.

Jones, M.A., Neuman, R. and Shyne, A.W. (1976) *A Second Chance for Families*, Child Welfare League of America.

Kahn, A.J. *et al.* (1972) *Child Advocacy*, Columbia University Press.

Keith-Lucas, Alan (1972) *The Giving and Taking of Help*, University of North Carolina Press.

Keller, Suzanne (1968) *The Urban Neighbourhood: A Sociological Perspective*, Random House.

King, J.F.S. (ed.) (1976) *Control Without Custody?*, Institute of Criminology, Cambridge.

Klein, Rudolf (1976) 'The politics of public expenditure: American theory and British practice', *British Journal of Political Science*, 6. pp. 401–32.

Knight, Lindsay (1976) 'Kids they couldn't foster', *CC*, no. 129, 22 September, pp. 19–21.

Knight, Lindsay (1978a) 'A crumbling foundation – action on the Act', *CC*, no. 201, 22 February, pp. 14–19.

Knight, Lindsay (1978b) 'Intake team: The hours of caring', *CC*, no. 210, 26 April, pp. 18–21.

Knight, Lindsay (1979) 'Children's guardian angels?', *CC*, no. 265, 24 May, pp. 22–3.

Lancet (1975) 'Editorial: The battered', 31May.

Lawson, Colin (1978) *The Probation Officer as Prosecutor*, Institute of Criminology, Cambridge.

Leonard, Peter (1976) 'Marx: the class perspective', *CC*, no. 123, 11 August, pp. 16–18.

Levy, Leon H. (1976) 'Self-help groups: types and psychological processes', *Journal of Applied Behavioural Science*, 12(3) pp. 311–12.

Lindemann, Erich (1944) 'Symptomatology and management of acute grief', *American Journal of Psychiatry*, 101, September.

Lishman, Joyce (1978) 'A clash in perspective?', *BJSW*, 8(3), Autumn, pp. 301–11.

Loewentstein, Carol (1974) 'An intake team in action in a social services department'. *BJSW*, 4(2), Summer, pp. 115–41.

McGrail, Stephen (1983), 'Room for improvement', *SWT*, 14(39), 21 June, pp. 12–13.

McGrath, Morag (1979) 'Planning for children in care', *SWT*, 10(29), 20 March, pp. 21–8.

MacVeigh, James (1982), *Gaskin*, Jonathan Cape.

McWilliams, William (1975) 'Research into community service orders', paper given to the South West Region of the National Association of Probation Officers, 17 October.

Marshall, Mary and Hargreaves, M. (1979) 'So you want to try GP attachment', *SWT*, 10(42), 3 July, pp. 25–6.

Mayer, John and Timms, Noel (1970) *The Client Speaks*, Routledge and Kegan Paul.

Melotte, C.J. (1976) 'Social workers' information on welfare benefits', Kirklees Social Services Department Research Section, Occasional Papers no. 10.

Meyer, Carol (1976) *Social Work Practice – The Changing Landscape*, (2nd edn) Free Press.

Millard, D.A. (ed.) (1975 and 1976) 'Shelton 1; and Shelton 2. Papers from a working probation office', Staffordshire Probation and After-Care Service.

Miller, E.J. and Gwynne, G.V. (1972) *A Life Apart*, Tavistock.

Mittler, Peter (1979) 'Social work services for the mentally handicapped', *SWT*, 10(43), 10 July, pp., 18–20.

Moroney, Robert M. (1976) *The Family and the State*, Longman.

Morris, Catriona (1984) *The Permanency Principle in Child Care Social Work*, Social Work Monographs.

Morris, Pauline and Beverly, Farida (1975) *On Licence: A Study of Parole*, Wiley.

Morris, Peter (1976) 'House with a view in Havelock Square', *CC*, no. 121, 28 July, pp. 14–16.

Mott, Joy (1977) 'Decision making and social inquiry reports in one juvenile court', *BJSW*, 7(4), Winter, pp. 421–32.

Nokes, Peter (1967) *The Professional Task in Welfare Practice*, Routledge and Kegan Paul.

Norman, Alison J. (1980) *Rights and Risk: Civil Liberty in Old Age*, National Corporation for the Care of Old People.

Oram, Eddie (1978) 'Compulsory admission to psychiatric hospital: legislation and practice', *SWT*, 9(42), 4 July, pp. 19–21.

Osmond, Robin (1980) Letter to *The Times*, 28 February.

Page, Raissa and Clark, G.A. (eds) (1977) *Who Cares? Young People in Care Speak Out*, National Children's Bureau.

Parker, Howard (ed.) (1979) *Social Work and the Courts*, Edward Arnold.

Parker, Paul (1978) 'Reaching out to a wider network', *CC*, no. 235, 18 October, pp. 21–2.

Parkinson, Geoffrey (1970) 'I give them money', *New Society*, vol. 15, 5 February, pp. 220–1.

Parsloe, Phyllida (1978) 'Some educational implications', in Stevenson and Parsloe (1978) pp. 329–59.

Parton, Nigel (1979) 'The natural history of child abuse', *BJSW*, 9(4), Winter, pp. 427–51.

Pearson, Geoffrey (1973) 'Social work as the privatized solution of public ills', *BJSW*, 3(2) Summer, pp. 209–27.

Perlman, Helen (1957) *Social Casework: A Problem-Solving Process*, University of Chicago Press.

Perlman, Helen (1970) 'The problem-solving model in social casework', in Roberts and Nee (1970) pp. 129–79.

Perry, Fred G. (1975) *A Guide to the Preparation of Social Inquiry Reports*, Barry Rose.

Pincus, Allen and Minahan, Anne (1973) *Social Work Practice, Model and Method*, F.E. Peacock.

Plant, Raymond (1970) *Social and Moral Theory in Casework*, Routledge and Kegan Paul.

Presland, John and Roberts, Helen (1983), 'Reaching those who need help', *CC*, no. 487, 10 November, pp. 19–20.

Prime, Ruth (1977) 'Report on a method of workload management and weighting', *SWT*, 9(15), 6 December, pp. 16–18.

Rapaport, Lydia (1970) 'Crisis intervention as a mode of brief intervention', in Roberts and Nee (1970) pp. 265–311.

Rashid, Stephen and Ball, Caroline (1984), *Mental Health, Disability, Homelessness, Race Relations*, Social Work Monographs.

Redford, David and Goodenough, Alan (1979) 'Learning interviewing skills', *CC*, no. 279, 30 August, pp. 27–8.

Rees, Stuart (1974) 'No more than contact', *BJSW*, 4(3), Autumn, pp. 255–79.

Rees, Stuart (1978) *Social Work Face to Face*, Edward Arnold.

Rees, Stuart and Wallace, Alison (1982), *Verdicts on Social Work*, Edward Arnold.

Reid, William and Epstein, Laura (1972) *Task Centred Casework*, Columbia University Press.

Reid, William and Epstein, Laura (eds) (1977) *Task Centred Practice*, Columbia University Press.

Reid, William and Hanrahan, Patricia (1982), 'Recent evaluations of social work: grounds for optimism', *Social work (NASW)*, July, pp. 328–40.

Reid, William and Shyne, Anne (1969) *Brief and Extended Casework*, Columbia University Press.

Roberts, R.W. and Nee, R.H. (1970) *Theories of Social Casework*, Chicago University Press.

Rogers, Carl (1967) *The Therapeutic Relationship and its Impact*, University of Wisconsin Press.

Rowe, Jane (1966) *Parents, Children and Adoption*, Routledge and Kegan Paul.

Rushton, Andree and Davies, Penny (1984), *Social Work and Health Care*, Heinemann Educational Books.

Rutter, Michael (1972) *Maternal Deprivation Re-assessed*, Penguin.

Sainsbury, Eric (1975) *Social Work with Families*, Routledge and Kegan Paul.

Salmon, Wilma (1977) 'A service program in a state public welfare agency', in Reid and Epstein (1977) pp. 113–22.

Scott, Mike (1982), 'Talking to learn', *SWT*, 13(37), 8 June, pp. 18–19.

Seebohm Report (1968) *Report of the Committee on Local Authority and Allied Personal Social Services*, HMSO.

Sharron, Howard (1982), 'A stitch in time', *SWT*, 13(18), 12 January, pp. 7–9.

Shaw, Margaret (1974) *Social Work in Prison*, HMSO.

Shaw, Stephen (1983) 'Crime prevention and the future of the probation service', *Probation Journal*, 30(4), December, pp. 127–9.

Shearer, Ann (1979) 'The legacy of Maria Colwell', *SWT*, 10(19), 9 January, pp. 12–19.

Sheldon, Brian (1977) 'Do you know where you're going?', *CC*, no. 165, 8 June 1977, pp. 13–15.

Sheldon, Brian (1981a) 'The Pavlov inheritance', *SWT*, 13(9), 3 November, pp. 8–12.

Sheldon, Brian (1981b) 'Crossing the bridge', *SWT*, 13(10), 10 November, pp. 10–14.

Simpkin, Mike (1979) *Trapped Within Welfare*, Macmillan.

Sinclair, Ian (1971), *Hostels for Probationers*, HMSO.

Smalley, Ruth (1970) 'The functional approach to casework' in Roberts and Nee (1970) pp. 77–128.

Smith, Cyril S. *et al.* (1972) *The Wincroft Project*, Tavistock.

Specht, Harry and Vickery, Anne (eds) (1977) *Integrating Social Work Methods*, Allen and Unwin.

Stein, Mike (1979) 'Children of the State', *SWT*, 10(28) 13 March, pp. 26–9.

Stevenson, Olive (1974) Editorial, *BJSW*, 4(1), Spring, p. 1.

Stevenson, Olive (1976) 'Social services as controllers', in King (1976), pp. 1–22.

Stevenson, Olive and Parsloe, Phyllida (1978) *Social Service Teams: The Practitioner's View*, HMSO.

Streathfield, David and Wilson, Tom (1979) 'Organising office information', *CC*, no. 275, 2 August pp. 16–18.

Sweet, Douglas (1981) 'From a hole in the wall', *SWT*, 12(45), 28 July, p. 16.

Takagi, Paul T. (1969) 'The effect of parole agents' judgments on recidivism rates', *Psychiatry*, 32(2) pp. 192–9.

Thoburn, June (1980) *Captive Clients*, Routledge and Kegan Paul.

Thomas, D.N. (1983) *The Making of Community Work*, Allen and Unwin.

Thomlinson, Ray J. (1984) 'Something works: evidence from practice effectiveness studies', *Social Work (NASW)*, 29(1), January/February, pp. 51–6.

Thorpe, David (1982), 'IT in theory and practice' in Bailey and Lee (eds), q.v., pp. 78–97.

Timms, Noel and Rita (1977) *Perspectives in Social Work*, Routledge and Kegan Paul.

Timms, Noel and Watson, David (eds) (1978) *Philosophy in Social Work*, Routledge and Kegan Paul.

Towle, Charlotte (1945) *Common Human Needs*, US Government Printing Office.

Townsend, Peter (1979) *Poverty*, Penguin.

Truax, C.B. and Carkhuff, R. (1967) *Towards Effective Counselling and Psychotherapy*, Aldine.

Truax, C.B. *et al.* (1968) 'Effects of therapist persuasive potency in individual psychotherapy', *Journal of Clinical Psychology*.

Tutt, Norman (1979), 'The nature and scope of control', *SWT*, 10(30), 27 March, pp. 19–22.

Vevers, Paul (1981), 'Bringing up baby', *CC*, no. 353, 26 March, pp. 12–13.

Wakefield, C.E. (1976) 'Intake', supplement to *CC*, no. 129, 22 September.

West, Jenny (1976) 'Community service orders' in King (1976) pp. 68–92.

Whittington, Colin (1971) 'Self-determination re-examined', *BJSW*, 1(3), Autumn, pp. 293–303.

Wilding, Keith (1979) 'Choosing Part III', *CC*, no. 277, 16 August, pp. 20–1.

Wilkin, David (1979) *Caring for the Mentally Handicapped Child*, Croom Helm.

Wills, D.J. (1967) *Spare the Child*, Penguin.

Winnicott, Clare (1964) *Child Care and Social Work*, Codicote.

Wright, Andrew (1984), *The Day Centre in Probation Practice*, Social Work Monographs.

Name Index

MacVeigh, James 163
McWilliams, William 79, 89, 189
Marshall, Mary 42, 208
Marx, Karl 11
Mayer, John 18, 22, 97, 135
Melotte, C J 228
Meyer, Carol 181
Miller, E J 86–7, 162, 175
Minahan, Anne 150, 152, 191
Mittler, Peter 37
Moroney, Robert M 36
Morris, Catriona 104–105
Morris, Pauline 93
Morris, Peter 120–1
Mott, Joy 89

Neuman, R 53
Nokes, Peter 33–4
Nottinghamshire Social Services
  Department 145
NSPCC 51

Oram, Eddie 112
Osmond, Robin 126

Page, Raissa 39
Parker, Howard 228
Parker, Paul 121
Parkinson, Geoffrey 97
Parsloe, Phyllida 48, 98, 198
Parton, Nigel 80
Pearson, Geoffrey 72
Perlman, Helen 160, 171, 181–2
Perry, Fred 88
Pincus, Allen 150, 152, 191
Plant, Raymond 153
Presland, John 38

Rapaport, Lydia 172, 174
Rashid, Stephen 113, 249, 251
Redford, David 75, 166
Rees Stuart 9, 20–3, 25, 135, 160
Reid, William 71, 158, 160–1, 172
Roberts, Helen 38
Robertson, Margriet 61, 63
Rogers, Carl 51
Rowe, Jane 91–92
Rushton, Andrée 208
Rutter, Michael 215–6

Sainsbury, Eric 18, 23, 53, 175
Salmon, Wilma 161
Scott, Mike 62
Seebohm Report 76, 94–5, 123, 131, 170, 205
Sharron, Howard 124
Shaw Margaret 52
Shaw, Stephen 129
Shearer, Ann 80
Sheldon, Brian 58, 60, 158–9
Short, Maggie 61, 63
Shyne, Anne W 53, 172
Simpkin, Mike 12
Sinclair, Ian 85–6, 206
Smalley, Ruth 171
Smith, Cyril S 118
South, Nigel 119
Stacy, G 55, 125
Stevenson, Olive 48, 76, 84, 101, 198
Streathfield, David 232
Sweet, Douglas 142

Takagi, Paul 72
Thoburn, June 108
Thomas, D N 131
Thomlinson, Ray J 174
Thorpe, David 73, 175
Timms, Noel 18, 22, 80, 97, 105, 135
Timms, Rita 80
Towle, Charlotte 181
Townsend, Peter 219
Truax, C B 53, 71, 185
Tutt, Norman 86

Valencia, Michael B 98
Vevers, Paul 59

Wakefield, C E 145–6
Walker, Hilary 12
Wallace, Alison 20–3, 25
Weber, Max 33
West, Jenny 56–7
Whittington, Colin 153
Wilding, Keith 111
Wilkin, David 122
Wills, D J 70
Wilson, Judy 67
Wilson, Tom 232
Winnicott, Clare 70
Wright, Andrew 189

Subject index